tumblr

Digital Media and Society Series

tumblr

KATRIN TIIDENBERG,
NATALIE ANN HENDRY, AND
CRYSTAL ABIDIN

polity

First published in 2021 by Polity Press

Polity Press
65 Bridge Street
Cambridge CB2 1UR, UK

Polity Press
101 Station Landing
Suite 300
Medford, MA 02155, USA

ISBN-13: 978-1-5095-4108-9
ISBN-13: 978-1-5095-4109-6(pb)

A catalogue record for this book is available from the British Library.

Library of Congress Cataloging-in-Publication Data
Names: Tiidenberg, Katrin, author. | Hendry, Natalie Ann, author. | Abidin,
    Crystal, author.
Title: Tumblr / Katrin Tiidenberg, Natalie Ann Hendry and Crystal Abidin.
Description: Cambridge ; Medford, MA : Polity, 2021. | Series: Digital
    media and society series | Includes bibliographical references and
    index.
Identifiers: LCCN 2021003003 (print) | LCCN 2021003004 (ebook) | ISBN
    9781509541089 (hardback) | ISBN 9781509541096 (paperback) | ISBN
    9781509541102 (epub)
Subjects: LCSH: Tumblr (Electronic resource) | Microblogs--United
    States--History. | Microblogs--Social aspects. | Online social
    networks--United States--History.
Classification: LCC TK5105.8885.T85 T55 2021 (print) | LCC TK5105.8885.T85
    (ebook) | DDC 338.7/613022314--dc23
LC record available at https://lccn.loc.gov/2021003003
LC ebook record available at https://lccn.loc.gov/2021003004

Typeset in 10.25 on 13pt Scala
by Fakenham Prepress Solutions, Fakenham, Norfolk NR21 8NL
Printed and bound in Great Britain by TJ Books Ltd, Padstow, Cornwall

For further information on Polity, visit our website:
politybooks.com

Contents

Acknowledgments

Studying tumblr used to be a lonely endeavor, so first and foremost we thank our friends in the research community, who supported the development of our ideas and worked with us on fieldwork and thinking about tumblr – of course, rarely sharing their tumblog addresses, but supporting us nonetheless.

We especially would like to thank: Kath Albury, Airi-Alina Allaste, Steven Angelides, Nancy Baym, Megan Lindsay Brown, Michael Burnam-Fink, Paul Byron, Earvin Cabalquinto, Alexander Cho, Edgar Gómez Cruz, Debra Ferreday, Robbie Fordyce, Ysabel Gerrard, Ben Hanckel, Matt Hart, Larissa Hjorth, Amelia Johns, Akane Kanai, Annette Markham, Anthony McCosker, Allison McCracken, John Carter McKnight, Kristian Møller, Susanna Paasonen, Daniel Reeders, Bryce Renninger, Brady Robards, Jenny Robinson, Julian Sefton-Green, Terri Senft, Frances Shaw, Daphanie Teo, Cindy Tekobbe, Emily van der Nagel, Son Vivienne, Katie Warfield, Rosie Welch, and Andrew Whelan.

We are grateful to the Association of Internet Researchers (AoIR) for organizing the best conferences ever and allowing the three of us to meet, and for our talented illustrator River Juno for lending us her expert skills and sharing with us her love for tumblr too. Thank you also to Mary Savigar, Ellen MacDonald-Kramer, and Stephanie Homer at Polity Press for your encouragement and patience to help us write about tumblr with a small t.

Katrin. I am grateful for the opportunity to have worked and written with Natalie and Crystal: the nuances in your ways of seeing the world, of making sense of it and of expressing yourself in writing have enriched and educated me, as a human and a scholar. I want to also thank Tallinn University, for the rector's grant that allowed me the privilege of writing time. My undying gratitude belongs to my research participants, in particular the open, kind, interesting, funny, and sexy people for NSFW tumblr, who let me in, shared their thoughts and lives with me, and helped nourish a research project that ended up spanning eight years.

Natalie. My research was generously supported by the Young and Well Cooperative Research Centre and RMIT PhD Scholarship, and grants from RMIT University and Deakin University. I am grateful for the support of a number of mental health and education organizations and services; here, they remain unnamed so as to protect the confidentiality of my research participants. I would also like to acknowledge the support of RMIT through my Vice-Chancellor's Postdoctoral Research Fellowship with the School of Media and Communication and the Digital Ethnography Research Centre. I am forever grateful for the nourishing writing support from Sarah Sentilles and the Right to Write community, and the tumblrs that introduced me to affect theory when I returned to studying after years away from theory. I especially thank my mother for unknowingly helping me get online in the first place, and Sam for helping me stay online through house moves, a new job, and a pandemic bedroom office, as well as Ida and Patrick for their warm welcome. Thank you, Sam, for sending me memes and bringing me dinners while I kept working late in the bedroom-office. Kat and Crystal, I still pinch myself that I was able to learn about writing and thinking for a book with both of you, during a pandemic nonetheless. Thank you both for caring, ranting, challenging, and rewriting together.

Crystal. I dedicate this book to COGY, in commemoration of our teenhood spent loitering publicly together in IRL places and gallivanting privately together on tumblr. I also write this book in memory of Carissa, who was my Super Cool Tumblr Guide. Thank you also to my precious anonymous digital penpals on tumblr, who have brought me much companionship and joy in the past decade, and to Sherman, for being in my life. I would like to acknowledge my colleagues in Internet Studies, and the School of Media, Creative Arts and Social Inquiry at Curtin University for their cheerleading, and the ARC DECRA Fellowship that supported my research and writing time. Finally, to Kat and Nat: I still cannot believe that we completed this book in the fragile months of the blessed year 2020. Alongside feeling tired and despondent from the state of The World, I was also coping with So Many Things, and could not have made these words without your companionship, comfort, and confidence. It has been an honor and a privilege to be enveloped by the rare combination of intellect and kindness inside both of you – I am so glad we are friends IRL (and maybe someday even mutuals on tumblr).

Prologue

I found tumblr some time in 2010. I was reading a lot of fanfiction and many of the stories used images "from tumblr," so I decided to find out what it meant. My first blog exists as twenty-five static snapshots in the Wayback Machine. Shutting down that first blog was a sudden and emotional decision and what remains of it fits. No coherent archive, rather a metaphorical stash of ticket stubs, candy wrappers, and phone numbers on stained napkins. My second blog is nine years old. My third and fourth were both set up for research. For each of these, I set up a new email address, and each is a new primary blog. This was the way of my first tumblr tribe, guided by a fervent commitment to avoiding context collapse.

–Katrin

I migrated sharing my personal "feels" and obsessions from music forums and sites like LiveJournal to posting diary-like fragments on tumblr. Those first posts are gone, manually deleted, but others endure. Each new blog marked a new project: excerpts from literature I loved, frustrated rants about the hardcore punk scene I was sort of in, screenshots of text conversations that were just too personal to go elsewhere. Like the boxes of letters, photos, and other personal archives under my bed, tumblr curates my passions and transformations. Now, my primary blog is too attached to a public early-20-something self, it is too exposing, not the tumblr self I am now. And yet this blog "follows" other blogs, this younger me, not the me in one of

my active secondary blogs. I wish I could swap which blog
is my primary.

—Natalie

I was introduced to tumblr when I mentored a group of
teenage girls in my youth group in 2008. My main blog is the
most respectable of the lot, but then one day I got bored and
stopped updating it. But this "old life" still haunts me every
time I open my tumblr mobile app, because my main blog is
still linked to another twenty-three side blogs. Where I post
depends on my mood in the moment. In one, I diary my grief
from missing my sister; in another, I curate pretty pictures
based on themes (fluffy birds, clouds at sunset, anime foods);
still others are memory capsules, like the time I made a post
every day for a month as a gift to a friend. Fingers crossed I
never lose my phone and have my tumblr lives exposed.

—Crystal

Introduction: tumblr, with a small t

> tumblr makes me want to have drinks with people I have never met and Facebook makes me want to throw drinks at people I already know.
>
> (Unknown)

This is a meme that made rounds on tumblr, gathering affirmations from people across different user groups and communities. Fans, queers, "snowflakes," sex workers, "horny people," teenage girls with flawless aesthetics, writers, artists: they all seemed to agree, that tumblr is very different from Facebook – and much, much better. The vernacular positioning of tumblr within the social media ecology did not stop at comparisons with Facebook. Another popular meme that has circulated on tumblr at various points in time is a still from the 1985 movie *The Breakfast Club*, where the five main characters – described in the film as: "a brain ... and an athlete ... and a basket case ... a princess ... and a criminal" – were labeled as LinkedIn, Facebook, tumblr, Instagram, and Twitter respectively. tumblr, unsurprisingly for anyone who has ever spent time on the platform, was cast as the basket case of the group.

These comparisons were not merely vernacular. In an early interview with the *New York Sun* (Martin 2007), tumblr's then 21-year-old "boy wonder," founder David Karp, rejected the comparison between both himself and Facebook founder Mark Zuckerberg, and the two social media platforms (David's Log 2008). Karp was cited as saying that it is "lame" when your online experience ends with Facebook, which "really falls short [as a] space on the Web to identify you." In the same breath, he also called YouTube "a miserable social experience" (Martin 2007). These little glimpses into popular and corporate imaginaries of tumblr open up our discussion of what tumblr is, how it works, and why so many people consider(ed) it special. We start with a journey through tumblr's history and ownership.

History, ownership, and vision

tumblr was launched in February 2007. In March, the press was calling it "delightfully simple," "blazingly fast," and "microblogging done right" (Lowensohn 2007). By the end of the year, US$750,000 had been invested in it and trade blogs called it "the darling of the New York startup scene" (Martin 2007). In the thirteen years since, tumblr has consistently had more active users than Twitter, Snapchat, Baidu, or LinkedIn. During its first months of operation, tumblr gained 75,000 users. By 2012, this number was approximately 147 million, doubling in 2013, doubling again to 594 million in 2017, and growing to 624 million in 2018 (Roser et al. 2020). But then, this figure suddenly plummeted to just 370 million in the first months after the NSFW (Not Safe For Work) ban (see Chapter 1) that went into effect in the final weeks of 2018 (Armstrong 2019). In the global ranking of leading social media platforms (Roser et al. 2020), tumblr was usually ranked fourth to sixth from 2013 to 2018 (although different reports have different numbers and rankings, so these statistics should be taken with a grain of salt). Beyond user numbers, tumblr has always boasted impressive user engagement metrics: it had enviable retention rates – 85 percent of the blogs on the platform updated regularly (Dannen 2009) – and was consistently reported to exceed other platforms in terms of time spent on the site (Perez 2013; Ratcliff 2014).

But statistics have limited usefulness when it comes to really understanding tumblr and its significance. There is even a tumblr meme that argues this point. It started in 2013, when a tumblr user commented on a broadly circulated myth that an average person swallows eight spiders a year, saying that the factoid is based on a statistical error, because "an average person eats 0 spiders per year. Spiders Georg, who lives in a cave & eats over 10,000 each day, is an outlier and should not have been counted." The post's popularity led to the setting up of a Spiders-Georg tumblr blog (Knowyourmeme 2020a), and became memorialized as the "statistical error" meme (memedocumentation 2017). In 2015, a now-deactivated blog posted: "according to USA Today, the average tumblr user spends 2.5 hours a month on tumblr," accompanied with a GIF of actress Mila Kunis laughing hysterically. This was reblogged with the statistical error meme, with added text that read "the average person spends 0 hours per month. We Georg, who live in caves & spend over 23 hours on tumblr each day, are outliers and should not have been counted." To say the sentiment resonated with tumblr users would be an understatement. The post has 1,159,527 "notes" (likes and reblogs) at the time of writing.

Most social media platforms are owned by private corporations, which inevitably serve corporate and not public interests, even when governed by laws and regulations. Platform owners' vision and governance choices often have profound, if unplanned, social, political, and cultural implications. We can recall highly publicized examples, such as Facebook and Cambridge Analytica's impact on the results of the 2016 US general election and the UK Brexit vote (Cadwalladr and Graham-Harrison 2018), or the role that fake news on WhatsApp – owned by Facebook as of 2014 – played in the Brazilian 2018 elections (Pereira and Bojczuk 2018). Similarly, it matters when tumblr suddenly bans NSFW content, as it did in 2018.

By tracking changes in platform ownership, we can trace the "power relationships" and identify "how institutional structures control social enactment" (van Dijck 2013: 37–9).

Directly linked to ownership is the owners' and other stake-holders' vision for the platform, as well as the public image it has among various constituencies – most notably, marketers, advertisers, end users, and trade presses. A platform's vision "involves its purpose, target user base and scenarios of use," and explicitly communicates what the platform "is supposed to do and, by extension, implies how it can be used and by whom" (Light et al. 2018: 889). In this section, we identify three phases in tumblr's vision, guided by changes in ownership. We review tumblr when it was an independent company (2007–12), when it was owned by Yahoo! and the corporations that subsequently bought it (2013–18), and, finally, when it was most recently sold to Automattic (2019–time of writing). While there is not yet evidence that Automattic will run tumblr differently from Yahoo!, the separation is based on the cultural imaginary of Yahoo! having "ruined" tumblr. We will come back to this shortly.

A brief note. You might have noticed that we do not capitalize the word "tumblr." We use the small "t" when we talk about tumblr as a social experience and a platform, and capitalize it when we discuss "Tumblr Inc.," the company that developed it. The small "t" is folkloric. It reflects how people across our personal and research experiences have referred to the platform since its inception. This preference for a lower-case "t," in turn, reflects the developers' design choices. tumblr's logo and app icon have both always used lowercase "t"s.

Independent tumblr

While Karp attracted investor enthusiasm and raised capital from the get-go, he was explicit about his focus being less on business and monetization and more on what he called the product. "I didn't care how the bills got paid, or about facilities or H.R. stuff," Karp is cited as saying in the *New York Times* (Walker 2012). Karp's vision for tumblr seemed to stand on the three pillars of ease of use, design, and creativity. tumblr's public facing texts (e.g., About page, FAQ, press clippings posted on the site) highlighted simplicity, customizability, interest-driven community, and creative self-expression. tumblr was positioned as making it easy to share "everything you find, love, hate or create" (tumblr 2007), an "effortless" way to "share" and "express yourself," because "everything" is customizable (tumblr 2008). In 2012, corporate rhetoric shifted toward prioritizing creativity. A "what tumblr is for" segment was added to the Guidelines, stating: "Tumblr celebrates creativity. We want you to express yourself freely and use Tumblr to reflect who you are, and what you love, think, witness, and believe" (tumblr 2012). In 2015, "witness, and believe" was changed to "standing for" but other than that the mission statement has, to date, remained unchanged. The tagline, too, was updated in 2012 to "Follow the world's creators" and has not been changed since. Karp's interviews during the period focused on ease of use and creativity. In 2009, he is cited as saying that "the world would be a better place if more people could find, love and create things more easily" (Dannen 2009).

Karp wanted tumblr to be "a product-orientated company" (Cheshire 2012) like Google or Apple, rather than a social graph-driven one like Facebook, YouTube, or Twitter. Those, he claimed: "are not tools built for creative expression," adding that "nobody is proud of their identity on Facebook" (Schonfeld 2011). Trade journalists and the experts they interviewed seem largely to accept Karp's vision of the period – tumblr was typically described by third parties as a stunningly simple, beautifully designed place for intelligent social networking and original self-expression. In terms of business, it was often called an investor darling guided by feeling. This focus on "product" paid off in terms of the site's popularity with users. Numbers grew rapidly, reaching a point that Karp described as "we made it on the map" by 2010 (Schawbel 2013).

Yahoo! tumblr

In May 2013, Karp sold Tumblr Inc. to Yahoo! for US$1.1 billion. In terms of communicating the platform's vision though, Karp remained true to creativity, maintaining that if they got it right with Yahoo!, tumblr would in five years "be home to the most aspiring and talented creators all over the world" (Lapowski 2013). Marissa Mayer, the CEO of Yahoo!, in turn publicly promised to "not screw it up," while also emphasizing the potential to bring in more money by selling ads. Under Yahoo!, Karp's comments on creativity shifted to emphasize creative expression of one's unique self, on the one hand, but also something enacted by an empowered "creative class" who will change the world (Lapowski 2013), on the other. Increasingly, curation was mentioned as a form of creation. Karp told the BBC that "curation is a new, more accessible way to express yourself" (Mason 2012). In 2014, he said that while other social media platforms are "giant direc-tories of profiles," tumblr gives people a community where they can be themselves, fulfilling the promise of the internet as "a space where you could really create ... an identity that you're really, truly proud of" (Hamburger 2014). Karp argued that, unlike the "Valley," where engineers are the shapers of the vision and the experience, tumblr is not interested in data-driven categorization of users, but, instead, instils a mindset that creators, empowered by tumblr, "are going to show us the way" (Hamburger 2014). However, tumblr's image among trade presses and marketing professionals started to waver. While many stories continued to highlight that tumblr was aesthetically superior and loved by its users, attention was shifting to its revenue-earning potential, as per Mayer's aim.

Although user numbers kept growing, tumblr's revenue appeared to come to a standstill (Fell 2014); by the end of 2014, Mayer, under pressure, publicly promised that tumblr would make more than US$100 million in revenue in 2015. She merged Yahoo! and tumblr's ad sales teams, placing both under a new executive, whose image as a "shark"[1] perhaps explains the mass exodus of tumblr employees that followed. A couple of months later, Mayer reorganized Yahoo!'s leadership, placing David Karp himself under Simon Khalaf. Khalaf would later gain infamy for showing up to a tumblr staff meeting only to perplex everyone with an announcement that tumblr would "be the new PDF" (Fiegerman 2016). Retrospectively, 2015 is marked as the year when Yahoo! completely derailed tumblr. In those retrospective imaginaries, the pre-Yahoo! tumblr is described as having been "the hottest thing on the internet," a platform that "built strong communities, launched Internet memes, led to countless book deals and helped shape the culture, online and offline," but also a "vibrant network of powerful cultural commentary," and one of the more beloved private tech companies in the world (Fiegerman 2016).

In June 2017, the telcom giant Verizon acquired Yahoo! – and tumblr with it. Later in the same year, it merged Yahoo! with its other acquisition, AOL, renaming the group OATH. Shortly after, tumblr's founder and "mascot" David Karp announced that he was leaving the company, but he did not confirm whether this latest acquisition was the reason. Karp's goodbye email further reinforced what tumblr's vision had been under his tenure, stating that he looks back "with so much pride at a generation of artists, writers, creators, curators, and crusaders that have redefined our culture, and who we have helped to empower" (Menegus 2017).

Automattic tumblr

In an attempt to make tumblr more palatable for advertisers, Verizon enhanced its filtering of sexual content in 2017, and by December of the next year it announced a plan to ban all sexual content from the platform (see Chapters 1 and 6). This generated, next to public uproar, a drastic drop (estimated at 30 percent in the first three months) in user engagement and traffic (Sung 2019), and spawned a crop of tumblr clones targeted at those with interest in sexually explicit content. By May 2019, news surfaced that Verizon was looking to offload tumblr. Pornhub expressed interest, but in August, Verizon announced a sale of the platform and the company to Automattic, the owner of the blogging platform WordPress. The price tag was less than US$3 million, a phenomenal drop from the US$1.1 billion that Yahoo! had bought it for. Automattic CEO Matt Mullenweg echoed the popular sentiment of tumblr being something beautiful but ruined by Yahoo!, and had a hopeful vision that under Automattic the "magic" and "frisson" that tumblr once brought to blogging could be reinvigorated. "I would love for tumblr to become a social alternative," Mullenweg said, while arguing that tumblr had always brought substance to social discourse and possessed a certain friendliness and supportiveness that other platforms lacked (Patel 2019).

Magic and frisson

But what was this "magic" and "frisson" that tumblr once brought? What are – or were – those engaged, invested users doing on tumblr? Why do or did they log on? Why are tumblr users and tumblr scholars so sure, when they say that tumblr is special and played a key role in the digital culture of the past decade? A strong pattern emerges from qualitative, immersive research. Conversations around fandom (Bourlai 2018; Burton 2019; Hillman et al. 2014), feminism (Connelly 2015; Keller 2019), LGBTQIA+[2] experiences (Byron 2019; Cho 2015a; Feraday 2016; Fink and Miller 2014; Haimson et al. 2019; Oakley 2016), and NSFW topics (Mondin 2017; Tiidenberg 2014a, 2020; Tiidenberg and van der Nagel 2020) are all highly visible on tumblr. So are the users' commitments to social justice (Burton 2019; Wargo 2017a) and mental health (Cavazos-Rehg et al. 2017; Hendry 2020a; Seko and Lewis 2018) while having those conversations. Further, across

these interests and commitments, users have told researchers
that their tumblr experiences are communal, consciousness-
raising, therapeutic, and educational (Chew 2018; Hendry
2020b; McCracken 2017; Tiidenberg 2014b, 2017). People
often feel that on tumblr they can truly be themselves
(Renninger 2014; Tiidenberg 2013). tumblr users seem to
be quite self-aware about the platform's role in their lives.
Posts listing "things tumblr has taught me" are so common
they can be considered a platform-specific meme (Figure i.1;
see Chapter 5 for a discussion on tumblr pedagogies, and
Chapters 6 and 7 on learning in specific groups and communities). Some of these lists are serious, others are funny, yet
others deeply sincere. Many are everything at once.

Figure i.1: Artist's impression of a now-deactivated blog post from 2015 listing
"Things tumblr has taught me," with approximately 30,000 notes. Art provided
by River Juno.

Most statistics show that tumblr's user base has always been predominantly composed of young people or millennials (variously recognized as born between the early 1980s to the late 1990s; Petrov 2020), with some growing up on the platform through their teen years into their twenties and thirties. In part, the youthful nature of the platform explains why it was a place for learning and for people to "find themselves" (see Chapters 2 and 5). This narrative of tumblr having had a profound transformative and educational impact on (young) people is reproduced by journalists. tumblr is credited with having "taught social justice to a generation of teenagers" (Sarappo 2018), "taught the world how to speak Australian" (Nye 2017), taught writers to write (Manley 2013), taught youth about nonbinary gender identities (Arscott 2018), and offered them "a means of survival" (Morris 2019). However, many of these narratives are veiled in nostalgia, deeming *circa* 2012–14 as tumblr's heyday and presuming that it no longer offers these things (Jennings 2020; Morris 2019). As tumblr researchers and authors of this book, we grappled with the same sentiment (we will return to the notion of "lost" tumblr and tumblr's demise in the Conclusion). Yet, the "#what tumblr has taught me" hashtag keeps returning results every time we conduct a search. A brief walkthrough (Figure i.2) shows that in 2020, tumblr users are still learning and still crediting tumblr with it.

Of course, tumblr is not a utopia. There are conflicts, arguments, toxic dog piling, and trolling between users (see Chapter 5 for a discussion on call-out cultures). The general consensus, however, seems to be that compared to most alternatives, tumblr has offered an inhabitable space for people and communities, especially those with minoritarian experiences, identifications, lifestyles, and values. As noted in the roundtable interview published in *The Ringer*, tumblr "felt friendlier than other famously weird internet zones like Reddit or 4chan. I still felt like I was on a cool detour, but I wasn't in the Wild West, you know?" (Bereznak et al. 2017).

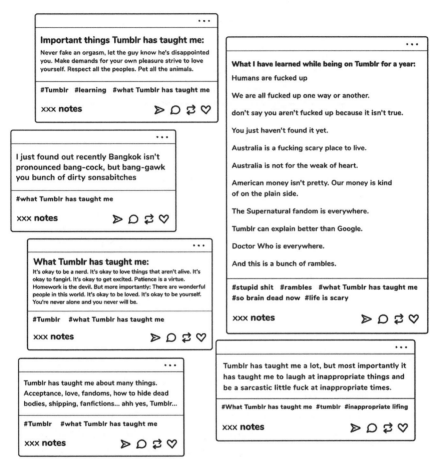

Figure i.2: Artist's impression of a collage of some posts under "#what tumblr has taught me." Art provided by River Juno.

Overall then, tumblr has been formative of the worldviews and identities of many (mostly young) people; has played a significant part in elevating conversations on gender, sexual identities, intersectionality, and cultural representations thereof; and has launched, or at least played an instrumental role in, various social movements, such as Occupy and Black Lives Matter (Baptiste 2017; Safronova 2014; Sutter 2011;

see also chapters in McCracken et al. 2020). Some think that tumblr's 2010 meme war with 4chan served as a direct precursor to the polarization that characterizes our current (online) opinion space (Rosenberg 2020).[3] Despite all of this, tumblr remained an obscure, cult-like subculture to nonusers, a space difficult to "crack" for marketers, and a platform to which little or no attention was paid by academics outside research on fandom or queer youth. Why?

tumblr is a silosocial platform

Social media are diverse, but public imaginaries of their functions and implications are dominated by Facebook. Scholarship too, is heavily skewed toward Facebook (given its popularity worldwide), and also Twitter (given its high accessibility for researchers to extract data via the API). Generalist discussions and critiques of social media therefore often presume that social media sociality[4] is profile-based and built on what is called the social graph and the ego network.[5] In the case of Facebook, egos in the graph are represented by profiles – descriptions of the account owner's social characteristics, often in the form of answers to questions, sometimes via predetermined options. This version of social media sociality is linked to individual connections and has been multiply critiqued in the past decade: as networked individualism (Wellman 2002), as people converging around someone's profile or interacting in dyads instead of converging around interests (Baym 2010), as leading to context collapse resulting from the inability to modulate one's self presentations to different audiences (Marwick and boyd 2011), as fostering a culture of connectivity instead one of connection (van Dijck 2013), or even as antisocial, because it discourages deliberation (Vaidhyanathan 2018).

The following are generalizations, of course, but they reflect dominant trends on platforms and, more importantly, dominant imaginaries about the platforms, which together converge into an increasingly popular narrative of a broken internet (Berners-Lee 2019; Phillips 2020). Facebook started out as a social ego network intended for interpersonal interaction, but has, according to American media scholar Siva Vaidhyanathan (2018), devolved into a network of amplified prejudices and predilections. Twitter, according to media and communication scholars Jean Burgess and Nancy Baym (2020: 13), remains unsure whether it should be a social network or an information network, and which of the two is a more valuable form of human communication, even if the founders themselves have framed the platform's transformation "from a me-centered, personal, and intimate Twitter, to a world-centered, public, and newsy one" as progress. Instagram, as argued by internet researchers Tama Leaver, Tim Highfield, and Crystal Abidin (2020), increasingly functions as a communication and commerce network, where sociality is template-based and communication rarely leads to collective experiences (Leaver and Highfield 2018). In contrast, tumblr's features, functions, governance, and user cultures – as we will go on to show – differ significantly from these popular platforms. tumblr is a social network, but not profile-based or legal name-linked, and welcomes multifaceted self-presentation; it is informative, but through educational rather than newsy ways; attention flows and converges on it but is linked differently to commerce than elsewhere.

As a result, a very particular, idiosyncratic form of sociality has emerged on tumblr. We call it "silosociality," because it is experienced through silos – experiential tumblrs imagined and enacted by users as somewhat apart from each other. Silos emerge out of and are defined by people's shared interests, but sustained through shared practices, vernacular, and sensibility. We conceptualize this in detail in Chapters 1 and 2. Silosociality is thus the cultural and experiential dynamic that relies on tumblr's features and governance (Chapter 1) but is (re)produced by how people imagine and do things on tumblr (Chapter 2). We argue that silosociality explains tumblr's pivotal role in shaping digital culture, but also fills a conceptual gap in existing social media analyses (see Chapter 2) and helps illuminate possible trajectories for the future.

What is in this book

While the book offers most when read in its entirety, we have taken care to include cross-references and to construct the chapters so that they can be read separately. The early chapters describe and explain the structure and broad logics of tumblr. Chapter 1 analyzes tumblr as a built, corporately owned space with particular features and functions, governed in particular ways. We highlight the features and functions used when setting up a blog, posting, reblogging, tagging, and interacting on the platform as well as the rules for acceptable behavior and intended use(r)s. Chapter 2 focuses on tumblr as a social space that has unique affordances, which lead to an emergence of a shared vernacular based on curatorial and multimodal expression, personal testimonials, and affinity-based participation, and a shared sensibility that is committed to social justice and safe spaces. We demonstrate how these three elements – affordances, vernacular, and sensibility – along with tumblr's features and rules, contribute to creating tumblr's silosociality. In Chapter 3, we look at attention flows on tumblr, analyzing the business model, the forms of commerce, and the discursive strategies of attention hacking used on the platform by Tumblr Inc., brands, celebrities, influencers, and everyday users.

Chapters 4–7 explore what we want to elevate as the key silos on tumblr. We discuss the *fandom* silo in Chapter 4, outlining how tumblr has always afforded fan cultures and describing fannish uses of the tumblr vernacular and sensibility in two less-researched fan communities – K-pop and the tumblr meta-fandom. In Chapter 5, we discuss the nuances of social media practices and sensibilities through the example of the *queer* silo. Here, we talk about social justice warriors, call-out cultures, tumblr pedagogies, and queer tumblr in terms of both a utopian bubble and an overwhelming vortex. The *NSFW* (sexually explicit) silo is discussed in Chapter 6. We open up with how safe spaces were built within this silo, and explore how these allowed people to experiment, accept themselves, diversify their standards, expand their tolerance, and find a socially just voice. In Chapter 7, we examine the *mental health* silo. While mental health professionals tend to position tumblr as problematic, even harmful, arguing that depression, self-harm, anxiety, and disordered eating are exacerbated on the platform, our participants' lived experiences paint a much more nuanced, ambiguous picture of freedom, validation, modulated visibility, and laughing about their own pain.

While these four silos emerge out of our own fieldwork and have consistently been named as having key importance by our tumblr-researching colleagues, we are mindful to avoid totalizing claims. The tumblr signposted by these silos is one – relevant, perhaps even dominant – version. But there are other culturally and geographically specific imaginaries of tumblr (e.g., in Japan, tumblr is commonly perceived as simply a site to host a creative's visual portfolios). In the Conclusion, we discuss whether tumblr is "dying," as some critics have been arguing after the NSFW ban, or simply mutating into something new. We discuss tumblr silosociality as offering education and escape, and finish with imagining silosocial futures for social media as such.

Our research methods

We have been researching tumblr since 2011. To understand tumblr practices, cultures, vernacular, and sensibilities, we have – between the three of us – conducted a decade's worth of multifaceted ethnographic fieldwork, comprising:

- observations across different tumblr silos and in various tumblr communities (network of eating disorder blogs, NSFW selfie community, East Asian NSFW tumblr communities, various K-pop fandoms, *Supernatural* and *Teen Wolf* fandoms and meta-tumblr fandoms, mental health blogs including Borderline Personality Disorder communities and art blogs related to mental health, queer tumblr);
- approximately one hundred individual interviews, approximately ten group interviews, focus groups, and creative workshops, and twelve image elicitation conversations with tumblr users;
- analyses of an uncountable number of tumblr posts, tumblr blogs, and hashtag conversations in English, Chinese, and Japanese, using content-, thematic-, discourse-, and narrative-analysis;
- hashtag and keyword mapping exercises; and
- participant observation in school and hospital settings.

To contextualize what is happening on the platform and how tumblr users make sense of it, we have studied tumblr as a corporately owned technical structure. For this, we have analyzed:

- hundreds of trade press and news articles, interviews with key tumblr employees, and marketing, pop culture, and technology blogs (e.g., Adweek, *The Atlantic*, Bustle, CNET, Fast Company, Forbes, Gawker, the *Guardian*, i-D, Mashable, *The New York Times*, Popsugar, *The Ringer*, TechCrunch, The Verge, Vice, *Wall Street Journal*, Wired);
- fourteen years' worth of tumblr's marketing (press releases, tag lines, app store descriptions) and governance (Terms of Service Agreements, Community Guidelines, Privacy Policy, About page, Help page, Staff Blog posts), texts procured using

Google search, the Wayback Machine, and updates logged on Github.

At moments of heightened attention to tumblr (e.g., the 2012 content moderation change, the 2018 NSFW ban, various changes of ownership), we have gathered – both manually and using automated scraping tools – content regarding tumblr that was sourced either from tumblr itself or via other social media sites (e.g., Buzzfeed, Facebook, Pinterest, Twitter, YouTube).

Finally, we analyzed tumblr features, functionalities, and interfaces across the years drawing from our personal research archives of fieldnotes and screenshots, the Wayback Machine, and conducted a systematic walkthrough of the platform and its app in 2020.

Our arguments rely on our extensive empirical work, but also dialogue with the research conducted by our colleagues. Wherever possible, we allow our research participants to speak for themselves, quoting interview snippets or reproducing sections of blog posts. Whenever we quote people we interviewed, we refer to them by research pseudonyms, as agreed in our informed consent negotiations. Where we reproduce images or posts, we follow three strategies. Publicly accessible, noncontroversial, widely shared content is reproduced as is, or anonymized. Where we have needed to depict a practice (e.g., the massive nested system of reblogs converging in a single post), illustrate the interface (e.g., notes showing all the likes and reblogs and comments), or reproduce contentious material (e.g., thinspo, NSFW content), we err on the side of caution and care – we use artist impressions to convey these visual practices or publish blog outtakes without linking them either to a tumblr username or to the research-based pseudonym linked to interview quotes. Where content is not contentious, but we have been uncertain about whether users would like their usernames reproduced, we have modified screenshots or commissioned artist impressions to preserve user or content confidentiality; however, where we have felt it important for the user to be acknowledged and credited for their creative contributions, we name them briefly.

Writing this book has been a labor of love and we are happy and grateful that you have chosen to come on this journey with us. Thank you.

I

tumblr structure

The way tumblr is set up – the likes and reblogs – provides the framework for constant feedback and support. It's easy to feel like I've been heard, appreciated, understood. We are connected with very intimate parts of ourselves and it makes it easier to see people's humanity and to be compassionate toward them. I know how hard it is to be so open and I appreciate that others do the same. I find myself responding in ways through tumblr that just wouldn't be socially acceptable in real life, and others do the same

(Katie: personal interview by authors, 2012)

The way tumblr is set up feels to me like it replicates a couple of significant modes of offline affiliation – the ability to "like" and "reblog" as well as comment feel to me like an analogue of some of the mirroring that happens between people who are working at attuning with one another in person. So, I would say it's just been a matter of feeling out shared likes and dislikes, and developing a sense that we share enough to have that kind of identification with one another. Or shared community identity, at any rate.

(Olly: personal interview by authors, 2012)

This chapter is about tumblr as a built space. We explore it as a platform that is wrought from computer code and design choices, owned and managed by corporate entities that have particular goals and sets specific rules for users. To do this, we analyze tumblr's features and functions first, and then discuss tumblr's platform governance by describing its most pertinent rules and how they are enforced. This chapter is written to be read alongside Chapter 2, where we continue to analyze how people imagine what they can do on tumblr and how they actually use it.

Features and functions

Features and functions of social media platforms can be thought of as "arrangements that mandate or enable an activity," (Light et al. 2018: 891). Broadly, both features and functions have been defined as indications of what people can do with a thing. A feature is literally "what users can do with a technology" (Markus and Silver 2008: 612), while what an artifact is for – and it is arguably always for something – is the artifact's function (Franssen et al. 2018). Social media platforms' features (e.g., a "heart" button) communicate and suggest actions (e.g., clicking it) as well as an assortment of possible meanings of those actions (e.g., "if I click it, I like it" – see Bucher and Helmond 2017).

While there are many features and functions on tumblr that are similar to those on other social media platforms, there are also those that are unique to tumblr, and still others that were pioneered on tumblr before becoming pervasive across the social media ecosystem. We start with a discussion of what setting up and posting on tumblr is like. This takes us through a brief description and history of the features and functions that deprioritize the social graph and invite multi-modality and personalization. We then discuss, in more detail, three clusters of features and functions that make tumblr stand out: (1) tumblr's signature reblog, (2) the tumblr-unique format for hashtags, and (3) the unconventional features and functions for on-platform interaction.

Setting up and posting

Setting up a tumblr account is easy: users only need to provide a functioning email address and state their age and, voilà, they have a blog. Tumblr Inc.'s designers and engineers try to help new users find "what're you into" (see Chapter 2) during the onboarding process. This directs users to curate their own blogs as interest-based spaces too. The blogs are not profiles, and whether any particular blog has a description at all depends on the chosen blog "theme"; these are available for free and for purchase in the tumblr "themes" catalogue. Further, those descriptions are completely open, filled out with any information that users deem relevant (see Oakely 2016 on self-labeling in About sections). After setting up one blog, users can set up as many "secondary" or "side" blogs as they want and toggle between their blogs from the same user interface. While only "primary" or "main" blogs (created upon account sign-up) have social features that allow following others, liking, and replying to posts, secondary blogs can be set to be private- and password-protected. A user cannot change a previously primary blog to private, or a previously secondary blog to primary (something often highlighted as a fault by users), so it is quite common for users to set up more than one primary account. Users with multiple (primary or secondary) blogs generally argue that this allows for multi-faceted self-presentation, audience segregation, and identity curation.

Types of blog posts invited via specific buttons are text posts, photo posts, quote posts, link posts, chat posts, and audio or video posts (see Figure 1.1 for tumblr's dashboard on a desktop). Visual content, in particular photos, is very popular (78.11 percent of posts in Chang et al. 2014). While most social media platforms allow sharing texts, links, and visual content, the tumblr "chat" post format is less common. Linguists Camilla Vásquez and Samantha Creel (2017) link the popularization of chat memes, especially the me-chat meme, across social media directly to this tumblr feature. Me-chat memes usually feature a pretend conversation between various facets of one's identity, like "past me" and "present me," or just two "me"s with incompatible goals

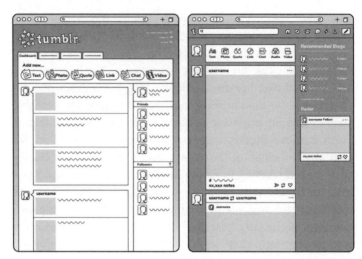

Figure 1.1: Artist's impression of the changing interface design of tumblr's dashboard. LEFT: 2007; RIGHT: current browser dashboard at the time of writing in 2020. Art provided by River Juno.

and desires, usually to a humorous or relatable effect (see Chapter 7).

While different types of posts continue to be differentiated and the "chat" post was still available via the browser-based Dashboard in 2020, the mobile interface has recently been updated to significantly alter the posting experience (Figure 1.2). The post icon looks like a pen, which feels less multimodal and more writing-centric and "bloglike." This possibly follows Automattic's acquisition, as the company is best known for the legendary blogging platform WordPress. Clicking on the pen icon gives further options of taking an image, uploading image or video from the camera roll, adding a link, making or choosing a GIF, choosing an audio file from Spotify or Soundcloud, and adding hashtags. However, the experience of tumblr is not just about posting but, more importantly, about consuming what other people have posted.

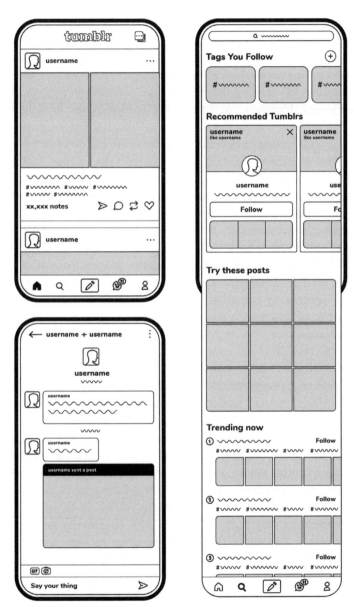

Figure 1.2: Artist's impression of the tumblr interface via the app on a mobile phone. Art provided by River Juno.

Reblogs

Users who set up an account can "follow" other blogs, upon which the content posted to those blogs converges into their "dashboard" feed. Following is not necessarily reciprocal, although bloggers within specific communities do follow each other and refer to each other as "mutuals" (see Chapter 3). Further, "lists" of whom one follows are not automatically visible to others, but rather, one has to select a blog theme that allows for it and choose to publish the list. Posts seen on one's dashboard can be "liked" by clicking the heart button (introduced in 2008), replied to by clicking the "reply" button (introduced in 2010), or reblogged by clicking the "reblog" button. Each user sees what they themselves have liked in the "likes" list, which is, again, hidden from others. All of the likes, replies, and reblogs of a particular post are summarily calculated as "notes," which is the primary metric of how much attention a post has generated on the platform.

To reblog is to repost someone else's post to your own blog, whether partially or entirely. Reblogging (and "following") were tumblr's original features from its launch in March 2007, preceding retweeting on Twitter[1] and sharing on Facebook. Reblogging has always been a central practice on tumblr, with less than 10 percent of content qualifying as original (Xu et al. 2014). Clicking on the reblog button opens someone else's post in a new window allowing the reposter to add to it or reblog it as is. All post types are rebloggable, so one might reblog an image with a caption, a text post, a GIF set with comments, or a set of nested, cascading threads of previous reblogs, wherein every next reblogger has added a comment or a sentiment (see Figure 1.3).[2]

Initially, only text could be added to reblogs, but a 2017 update made adding images possible, which led to long intertextual image threads. Authorship of the original post as

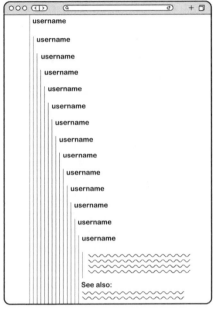

Figure 1.3: Artist's impression of an example of a cascading multi-reblog post on tumblr. Art provided by River Juno.

well as the content added in previous reblogs can be deleted from the body of the post. Perceptions of such deletion vary across users. For some it is an affront, while for others it is a perfectly natural aspect of curation. The source of the original post, as well the blog from which it was most recently reblogged, remains embedded in the code and visible at the top of the post even when the information is deleted from the body of the post.

These features make authorship and curatorship visible, which has further social implications. Interacting with other people's content via reblogging deincentivizes trolling and increases accountability for one's words (Renninger 2014). Fieldwork across different user groups has shown that people tend to reblog content they agree with or appreciate, because reblogging out of hate publishes the disliked content on one's own blog (Kanai 2015; Shorey 2015). Reblogging has taken on myriad additional meanings on tumblr. It fosters dialogue, consciousness-raising, and community creation (Connelly 2015; Marquart 2010), and allows the shy to express themselves (Salmon 2012). But it is also used to curate, reappropriate, frame, and remix – as one of media scholar Alessandra Mondin's (2017) research participants said, "the way a lot of tumblr bloggers reblog things makes them feminist and/or queer" (see Chapters 5 and 6). Further, media scholar Akane Kanai (2019) has argued that reblogging is a form of phatic communication that articulates a sense of connection and retains sociability instead of, or in addition to, directly exchanging information. It is common for tumblr users to start a relationship by reblogging each other's content with thoughtful commentary or funny compliments.

Reblogging is also an affective practice. Digital media anthropologist Alexander Cho (2015a) describes reblogging through Paasonen's (2011) notion of "resonance" and his own notion of "reverb," both of which highlight the sensation of intensity and affect involved in noticing and choosing to reblog posts, but also in demarcating the quality that makes some posts so rebloggable. Kanai (2017) adds "relatability" to the types of affect that drive reblogging. Relatability builds publics of like-minded users, who relate to each other's daily experiences. All three – resonance, reverberation, and relatability – are experienced based on one's life circumstance, thus bringing together people with similar experiences of, among other things, marginalization or discrimination, contributing to emergence of what we call silos (see Chapter 2).

Tags

The only thing that does not automatically travel with a reblog are prior "hashtags" (usually called just "tags" on tumblr). Hashtags are user-generated, but machine-readable descriptive labels, which make content searchable, injecting it into the platform's attention flows (see Chapter 3). But hashtags also have metacommunicative (Zappavigna 2018) and social functions, which allow people to gather around issues or affect (Papacharissi 2015; Rambukkana 2015). Special characters and spaces in hashtags are typically not allowed on other platforms. tumblr, however, has always allowed spaces and all non-comma punctuation marks within hashtags. This means that, on tumblr, a tag might be, and often is, an entire sentence. tumblr tags are thus uniquely multifunctional; they are used for self-reflexive, or emotional "behind the scenes" commentary, for making explicit LGBTQIA identity statements (Oakley 2016), for respectfully commenting on a popular post without cluttering it (Bourlai 2018), for avoiding conflict by making pre-emptive apologies (Neill Hoch 2018). Of course, as elsewhere on social media, there are plenty of keyword tags on tumblr (see Chapter 7 on mental health tags). These allow searchability, archiving, and filtering, as well as locating shared interests (Bourlai 2018; Mondin 2017).

Interaction

By 2020, tumblr had multiple features for users to interact with each other, developed and rolled out at various moments in time. In 2009, the "submissions" feature was introduced, allowing other users to submit posts for publication on someone else's blog (staff 2009). Each blogger can choose which format they accept submissions in, and whether or not to publish sent submissions. When introducing submissions, tumblr linked the feature primarily to artists submitting their artwork; however, it has been used by many other groups, including the NSFW communities, where soliciting and sending nudes via submissions was common. Another early (2010) feature of interaction on tumblr was "asks." tumblr users can set their asks to accept questions and comments anonymously or only from other tumblr users. At times, anonymous asks are used by those who read and follow tumblr blogs via a browser and do not have an account themselves. At other times, tumblr users choose to anonymize themselves specifically for using the asks, either to ask embarrassing questions, to joke, or (more rarely) to be mean. Because of the gray anonymous user icon accompanying such asks, the vernacular name for anonymous ask senders is "Grayfaces." Asks are responded to by publishing them with an answer, or by responding to them in private. In both cases, the original message disappears from one's asks, which complicates conversation. In the early 2010s, it was common for people to start interacting via asks and then move the conversation off tumblr, into email or a separate chat app. Asks was explicitly framed by tumblr staff as "a one-off Q&A, not a two-way conversation" (tumblr Help Center 2020a) linking it to their vision of tumblr as a space for creators, who are bound to have followers or fans. The latter brings us to yet another interactional feature, rolled out in 2010 – "fan mail." This allowed users who had followed someone for at least forty-eight hours to leave feedback, which, unlike asks and submissions, could not be published, and, unlike privately replied asks, stayed in the receiver's mailbox after being responded to. Fan mail was described as a "private commenting system between the blogger and the reader, that doesn't involve other visitors" (Panzarino 2012). Finally, in 2015, after years of requests from users, "messaging" was introduced. Messaging is only possible between logged-in users and cannot be anonymous. Fan mail was later discontinued in favor of messaging.

In November 2019, tumblr rolled out "group chats," which are only available on the mobile app. To some user criticism, group chats are public by default and cannot be set to private. Anyone can see messages within the chat, but to be able to send messages, one has to be approved as a member. Group chat messages expire after twenty-four hours, seventy-two hours, or a week, as chosen by the group chat "owner."

All mobile chat groups have to follow tumblr's central Community Guidelines, although some have additional rules described in the chat description (e.g., "feel free to observe or participate, don't worry, we don't know what we're doing either"; "DM your information to get accepted"). Group chats hold a maximum of two hundred participants, and the more popular chats often migrate to Discord servers to allow more people in, and because "chat functions in tumblr are super basic" as reported to us by a moderator in a group chat we observed. tumblr's aim in adding this feature seems to be to allow "niche communities" to "create dedicated spaces to talk about their interests instead of simply reblogging someone else's post" (Alexander 2019). Uploading images and GIFs is not possible in group chats. The conversations in the group chats we observed usually consist of sharing links to tumblr posts, memes, or Archive of Our Own fanfiction stories, and discussing those. Parody chats (e.g., "we all pretend to be middle-aged moms") only discuss issues in character. A user only sees the chats they are part of and those recommended by tumblr, while a directory of all group chats is not available at the time of writing.

Finally, it is important to understand how the "reply" function differs from the typical (public) commenting feature. David Karp has expressed a view that comments bring out the worst in people (Walker 2012), so he purposefully omitted that functionality, articulating reblogs, fan mail, or replies as its substitutes in various interviews. Replies were introduced as beta in 2010 and were generally loved by users. They were discontinued in 2015 to roll out messaging, but brought back in 2016. Bloggers can choose whether they want to enable replies. In the early years, a blogger had to turn replies on from the settings menu. Now, a user can select who they want to be able to reply to their posts (everyone, those whom one follows, or those who have been following one for at least a week). Replies are only available to logged-in users via the dashboard. tumblr's Help page describes replies as a "way of responding to a post that's more specific than a like, less of a commitment than a reblog, and more public than a message" (tumblr Help Center 2020b).

Governance

While the features and functions of tumblr tell us about the platform at a level of the interface, tumblr's governance tells us how the platform is structured more broadly, and how and what Tumblr Inc. thinks users should be able to do. Platforms are governed by laws, regulations, general industry logics, and their owners' vision, but they also govern us, their users, by setting explicit rules, making design and functionality choices (e.g., defaults and mandatory fields in profiles), and policing our behavior for compliance (see van Dijck 2013; Gillespie 2018; Light et al. 2018). The central piece of legislation governing American-owned social media platforms, including tumblr, has been Section 230 of the US Communications Decency Act (CDA 230). It states that internet intermediaries – including social media platforms – are not liable for their users' harmful speech, yet are allowed to regulate it as they see fit, without losing this "safe harbor" from liability.[3] While CDA 230 has consistently been heralded as the cornerstone of internet innovation and free speech, it has also been critiqued for letting social media platforms off the hook on a false premise that they are not shaping, amplifying, and suppressing content for profit (Marwick 2017). Here, we discuss how participants, practices, and content are moderated on tumblr. We follow this with a brief discussion on how algorithms are used in content moderation.

Moderating participants and practices

Between 2007 and 2012, tumblr's Terms of Service were, as is common for social media platforms, written in impenetrable legalese. Back then, a "subscriber" was described as someone at least 18 years of age. In 2012, tumblr added humorous, accessible "translations" to sections of their Terms of Service agreement and their Community Guidelines. The age of eligibility was lowered to 13, and the following explanation was added: "You have to be at least 13 years old to use Tumblr. We're serious: it's a hard rule, based on U.S. federal and state legislation, even if you're 12.9 years old. If you're younger than 13, don't use Tumblr. Ask your parents for an Xbox or try books." By 2020, tumblr's rules regarding age depended on the users' location, echoing the differences in law. tumblr users thus now have to be at least 13, or at least 16 if they live in the EU (there is flexibility depending on the data-processing consent age limits in particular European countries), and at least 18 to access blogs self- or platform-flagged as "explicit"[4] (tumblr Help Center 2020c).

tumblr has never made any prescriptions about usernames beyond stating, since the 2012 update to the Community Guidelines, that "Tumblr's URLs (usernames) are for the use and enjoyment of our users" and should not be hoarded, traded, or sold, nor registered for the purpose of imperson-ating someone. The 2012 accessible translation added to this that, "if you want to parody or ridicule a public figure (and who doesn't?), don't try to trick readers into thinking you are actually that public figure" (Community Guidelines update 2012). Setting up an account has only ever asked for a functioning email address and your age; tumblr has always accepted pseudonymity. The 2012 Community Guidelines also introduced "non-genuine social gesture schemes" (artifi-cially enhancing one's follower count), "mass registration and automation," "unauthorized sweepstakes or giveaways," as well as fraud and phishing into the list of "What tumblr is not for."

Moderating content

Most social media platforms prohibit or limit representations of sex, pornography, violence, obscenity, self-harm, and illegal activities, and posting content that functions as hate speech and harassment (Gillespie 2018). Of course, how stringently different platforms police the adherence to this list varies quite a bit. In 2012, tumblr staff posted plans for revising their Content Policy "against self-harm blogs" and proposed the removal of "active promotion of self-harm," including content that glorified or recommended self-injury, suicide, or eating disorder techniques. Users were invited to provide feedback on the policy change and the response was intense, immediate, and conflicting. In less than a week, the post received more than 25,000 notes (staff 2012a). Responses conveyed the move as, variously, stupid and dangerous; unfair ("what about other blogs that promote alcohol and drugs?," "It's still okay to have a racist blog on Tumblr"); exclusionary ("will target primarily women"); unproductive and potentially harmful ("some things need to be talked about"); well-intentioned but misguided ("taking away another safe space"); urgently needed and smart; and impractical ("where does Tumblr plan to draw the line between what is acceptable and what is not?") (staff 2012a). In their follow-up post, Tumblr Inc. seemed to have consulted with the National Eating Disorder Association and taken some of the user feedback on board, as they promised to find a balance between removing content, but keeping tumblr a place "where people struggling with these behaviors can find solace, community, dialog, understanding, and hope" (staff 2012b). Unlike Instagram, and perhaps as part of this promise, tumblr did not remove particular tags and started, instead, showing a PSA ("public service announcement," i.e., information on resources and support organizations) asking "Everything okay?" on search results for particular keywords and hashtags (see Figure 1.4[5]). While the impulse is admirable, the reality of the situation is much more complex. Users have dynamic and ever-developing techniques for circumventing hashtag moderation, and platforms' automated recommendation systems still circulate self-harm content (Gerrard 2018). Clicking through the PSA

Figure 1.4: The public service announcement (PSA) returned when one searches for "proana" on tumblr. Screengrab by authors.

and behaving on the platform as interested in self-harm will result in tumblr suggesting self-harm blogs to follow.

Scholars focused on sexual social media have remarked that American-owned platforms seem to presume that, in the list of offenses we started this section with, sexually explicit content will deter advertisers the most (see Paasonen et al. 2019; Tiidenberg and van der Nagel 2020).[6] It is perhaps unsurprising that just as David Karp's attitudes toward advertising differed from many of its competitors (see Chapter 3), so too did Tumblr Inc.'s early approach toward moderation of sexually explicit content.

tumblr's early Content Policy and Guideline documents contained a single sentence claiming that those who regularly host and upload sexual videos would be suspended. The 2012 update to Community Guidelines elaborated by setting two rules: users who "regularly post sexual or adult-oriented content" were asked to flag their blogs as "Not Suitable For Work ('NSFW'),"[7] and users are welcome to embed links to sexually explicit video, but should avoid uploading, because tumblr is "not in the business of profiting from adult-oriented videos and hosting this stuff is fucking expensive." The call to self-label ushered in the first version of the so-called Safe Mode, where the content of the blogs, which had been self-tagged as NSFW, was filtered out from the dashboards and search results of those users who selected that option. In 2012, Karp went on record saying he is not "into moderating" NSFW content and that tumblr is "an excellent platform for porn," which he does not "personally have any moral opposition to" (Cheshire 2012). After the sale to Yahoo! in 2013, tumblr started tinkering with the visibility of sexual content in what Gillespie (2018: 173) has described as an attempt on Yahoo!'s part to both let "tumblr be tumblr" as well as sell ads. When invited to comment on the matter by talk show host Stephen Colbert, Karp maintained that tumblr had taken a pretty hard line on freedom of speech, arguing that he did not want to "go in there to draw the line between" art and behind the scenes photos of "Lady Gaga and like, her nip" (Dickey 2013). The Community Guideline clauses regarding NSFW content remained the same throughout updates in 2015, 2016, and 2017, although a link to "report unflagged NSFW content" was added in the 2016 update (tumblr 2016). In 2017 a stricter Safe Mode was introduced. The new system was quite complex, filtering blogs that were self-, moderator-, or automatically labeled as NSFW from the external and internal search results of all non-logged-on users and all logged-on users who were under the age of 18 (see Chapter 6).

In late 2018, to the great shock of tumblr users and scholars, Tumblr Inc. announced that it was banning all "photos, videos, or GIFs that show real-life human genitals or female-presenting nipples, and any content ... that depicts sex acts" to "keep the community safe" (staff 2018). The source of this sudden and radical change is twofold: the US Senate passed the twin bills of FOSTA/SESTA (Fight Online Sex Trafficking Act and Stop Enabling Sex Traffickers Act) amending the CDA 230 to allow internet intermediaries to be held responsible for "promoting or facilitating prostitution" or "knowingly assisting, facilitating or supporting sex trafficking,"[8] and tumblr's mobile app was briefly banned from Apple's App Store on the basis of claims that child pornography had been found on the site.[9] LGBTIQA+, fandom, sex worker, artist, and academic circles pointed out that the ban would destroy a unique, safe, and empowering space that many often-marginalized individuals and groups used for exploration of self and sexuality (Ashley 2019; Liao 2018).[10] Despite experts' and users' suggestions that there are better ways to deal with presumed child porn and increasing porn-bots,[11] or that perhaps the growing subsection of racist hate speech warrants attention (Tiidenberg 2019a), Tumblr Inc. went ahead with the ban as planned.

Although many users hoped that the NSFW ruling would be reversed under Automattic, CEO Mullenweg refuted that hope by citing the app stores' intolerance of NSFW content as the reason for the ban (Patel 2019). Sexually explicit content is still present on the platform, though its make-up and volume has changed. Based on our experiences, original visual content created by tumblr users themselves, often of themselves (see Chapter 6), is nearly gone. What remains is pornographic content: GIFs, videos, and still images from porn, which are much more explicit than selfies with female-presenting nipples ever were.

Algorithms

Algorithms are increasingly used to police user compliance to platform rules, but more broadly they shape flows of information, assign meaningfulness to content, and mold our participation in public life (Gillespie 2012; Langlois 2012). However, algorithms are usually invisible. They become noticeable to everyday users, when there are shifts in how they organize information, show or hide content, increase or reduce the visibility of the user's own content, recommend accounts or posts, or insert moneyed speech into one's line of sight. As algorithms themselves tend to be proprietary, researchers study their implications via users' algorithmic imaginaries (Bucher 2017) or algorithmic lore (Bishop 2020). This is what we will do to describe users' perceptions of and experiences with tumblr algorithms over the past decade.

tumblr's algorithms were experienced as comparatively unobtrusive until 2017. We link this to Tumblr Inc.'s particular approach to advertising and classifying users – up until 2015 they almost performatively refused targeted advertising (see Chapter 3). But it can also be linked to tumblr's vision, responses to user criticism. and historical "spam" problems (Perez 2011). There have almost always been spaces within the tumblr interface for recommended content, but users' reactions to it have been ambivalent. The now-defunct "spotlight" was introduced in 2011 and clearly articulated by tumblr, and experienced by users, as editorial and not algorithmic (staff 2011). Being featured on Spotlight was generally considered a good thing by users. In 2010 and 2011 even NSFW blogs could get recommended, if they were popular and original enough. "Radar" has been around since at least 2010 and "Recommended blogs" since 2011 (we were unable to precisely date these features). Users have imagined both to combine editorial and algorithmic techniques. There were many posts on and off tumblr articulating either how to increase one's chances to be featured in those spaces (e.g., tagging content with the #RadarPlz hashtag), or how to use a variety of browser add-ons to suppress them from one's Dashboard experience (see Chapter 3). Until the introduction of "Best Stuff First" in 2017, tumblr did not (noticeably) reorganize what users saw on their dashboard (staff 2017). Since 2020, tumblr recommendations have been made across sponsored posts, blogs, searches, and tags, which are demarcated as "sponsored." Within the mobile app there are additional categories of "recommended group chats," "recommended for you," and "watch on tumblr."

An early case of algorithmic imaginary (Bucher 2017) emerged after tumblr's 2012 policy against self-harm blogs. We noticed vernacular techniques circulating for backup hashtags and otherwise circumventing the algorithms among some thinspo blogs (Kanai et al. 2020; see also Chapter 7). Users' imaginaries of tumblr algorithms shifted more drastically with the 2017 Safe Mode, when algorithms were obviously and intrusively employed to filter content (see Chapter 6). Certain keywords, which returned results via browser, returned nothing on mobile apps because of app store restrictions. This included "#gay," because the data that the filtering algorithm was trained on had determined that the hashtag often accompanied pornographic content, but the LGBTIQA+ community rightfully interpreted this as an outright attack. tumblr managed to placate users by reversing some of the changes, promising to work on more intelligent solutions for battling porn bots and filtering content, and primarily by demonstrating that they were listening. Their resolution of this particular governance conflict showed that they understood that moderation involves a politics of visibility (Gillespie 2018), which in the case of sexual self-expression often follows the fault lines of systematic marginalization (e.g., disenfranchising the LGBTIQA+ community).

This understanding seemed to have evaporated by the time of the NSFW ban in 2018. tumblr's Help page claimed that the new ban was enforced through a "mix of machine-learning classification and human moderation from our team of trained experts," wherein appeals regarding misflagged posts would be reviewed by humans (tumblr Help Center 2018). tumblr's classification algorithms (usually referred to as flagging algorithms or flagging bots in vernacular discourse) were shockingly bad and the public backlash against them spanned platforms (Tiidenberg 2019a). While differentiating permitted nudity (mastectomy or gender-confirming scars, breastfeeding) from prohibited nudity ("female presenting nipples," any depictions of sex) is indeed a matter of contextual awareness, which automation is bound to fail at, tumblr's algorithms flagged images of food, knitting, and Joe Biden. Based on industry standards of image recognition, this was a spectacularly poor performance. Trade press and experts speculated that it stemmed from tumblr having trained their algorithms on insufficient datasets, using inaccurate platform models or weak classifiers; further, tumblr's new, black box algorithms were presumed to have identified patterns between objects in images that the developers did not teach it to identify, which led it to mistakenly flag content (Matsakis 2018). This led to users speculating and experimenting with various visual-aesthetic and discursive-logistic workarounds for circumventing tumblr's image recognition algorithm. A networked and loosely shared pool of algorithmic imaginaries and hacks emerged, where, in order to hide from the algorithmic gaze, bloggers would take sexy selfies in flesh-colored silk stockings or bodysuits, cover nipples with stickers or digital special effects (Figure 1.5), and superimpose text or QR codes onto the images.

At the same time, viewers were asked to refrain from liking, reblogging, or replying to posts, in the hope of remaining hidden from the algorithm. After the initial period, when flagged posts were equipped with a reporting button to address the mistakes, all flagged posts and blogs were forcibly made private, essentially rendering them invisible and inaccessible to everyone but the author. NSFW content hashtagged with culturally specific NSFW Chinese or Japanese words or in Chinese or Japanese characters ("#変態" or "hentai" and "#露點" or "ludian," connoting exposed private parts) remained on the site for a couple of months longer, but

Figure 1.5: Artist's impression of how some tumblr users are using emoji to cover nipples and circumvent flagging, while still being able to share nudes. Art provided by River Juno.

was eventually removed as well. Needless to say, tumblr's algorithms were no longer experienced as unobtrusive after that.

Conclusion

This chapter mapped how tumblr has been built, the features and functions that enable bloggers to create, post, reblog, and interact with each other, as well as how tumblr is governed and how bloggers are managed by the platform. In our research, our participants have continued to stress that tumblr is a unique platform, distinct from others that enact more punitive or restrictive moderation (even following tumblr's porn ban) or those that demand particular identifications or self-presentation based on real names and individual profiles. In the following chapter, we pick up this line of inquiry to map how tumblr bloggers' perceptions and uses of the platform birthed a variety of cultures, a recognizable vernacular, a shared sensibility, and a very specific form of sociality.

2

tumblr sociality

Eric: tumblr is great in bringing out niche/cult followings for things

Anna: And tumblr is hard to break up with. I know one person who has left and has allegedly not created a new blog, but he keeps reading my blog still, so it doesn't even count. And then I know like 10 people who have left and keep coming back

Nadine: Yeah, tumblr is weirdly addictive and the people become strangely intimate.

Luna: But that's it tho, isn't it ... tumblr is hard to break up with ... because you have your people whom you love and you have your relationships and you often take them elsewhere too, like email or skype or whatever, but if they then leave tumblr it's not the same

Nadine: It's strange when people leave

Luna: Their blog and your blog are an extra layer of that relationship. I kind of feel that I have relationships with my tumblr friends and then I have a relationship with tumblr. With like ... the ability to throw bits of myself at the wall and know that someone will engage with the splatter in an open and non judgy way

Nadine: Yeah, when I first found tumblr, I like literally had nowhere else to really express this stuff. And so it was a really good outlet

Eric: tumblr is an outlet for whatever you want, be it a specific area like sex or music or be it a more general "here's me and here's you" way

Anna: And I think its fun to look back at your blog overtime, like archaeology

(Outtake from group interview by authors, 2015)

This chapter analyzes tumblr as a social space. We focus on how the platform is used by people who – while stewarded, incited, or restrained by its vision, governance protocols, features, and functions (Chapter 1) – perceive and use the platform in diverse ways, not all of which adhere to what the developers intended. We explore how people imagine what they can do on tumblr (affordances), what tumblr-specific styles and genres of communication emerge (platform vernacular), and how users evaluate each other's behavior (platform sensibility). All of this leads to and explains tumblr's very distinct silosociality, which this chapter also conceptualizes.

tumblr affordances

In order to explain how people's practices and platform structures interrelate, the concept of "affordances" is increasingly used. At its most basic, affordances are the possibilities of action, describing "what material artifacts, such as media technologies, allow people to do" (Bucher and Helmond 2017: 235). Platform affordances shape and constrain how people use platforms and what the sociality on those platforms looks and feels like. Affordances are always perceived. Recent work also takes care to distinguish affordances from objects, features, or their outcomes (Evans et al. 2017), while reminding us that affordances have range; variably requesting, demanding, allowing, encouraging, discouraging, or refusing specific actions (Davis and Chouinard 2017). For example, due to the rules and features we discussed in the previous chapter, tumblr encourages pseudonymity, while Facebook refuses, or at least strongly discourages it. tumblr's signature reblog button is not an affordance, despite sometimes being cast as such. However, it is a feature that affords speedy and wide circulation of content. The affordance emerging from the reblog feature is thus scalability (sometimes also called "spreadability").

Most platforms seem to have the same high-level affordances (Bucher and Helmond 2017) like persistence, replicability, scalability, searchability, and anonymity (boyd 2010; Halpern and Gibbs 2013). However, if different platforms are used in ways that lead to different outcomes, there have to be some differences in their affordances. Scholars have focused on various outcomes in their discussions of tumblr, proposing that tumblr affords counterpublic communication (Renninger 2014), expressions of queer affect (Cho 2015a, 2015b), nonbinary gender labeling (Oakley 2016), polyvocal and inter-textual expressions of humor and relatability (Vásquez and Creel 2017), imagined intimacy (Hendry 2020b), feminist self-expression (Kanai 2017; Ringrose and Lawrence 2018), and trans* transitioning (Haimson et al. 2019).[1]

However, no systematic effort has so far been made to map tumblr's affordances and how they are distinct from those of other platforms. Based on our analysis of tumblr, we argue that it affords:

- *High pseudonymity*, meaning it is easy to remain pseudonymous on the platform. This is possible because tumblr asks for minimal personal information, allows multifaceted identity presentations via secondary blogs, and permits pseudonymous accounts. The affordance of high pseudonymity plays a crucial role in users feeling that they can communicate safely and in an open manner.
- *High scalability*, meaning there is high potential for content to spread and reach various audiences. This is primarily made possible by the reblog button, the features that de-prioritize the social graph and the ease of making a variety of post types that circulate various content. High scalability facilitates networks and practices geared toward shared interest and affect. It is important to note that tumblr content has high cross-platform scalability as well; Facebook pages, YouTube videos, listicle websites like Buzzfeed often create content by curating tumblr posts (see Chapter 3).

- *Low searchability*, meaning that things are, because of the conversational tags, poor search features, and no formal grouping structures, difficult to find for the uninitiated. Further, the prevalence of reblogged content and the lack of copyright or intellectual property enforcement makes authorship collaborative (Cho 2015b; Munteanu 2017). Together, this "grants users a sense of freedom ... you just keep going without knowing what you're going to find" (Keller 2019: 8).
- *High multimodality*, meaning that content and conversations on the platform are in the form of text, image, video, GIF, meme, link, tag, etc. This is possible because uploading multimodal content is made easy and as copyright is not enforced.
- *High interactivity*, meaning primarily that users interact with each others' ideas and content, but also with each other via the nuanced ecosystem of interactional features and functions described in the previous chapter, and because they actively reblog each others' content. Pseudonymity, the prevalence of secondary blogs and the reblog feature further encourage interaction between strangers.
- *Low reactivity*, meaning that while interaction, especially with content and ideas, is encouraged by the platform, knee-jerk reactions and signposting of sentiments cannot be easily registered and collated. This is because tumblr collapses the quick reaction buttons (e.g., "hearts" on Twitter; "like," "love," "laugh," "wow," "sad," "angry" emoji on Facebook) and metric counters (e.g., number of "upvotes" and "downvotes" on Reddit; number of "likes" on Instagram) that are popular on other mainstream Silicon Valley platforms into a singular number of "notes." tumblr also refuses public comments; instead, the platform encourages engaging and interacting (rather than merely reacting to) with other people's content through reblogs and replies.

- *High nonlinear temporality*, by which we mean that due to the reblog feature, nonreciprocal Follow, unobtrusive-seeming algorithmic manipulation and lack of formal grouping structures foster "unfamiliar modes of temporal engagement" (Fink and Miller 2014), leading to the "reverb" (Cho 2015b) and "both an ephemeral and timeless feel" (Popova 2017), where some posts recirculate forever, others blink briefly before being forgotten, and many (networks of) blogs still function as archives.

We suggest that a set of affordances with ranges (high or low) communicates which actions tumblr is perceived as encouraging or demanding and which as discouraging or refusing. A set of affordance variability rather than a blunt list of affordances is a more fine-tuned tool for making sense of platforms as social spaces and for understanding how platforms differ from each other. The set of affordances we put forward have encouraged actions, practices, and meaning-making that have, since the start of tumblr, converged into a recognizable platform vernacular, to which we now turn our attention.

tumblr vernacular

Each social media platform has a vernacular: a combination of communication practices, conventions, and registers of meaning and affect, which emerge from platform affordances and their mundane, everyday enactment in practice (Gibbs et al. 2014: 257). Just as most social media platforms have the same high-level affordances, so too do most platform vernaculars involve audience-aware self-expression (Shifman 2016), collaborative creation (Östman 2012), and registers of consumability and authenticity (Marwick and boyd 2011). However, each platform's vernacular has to be unique enough to be recognizable to users and sometimes even nonusers of that platform. Leaver et al. (2020) refer to this as "templat-ability," where, if users recognize and are able to replicate the platforms' template of participating and communicating, they are able to tumblr, Instagram, or Facebook (as verbs) in accordance with the local logics, grammars, and norms of those social spaces. Arguing that a platform has a recognizable vernacular does not mean that all communication within that platform follows the same style, logics, and registers (Warfield 2016).

We suggest that tumblr's unique and recognizable platform vernacular comprises communication practices that are *curatorial, multimodal,* and *multiply literate*; communication conventions that rely on affective investments and *personal testimonials*; and registers of meaning and affect that are, first, very *affective* – this has always been a platform of "feels" – but more specifically, based on shared *interest* and *affinity*. We will briefly discuss all of these.

Curatorial

We cast most of what people do on tumblr as social curation, which is often described as consisting of (1) discovering and selecting content, (2) cataloguing it, and then (3) interpreting, framing, and sharing it (Clark and Aufderheide 2009; Lupfer et al. 2016; Potter 2015; Seitzinger 2014). A blog can be a tightly curated performance, or a loosely curated collection of stuff that might have nothing more in common than that it was all selected, framed, and shared by one person. How tightly or loosely people curate depends on whether they curate for expressive purposes like self-presentation and privacy management, inward-facing purposes like selective looking (Davis 2017) or to make personal yet collaborative "(trans)personal/(trans)media archives" (Munteanu 2017: 148). Similar to art curation, social curation on tumblr can imbue objects with new significance, extending their circulation or catapulting them from obscurity (Villi 2012). Being reblogged by a popular tumblr user can vastly enhance the visibility of any blog post (see Chapter 3). Skillful curation is appreciated on the platform as a form of vernacular creativity (Burgess 2006), with many of the more popular blogs having made their name by curating rather than creating original content.

Further, curation allows expression by proxy (Seitzinger 2014), often in face-saving ways (see Chapters 6 and 7). Posting something someone else has made as a stand-in for one's own thoughts or feelings mitigates risk and thus encourages being open and even vulnerable about one's experiences (Hendry 2020b; Shorey 2015; Tiidenberg and Whelan 2017). As mentioned in Chapter 1, when we introduced the reblog, tumblr curation is often used to reimagine and reappropriate content in order to reframe it. This can function as curatorial activism (Reilly 2018), but can also – when such curation happens in a constantly moving flow – birth a new mode of "aesthetics of circulation" (Tedone 2017). Curating on tumblr thus generates a particular flow of aesthetics and affect. Media scholar Dinu Munteanu (2017: 146–8) has described it as the making of "psycho-aesthetic points," to collaboratively "calibrate and continuously stylize" communal discourse. This makes it possible – and here Munteanu cites Martinon (2013) – to jailbreak pre-existing frames, invent new points of departure, create allegiances against social ills, renew one's own subjectivity, do politics, and maintain community.

Multimodal, multiliterate, and affective

tumblr users engage with ideas and content through extreme close reading of cultural texts (Gürsimsek 2016), but collapse "boundaries between affect and social critique" (McCracken 2017: 152) in their interpretations of and reactions to that content. Things are "good" or rebloggable on tumblr, because they feel right, not because they meet some "objective" standards of quality. Thus, tumblr vernacular is multimodal

and remix-driven, but fueled primarily by affective investments and political stakes rather than "cultural hierarchies of
'quality'" (McCracken 2017: 152).

In order to recognize, "get," and be able to participate in
tumblr vernacular, one needs a combinatory literacy (Kanai
2019). It spans pop culture literacies (i.e., knowledge of
TV shows, pop music, memes), transmedia literacies (i.e.,
GIF making), ideological literacies (i.e., sensitivity to social
justice and intersectionality), representational literacies (i.e.,
an antiracist, antisexist stance in assessing pop-cultural representations), and affective literacies (i.e., a shared imaginary
that allows a joke to work, or disapproval to be expressed),
in addition to whatever interest-driven literacy is needed to
partake in a particular conversation or silo. This is why it
usually takes some time and commitment for people to really
get into tumblr. You have to (l)earn it.

Expressed through personal testimonials

Almost everything on tumblr is expressed through personal
narratives and experiences (McCracken 2017). People talk
about fandom, identity, everyday life, sex, health, or politics
by sharing personal experiences, thoughts, dreams, and
anxieties. Even jokes and memes are often in first-person
narrative form – we talked about me-chat in Chapter 1, will
discuss #gpoy and #me posts in Chapter 6, and doublevoicing
in #fp chat memes in Chapter 7. This style of communication tends to trigger affective responses and mobilize
social attitudes and political impulses and invite responses
that "reference a shared social imaginary" (Kanai 2019: 72).
The style of personal testimonials varies. In some groups
and communities, negative affect is tempered with humor
in order to practice a carefully curated form of relatability. In
others, a raw, confessional, or even "overshary" style is evident
(Haimson et al. 2019; Seko and Lewis 2018; Tiidenberg and
van der Nagel 2020).

Interest and affinity based

People's experience of tumblr is first and foremost interest-driven. Most users will have found tumblr as they were searching for information, conversations, or content pertaining to an interest they often felt was difficult to satisfy elsewhere. Because of this, the (imagined) shared interest breeds affinity and even a sense of community. This is why people often refer to their tumblr as a community or speak of a specific tumblr. "Queer tumblr is upset today," someone will say, or "the latest episode broke the SPN [*Supernatural*, the TV show] tumblr."

Together, these elements make up the communication styles, norms, and practices that are recognizably tumblresque, but not in a universal, monolithic way across the platform. There is variation in how different groups enact curation, multimodality, multiliteracy, affective investments, personal testimonials, and interest-based affinity. To illustrate this: fans curate multimodal posts that express their affective investment in their particular fandom, such as K-pop (see Chapter 4), while tumblr users with mental health concerns share personal testimonials about their emotional experiences, which are multimodal and remixed to allow sharing not only "what" they have experienced, but "how" it feels to live with mental health challenges (see Chapter 7). In both cases, the dominant register of meaning and affect stems from a shared interest and affinity, but the literacies needed to partake are different, as is the focus of the personal testimonials and the style and functionality of the multimodality of content.

tumblr sensibility

Finally, tumblr as a social space is shaped by a shared sensibility, which is the dominant way of making sense of, and assigning, moral value on the platform. It comprises *shared norms* (which are users' learned rules for acceptable and unacceptable behavior; Parsons 1951), *ethics* (which is how users relate to themselves; Foucault 2005), and *small-p politics* (which are the "small-scale, often individual decisions and actions that have either a political or ethical frame of reference (or both) and remain submerged in everyday life"; Bakardjieva 2009: 96). The shared sensibility is a part of tumblr's vernacular, so we could have addressed it in the preceding section, but the fact that norms, ethics, or politics are part of tumblr's recognizable vernacular – and arguably not such a recognizable part of Facebook's or Instagram's[2] – is why we have decided to discuss them separately. Yes, people adhere to norms of self-presentation and interaction on every platform, and these reflect broader cultural norms amplified by platform rules and moderation policies. But we argue that on a level useful for analyzing platforms as social spaces, most do not share norms, just like they do not form a singular community. Rather, they host many groups and communities with different norms. Now, this is also true for tumblr. There are various fan, queer, mental health, and kink communities, but also queer fan communities, communities of people living with borderline personality disorder, queer mental health communities, kinky social justice communities. These have different localized norms regarding spoiler alerts, trigger warnings, acceptable questions, compliments, comments, feedback, body positivity, sexual explicitness, etc. We argue that above these, tumblr has a broader recognizable normative, ethical, and political sensibility, which can be described as an *orientation toward social justice* (see Chapter 5) and a related commitment to maintaining one's experience of tumblr as a *safe space* (Muise 2011; Wood 2008).

This sensibility speaks through the elements we listed as making up its "vernacular." Content and conversations on tumblr often disrupt cultural production hierarchies and encourage ethical or political metanarrative construction

(Fotopoulou and Couldry 2017). This can be seen in the fandom tumblr (see Chapter 4). Further, tumblr users practice "curatorial activism" (Reilly 2018), where lesser-known or radically different stories and histories are purposefully highlighted to decenter institutionalized racism, sexism, and homophobia. This is the case in the NSFW tumblr (see Chapter 6). Affinity is sometimes born of shared norms, ethics, or politics, as is the case with some queer and mental health communities (see Chapters 5 and 7), but even when it emerges from a shared interest (e.g., loving K-pop or practicing ethical non-monogamy), groups will develop a shared ethical or a political sensibility. In those cases the community's social justice orientation might be enacted through discursive and activist efforts around issues of copyright, cultural representation, acknowledgment of intersectionality in identities, heteronormativity, body normativity, queer rights, or any entanglements thereof. This helps maintain what the users feel is a safe space, which, in turn, has been shown to lead to more radical political (Keller 2019), and more vulnerable-personal (Tiidenberg 2017; Tiidenberg and Whelan 2019) self-expression. Safe space experiences thus reinforce the commitment to social justice, and vice versa.

While a shared sensibility focused on social justice and safe spaces may sound like something that leads to uniformly positive experiences, it can tip over into what has been described as toxic call-out culture or harassing users deemed "problematic" (examples in Chapters 3, 4, 5, 6, and 7). While fighting racism and sexism and critiquing queer representations is the norm on tumblr (Morimoto 2018), this commitment to highlighting social wrongs can lead to harassment and even bullying (see Chapter 5 for a case study of fanartist *Zamiio70*). Maintaining a boundary between communication that creates inclusive and safe spaces, and that which transforms into overzealous and unempathetic dogpiling, can be difficult. Further, tumblr's shared social justice orientation has become not only its recognizable calling card, but also a source of ridicule (see Chapter 5 for analysis of the social justice warrior discourse).

Silosociality

We suggest that the best way to make sense of tumblr as a social space is via the concept of *silosociality*. Tumblr users experience tumblr in silos[3] that are defined by people's shared interests, but sustained through inward-facing shared vernacular and sensibility, made possible by tumblr's features, functions, and rules (see Figure 2.1). In later chapters, we will take a closer, empirical look at fandom (Chapter 4), queer (Chapter 5), NSFW (Chapter 6), and mental health (Chapter 7) silos. These are not the only silos on tumblr, and each of them may contain subsilos and communities. However, as noted in the Introduction, these four are, according to our own and our colleagues' fieldwork, large as well as noticeable both on tumblr and outside it, and thus best characterize both tumblr as a platform and silosociality as a concept. Silos are users' experiential tumblrs, and silosociality is about feelings of connection rather than metric-driven connection. We think of silos here as containers for how people feel on and about tumblr. Silos *feel* separate, and that is the point.

What are silos?

Silos have taken on a negative connotation in business discourses, as the word has been used to indicate how some groups or departments isolate themselves from others within an organization, thus hindering communication and cooperation. We would like to wrestle the word back from the market-based and efficiency-driven discourse and use it in its base meaning of "something deep, intended for storing valuable stuff." While grain silos are usually sealed, coal, sand, and silt silos are not. When we talk about silos on tumblr, we want to highlight that these are *felt* and *imagined*

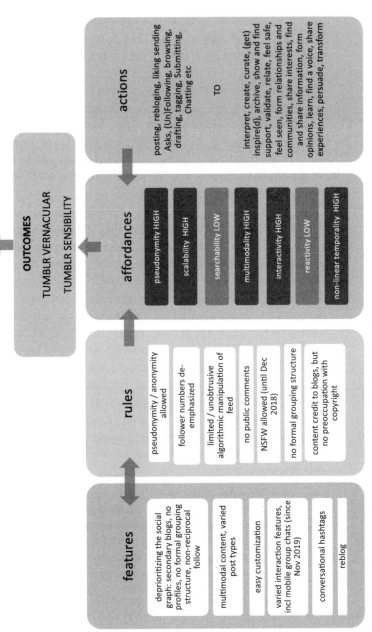

Figure 2.1: A diagram mapping out tumblr silosociality. Image by authors.

and experienced as somewhat sequestered from each other. That is why they feel so nice. That is why they are referred to as safe spaces. That is why they offer a sense of escape. That is why each one needs to be learned separately. tumblr silos are not hermetically sealed; moving from one to another is obviously possible, but it takes a certain amount of effort and insider knowledge. Inside silos, tumblr users display cohesive reblogging practices and often publicly reference their relationships to other users (Neill Hoch 2018). They imagine an audience that is literate in the local shared vernacular (Dame 2016).

People within silos have put in the effort to find others, with whom they share something they consider important – an identity, a lifestyle, an attitude, love for a fictional pairing. They have learned the vernacular and they accept the shared sensibility. But silosociality is also what makes tumblr disorienting to newcomers, who have described joining the platform as "being blindfolded and feeling your way through a new room" (Cho 2015b: 66), or where it is "hard to keep track of where everything goes and where everything comes from" (Munteanu 2017: 137). If a first-time user does not find something that sparks their interest or affinity with others, and consequently a silo, they often leave the platform. The effort needed to "get" it then doesn't seem worth it. Illustrating this, in one of our projects, 16-year-old Cleo described how, in 2015, she found tumblr too overwhelming, and never returned:

> Cleo [*laughing*]: I had tumblr for about a day. So I created it, and I tried to change my profile picture to a picture of a rabbit. But then I don't know what was happening, and I just kept reblogging this picture of a rabbit. I was getting overwhelmed by this stage, because I didn't know what was happening ... my profile picture wasn't changing and I couldn't find the log out button. So that was, that was the end of that for tumblr and I. There was too much going on for me.

If, however, a user finds something that sparks their interest, they still need to put in the time and the effort to get acquainted with tumblr's functionality, its vernacular and understand the shared sensibility. This is not obvious, and our participants do have experiences of failing in this. However, the drive to try again after failing further illustrates the power of the affinity we are trying to describe here. Dan, an American man in his early forties, commented on his first attempt at NSFW tumblr:

> Dan: I just posted things with no idea on how someone would read it. When I finally figured out people "follow" each other I tried doing that. But unfortunately, I was like the Anons I rage against today. "Here's my cock, show me your boobs." Yeah – I did that. And I got angry about it, when it didn't work, and said some not nice things to someone. I deleted that blog that day and started this blog minutes later. Thankfully that woman kept checking on me and re-followed me once she realized I learned my lesson. She's one of my best unknown tumblr friends now.

Tumblr Inc. recognizes how feeling disoriented can turn new users away from the platform. Over time tumblr's designers and engineers have reoriented the onboarding process to help new users not only to customize their blogs, but to start out with first following some blogs to make sure their dashboard has some interesting stuff on it (see Chapter 1).

Primarily, it is important to understand that silosociality is not about the separation of content or even users – it is about the separation of *context*. This means that silosociality makes very little sense on the level of a single post. A post is not silo-specific. Posts are reblogged, shared, remixed, and remade across the platform. One blogger, too, may belong to multiple silos – usually with different blogs. Toggling between them is the imaginary climbing out of one silo and into another. This means that when people move across and between silos, they often need to pay attention to the local variations of vernacular and sensibilities for that silo.

How does silosociality function?

Silos can lead to an ambivalent "love/hate" relationship with tumblr. This is because affect and affinity concentrate and intensify within silos. Silos offer people a sense of escape, belonging, and relief, and function as spaces of intense learning, sometimes in ways that increase people's agency. Imagine it like this: tumblr's affordances of pseudonymity and multifaceted self-presentation and its vernacular of personal testimonials and affective engagement create a sense of safe space and intensify the experience of affinity and escape. This intensity – when paired with the fact that interest-based silos often allow people to converge around topics they cannot discuss elsewhere, and that silos often validate and celebrate what users have been discriminated for or embarrassed about – makes the silo feel important for one's well-being, identity, and politics, and thus worth maintaining or protecting. This, in turn introduces call-outs, virtue-signaling, and normative performances of the "right way" of being in order to protect or maintain that experience.

We are not the only ones who have noticed this. Media and gender scholar Andre Cavalcante (2019: 2) has described queer tumblr both as a bubble that increases and sustains users' "political agency, possibility, community, and hope," and as a queer vortext of too-intense social interactions, information bubbles, and potentially dark or harmful niche communities. The feminist teenage girls researched by media scholar Jessalynn Keller (2019), in turn, used the notion of a black hole to describe their social justice tumblr.

This is why research that relies on scraping data combined under a tumblr tag can only ever be the beginning of making sense of tumblr, and why tumblr was, for years, understudied and difficult for Tumblr Inc. to monetize. tumblr was simply composed of too many worlds that rarely spoke with each other and could not be streamlined into a coherent brand-safe and brand-aligned space for corporate monetization. It is why the ability to curate tumblr became a legitimate genre and a source of popularity – evidenced in the wide spread of tumblr content on Facebook or Twitter, or in Buzzfeed listicle articles (see Chapter 3). You need to dive deep to uncover the good stuff. The only way to access, "get," and leverage silos is by being a part of them, and that requires literacy, which is only achievable through immersion. By current standards of social media, this is a somewhat slow process. Silosociality functions like an affective, discursive, intuitive gate (Cho 2015b: 66), because while most tumblr blogs are publicly accessible, there is no blueprint for how to find and experience things, or to discover what is out there in the first place.

Broader implications of silosociality

We argue that tumblr is characterized by silosociality, that it stands out within the ecosystem of social media because of silosociality, and that it is silosociality that made tumblr into a shaping force of twenty-first-century digital cultures. Conceptually, silosociality has similarities to what others have discussed as online communities, networked publics, affinity spaces, back places, social worlds and arenas, but does not neatly map onto any of these.

Silos are similar to online communities, but while communities consist of people who share a sense of space, activities, and identities, form close relationships, and offer each other social support (Baym 2015; Tiidenberg and van der Nagel 2020), not all silos do so. But silos can and sometimes do include communities (see Chapter 6 for an example of a sexy selfie community that is part of the NSFW silo). Silos are, for us, communal, but broader and looser than communities. While networked publics and online or digital communities have been used interchangeably, technology scholar danah boyd (2010: 39) refers to networked publics as "the space[s] constructed through networked technologies and ... the imagined collective that emerges as a result of the intersection of people, technology, and practice ... they allow people to gather for social, cultural, and civic purposes, and they help people connect with a world beyond their close friends and family." Although tumblr silos may be examples of networked publics (especially, perhaps, intimate or affective networked counterpublics), we feel that networked publics are more transient than silos, more often rely on a technological boundary (a forum, a hashtag), and have fewer shared imaginaries like the vernacular and sensibility we described. Silos, in our thinking, are more affectively and experientially coherent and more stable than networked publics.

While theories of subculture emerging from the Chicago School and the Birmingham School (Gelder and Thornton 1997), as well as subsequent post-subcultural iterations including "neo-tribes" (Maffesoli 1996), also share qualities with silos, we want to center on how, as a platform, tumblr configures possibilities of sociality. This, we argue, is missing from debates about (post-) subcultural analyses of socially mediated sociality. Neo-tribes refer to groups of people who cohere around a sense of closeness and shared practices where the boundaries are fluid and membership is transient (Hardy et al. 2018). Similarly, silos share closeness and while their boundaries are surmountable, we would not define them as porous. Silos are also clearly tumblr afforded, while neo-tribes and subcultures are mostly defined as emergent from broader cultural hierarchies and dynamics.

Erving Goffman's "back places" (distinct from "backstage") could also be used to understand silos as spaces of like-others, "where persons of the individual's kind stand exposed and find they need not try to conceal their stigma, nor be overly concerned with cooperatively trying to disattend it ... the place is likely to provide an atmosphere of special piquancy" (1963: 81). While Goffman positions back places as spaces of ease, we stress that silos may offer reprieve or escape from everyday and mediated stressors, but they are not necessarily always spaces of ease or freedom. Additionally, not all silos are responses to shared stigma, which means that for us, silos may hold back places, just as they may hold communities, but are not back places themselves.

We could, in line with grounded theory thinkers (Strauss 1978), make sense of tumblr silos as "social arenas" made up of multiple, and sometimes contradictory, "social worlds." Social worlds are shared relational, discursive spaces, which, when organized "ecologically around issues of mutual concern and commitment to action" comprise an arena (Clarke and Star 2008: 113). However, in our reading, the framework of social worlds and arenas presumes too much collective action for us to feel comfortable about taking over the concepts wholesale.

Finally, there are notable parallels between what we describe as silosociality with what linguistics scholar James Paul Gee (2004) calls "affinity spaces," and what Ito et al. (2018) describe as "online affinity networks." For Gee, affinity spaces are places "where people affiliate with others based primarily on shared activities, interests, and goals, not shared race, class culture, ethnicity, or gender" (2004: 67). He studied affinity spaces in gaming and applied what he observed to learning, arguing that affinity spaces encourage knowledge sharing, as they do not segregate participants by experience levels and allow everyone to create and value individual, distributed, dispersed as well as tacit knowledge. Ito et al. distinguish between "friendship-driven" modes of connection on Facebook or instant messaging apps, and "interest-driven" participation on platforms that allow for different forms of content creation, sharing, curation, and identity building. tumblr users too, experience silos as sites of affinity, interest, and learning, but we think that silos center affect more than affinity spaces do, and allow for the possibility of race, class, ethnicity, or gender being the force that affinity sticks to.

We offer the concept of silosociality as a contribution to the field of social media studies beyond understanding tumblr proper. Our argument is that tumblr's silosociality helps us to critically re-think social media, interrogate how it is structured, see what kinds of sociality its structures encourage, and understand what (unintended) consequences this may lead to. Early internet researchers and their research participants spoke of the web at the turn of the century as an escape from various constrictions, injustices, or the mundane tediousness of everyday life (Baym 2000; boyd 2014; Markham 1998; Waskul 2007). tumblr users have persistently reported the same; however, they frame their tumblr silos as also offering escape from the rest of social media and the rest of the internet. The sins and scandals of popular social media platforms collapse into a collective imaginary of a tiring, noisy, manipulative space that is more often than not toxic to those already marginalized because of their race, gender, sexual identity, ability, or political beliefs. tumblr experienced through silos is the escape.

Silosocial media emulates the smaller, more manageable, at least partially self-regulating and self-moderating communities of the early internet. It runs a lesser risk of context collapse, making it a more pleasant, safe-feeling, creative-seeming, and justice-oriented social space for users. It does not lock people into group structures, allowing for freshness and openness that comes with affinity-based interaction. Silosociality looks inwards rather than outwards; it is about consolidating content and practices, rather than focusing on the broadest possible distribution, circulation, and sharing. This is not to say that sharing posts is irrelevant to silosociality – reblogging is central to the platform – but rather that silosociality generally orients users to contextual sharing within their silo.

Dominant social media platforms have become incomprehensibly huge. They variously have very low barriers of entry and rarely afford group sociality; they foster information disorder and attention manipulation and enforce inescapable real-name connectivity and pervasive corporate and governmental surveillance. In contrast, our research participants articulate being able to slip into their tumblr silo as a pleasure, a relief, and a "life saver." Even if many of tumblr's populace have moved on, silo-like places that allow one to escape from the world and the more demanding or manipulative corners of the internet will continue to be invaluable. Silosocial experiences and connections are likely to persist beyond tumblr. Silosociality, arguably, is a potential route forward for social media as an industry, faced as it is with increasingly critical, publicity-weary and surveillance-fatigued constituencies, where the only escape seems to be digital detox or disconnection. Of course, how silosociality can or will extend into the future, and whether the platform economy will break it, remains to be seen (see Conclusion).

Conclusion

tumblr as a social space has afforded an emergence of a shared vernacular and sensibility, which shape how tumblr is used and what it feels like. We argue that this produces tumblr's unique silosociality and contributes to how people imagine tumblr to be oriented toward social justice. tumblr's silosociality allows users to escape the demands of other platforms. However, silos carry an intensity, which means that they are not necessarily utopias devoid of conflict or toxicity. We come back to the challenges of silos throughout the book. In the next chapter, we discuss how attention works on tumblr for Tumblr Inc.

3

fame

The idea of being "tumblr famous" has always been baffling. For one, most of our tumblr experience has indicated that while posts and tumblogs do go viral, they are usually not celebrated or noticed beyond having their username indicated in tiny font at the top or bottom of a post. tumblr culture has also been largely pseudoymous, which makes claims to fame and celebrity feel futile. And yet, our dash is often peppered with tumblr memes in which users proudly speak of the "double lives" that they lead, between the highs of having "tumblr fame" and the lows of being "alone and unknown" offline. What is "tumblr fame"? What does it mean to be "tumblr famous"? Is there money in it? Where is the money on tumblr?"

(Katrin Tiidenberg, Natalie Ann Hendry, and Crystal Abidin)

In this chapter we explore how attention is capitalized on tumblr. We look at the flows of attention that emerge from the platform as a *built* space (see Chapter 1), the platform as a *silosocial space* (see Chapter 2), and the attention-hacking techniques that the platform affordances sponsor. We explore how platform vernacular and sensibility are used to skillfully (and less skillfully) direct where, how, and when attention flows. We argue that on tumblr, specific discursive techniques of self-expression are used to harness attention and sometimes these techniques become adver-tising templates. We then discuss three types of commerce that explain tumblr as a commodified space: platform commerce, which is essentially tumblr's business model; brand commerce, which is when corporate entities try to earn profit as middlemen of tumblr attention; and vernacular commerce, where individual users somehow capitalize on their tumblr skills.

Attention flows

As mentioned in Chapter 2, users experience tumblr through their silos. Attention is born in and flows through silos most easily, although it also flows across silos and even out of and into tumblr, carrying trends and content. Unlike on most other popular social media platforms, algorithmic interference and gamification is rarely imagined as playing an important part in attention flows on tumblr. Rather, our fieldwork has indicated that jacking into a silo or wrestling attention away from one requires a degree of vernacular literacy, eloquence, or wit. Like everything else on tumblr, orchestrating attention flows on the platform relies on users' abilities to *get* tumblr. tumblr has its recognizable techniques and taxonomies of stickiness, which rely on the platform vernacular and sensibility (Chapter 2) and which become observable in what we call discursive strategies for attention hacking.

Discursive strategies for attention hacking

To explain how attention flows on tumblr, we build on previous work undertaken by Crystal Abidin on tacit visibility labor, or "the work individuals do when they … curate their self-presentations so as to be noticeable and positively prominent" among various audiences (2016a: 5), but which is "so thoroughly rehearsed that it appears as effortless and subconscious" (2016b: 10). Unlike studies on algorithmic visibility (Bucher 2012: 116), this focuses on the "analogue affective labor [that] ordinary users perform to be noticed" (Abidin 2016a: 5). On tumblr, visibility labor is undertaken through discursive strategies that users have fashioned out of their vernacular literacies and their mindfulness of the shared sensibility. We illustrate six such strategies via a series of exemplary and highly reblogged posts.

Linguistic wit

tumblr's multimodal, remixed, and multiply literate vernacular (see Chapter 2) is often fashioned into a strategy of *linguistic wit*, drawing on skills such as paralanguages or "the non-lexical component of communication by speech, for example intonation, pitch and speed of speaking, hesitation noises, gesture, and facial expression" (Lexico 2020);[1] code-switching or "the use of one dialect, register, accent, or language variety over another, depending on social or cultural context, to project a specific identity" (Dictionary.com 2020); vernacular creativity or "the wide range of everyday creative practices ... practiced outside the cultural value systems of either high culture or commercial creative practice" (Burgess and Green 2009: 25); and social steganography or "hiding messages in plain sight by leveraging shared knowledge and cues embedded in particular social contexts" (boyd 2014, 65) for users to encode, convey, decode, and receive multiple layers of meaning from a single post. In Figure 3.1, the first blogger posits that a hallmark of "millennial culture" is the ability to have "two wildly different conversations with the same person on two different apps at the exact same time." To this, a second blogger reblogs an illustration of two concurrent conversational threads: The first is a deliberate misspelling of "cheese burger" and is meant to connote a subgenre of "dank memes,"[2] and the second is what appears to be a deeply emotive confession of struggles with trust. Such parallel conversations conventionally happen between tumblr mutuals, who maintain ongoing conversations on both their more public "main" tumblogs or other, real-name based social media, and the more secretive "side" tumblogs.

Figure 3.1: Artist's impression of a tumblr meme displaying linguistic wit native to tumblr, originally sighted by the authors in posts from *transjemder* and *poorlytimed*. Art provided by River Juno.

Call-out culture

tumblr's vernacular of personal testimonials and the shared sensibility of social justice commitments (see Chapter 2) supports an emergence of a *call-out culture*, asserting that the most socially aware and informed users should be attuned to structural inequalities and social faux pas (see also Chapter 5 on the discussion on how call-out cultures can go bad). In Figure 3.2, the first blogger begins a conversation calling out users for reblogging "sylvia plath poetry" as they perceive her work to be "anti black" and "anti Semite" (*sic*). To this, the second blogger extends the discussion with details about where the poet has displayed anti-Semitic language, and another blogger further

Figure 3.2: Artist's impression of a post depicting instance of call-out culture on tumblr, originally sighted by the authors in posts from *rottenlesbian*, *tomibunny*, and *snakegay*. Art provided by River Juno.

extends the conversation with a clickthrough link to a source as supporting evidence. Such collaborative and corroborative call-out cultures on tumblr engage networks of users to chime in with contributions and resources to build a convincing case, encouraging information gathering, independent and networked research, and productive dialogue. Such behavior also normalizes the practice where users are presented with (new) information to consider, can be persuaded to change their opinion, and have the space to acknowledge this change without a sense of shame.

Perpetual arrested development

tumblr's young user base, the vernacular of personal testimonials, and the commonality of learning experiences (see Introduction, Chapters 1 and 5) are reflected in the discourse of *perpetual arrested development*, where users openly articulate that they still feel that they are learning to grow into the responsibilities and burdens of adulthood – a rite of passage commonly parsed as "adulting" or "how to adult" in tumblr speak. Such tips are addressed to an imagined audience of the same age-cohort, often framed as in need of this networked peer learning, because they have been neglected by their parents and the institutions that are supposed to prepare them for independent life. Figure 3.3 demonstrates users making

Figure 3.3: Artist's impression of a typical post on tumblr compiling list of "how to adult" resources, originally sighted by the authors in a post from *apparentjpg*. Art provided by River Juno.

the time and effort to curate links to resources to learn "how to grow the fuck up." For instance, a tumblr blogger's post includes serious topics like "what the hell is a mortgage?," practical guidelines like "first apartment essentials checklist," and more light-hearted hobbyist advice like "how to care for cacti and succulents." Other highly reblogged exemplars have sometimes toyed with parody and humor, by addressing tumblr users as if they were low-functioning "babies" and giving advice such as "how to walk" or "how to exist."

Self-care

tumblr's vernacular of personal testimonials drives a culture of validating and listening to others' personal experiences, which encourages a discourse of *self-care*, demonstrating inclusivity to all needs and abilities, at times to the point of toxic positivity (see Chapter 7), mere lip-serve, or slacktivism. In Figure 3.4, this gestural placation is depicted by a

Figure 3.4: Artist's impression of a tumblr post depicting tumblr's culture of gestural placation, originally sighted by the authors in a post from *180mph*. Art provided by River Juno.

blogger who juxtaposes the gravity of a crisis such as "world war 3" against the shallow advice sometimes dished out by tumblr users to "drink 8 cups of water a day" (Figure 3.5). This sentiment is often exaggerated with posts where tumblr users randomly reblog content with the reply "you are valid" as a solution to an otherwise easily solvable issue. While tumblr can be a goldmine for genuinely helpful tips and guides for self-care, especially around LGBTIQA+ concerns (see Chapter 5), feelings of sexual isolation (see Chapter 6) and mental health issues (see Chapter 7), this parody post exaggerates a tumblr culture that overtly focuses on oneself and one's body as the focal point for resolving issues and crises of every degree. It highlights an "individualizing" or "psychopathologizing" (see Chapter 7) ethos in which tumblr users are expected to personally take on the burden of fixing

Figure 3.5: Artist's impression of a typical tumblr conversation in which users ironically "solve issues" by disregarding them and refocusing on gestural self-care instead. Art provided by River Juno.

systemic problems, and an "isolating" pathos in which tumblr users can appear extremely invested in their silos to the point of being detached from "the real world."

Self-deprecation and helplessness

While providing a safe space for some marginalized populations and discourses, tumblr has simultaneously been accused of fetishizing, celebrating, and amplifying negative feelings of *self-deprecation and helplessness*. Figure 3.6 borrows

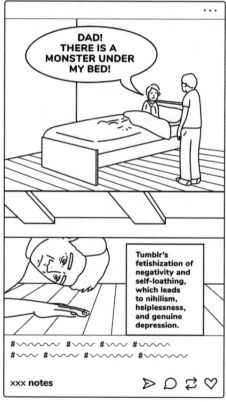

Figure 3.6: Artist's impression of a popular meme circulating on tumblr to depict its culture of self-deprecation and depression. Art provided by River Juno.

from a meme template in which a son calls out to his father
to check for "a monster under [his] bed," only for the father to
discover issues that are far more terrifying and troubling than
a frightening creature. In particular, this meme posits that
tumblr's "fetishization of negativity and self-loathing" leads to
"nihilism, helplessness, and genuine depression." It reflects
a longstanding sentiment that while mental health silos can
be candidly supportive spaces and networks for some users,
others become conditioned to adopt these negative feelings
as part of their foray into this silo (see Chapter 7). Figure
3.7 further demonstrates this through tumblr influencer

Figure 3.7: Artist's impression of prominent tumblr user *troyesivan* calling out
the fetishization of mental health issues on the site, originally sighted by the
authors in a post from *troyesivan*. Art provided by River Juno.

and singer-songwriter celebrity *troyesivan*'s call-out of tumblr users fetishizing mental health issues.

Queer normativity

Finally, tumblr fosters *queer normativity*. In general, tumblr is a platform that is welcoming to LGBT users and cultures, having been cited by generations of queer people as a safe space, where they learned a lot, found a voice, experimented with facets of their identity, and figured themselves out. However, this validation is often experienced as a super intense affective utopian bubble, that may for some become too much (see Chapter 5). Figure 3.8 is a screengrab from a Japanese anime series in which a character announces, "I don't understand straight people," indicating both the tacit

Figure 3.8: Artist's impression of a popular meme, depicting a screengrab of a Japanese anime that was repurposed as a highly reblogged tumblr meme, to express tumblr's culture of queer normativity. Art provided by River Juno.

presumption that tumblr is *the* queer platform and inverting the heteronormativity of most other spaces (Cover 2018).

These discursive strategies are everyday manifestations of the shared vernacular, but are also a form of visibility labor (Abidin 2016a) used by everyday users, microcelebrities, savvier celebrities, and the more tumblr-literate brand advertisers to generate or direct flows of attention. We now turn to how attention is commodified and monetized on tumblr. While doing so, we will occasionally return to the discursive strategies discussed here and review how they are used in some common templates for inserting and astroturfing advertising into tumblr silos.

Commerce on tumblr

Commerce on tumblr is best conceptualized in three categories: platform commerce, brand commerce, and vernacular commerce. *Platform commerce* is essentially Tumblr Inc.'s business model; it comprises the company's institutional and corporate endeavors to monetize its platform. *Brand commerce* considers how intermediaries like brands (with products and services to market) and agencies (with digital ad spaces and influencers to manage) participate on tumblr's platform to insert themselves into the attention flows to foster monetization and extract value as middlemen. *Vernacular commerce* is a term we use for all the strategies and practices enacted by individual tumblr users to generate potential for monetizing.

Platform commerce, the business model

All social media platforms' business models rely on maintaining a delicate balance between users' trust and owners' monetizing intentions (Clemons 2009; also cited in van Dijck 2013). While most American social media platforms founded in the second half of the 2000s feared user intolerance of, and avoided, commercial activities like pop-up ads during their first few years, Tumblr Inc. can be argued to have approached ads with greater reticence than its peers.

E-commerce

Typically, social media platforms' business models are based on advertising and exploitation of user data and metadata (van Dijck 2013). In the early years, during what we called "Independent tumblr" in our Introduction (2007–12), Karp's idea for earning revenue was based on an almost performative rejection of embedded advertising and user analytics, which Facebook, Twitter, and Google were all experimenting with, and which have now become the industry default. "We're pretty opposed to advertising," Karp told the *LA Times* in 2010: "it really turns our stomachs" (Milian 2010). When Karp deemed tumblr as a product to be advanced enough to finally start focusing on making money (Eaton 2010), his idea was to set up a marketplace akin to Apple's App Store, where users could buy low-cost items like designed themes for their blogs, stickers, etc. Tumblr Inc. also launched a digital merchandise store, "tumblrmerch," where it used to sell tacos (that were perpetually sold out; aaawhyme 2017), tote bags, caps, sweatshirts, and net neutrality badges among other trinkets (alexander 2017).[3] The earliest aspirations for tumblr's platform commerce thus focused on e-commerce.

By 2012, the approach had been slightly refined. Whenever asked about the business model, Karp mentioned the marketplace, on the one hand, and blog promotion – where users could pay US$5 to have one of their posts pinned at the top of their followers' blogs – on the other (this feature was discontinued in 2013, because users hated it). Karp believed his approach would make tumblr "wildly profitable," because there were no other "platforms for creators to promote themselves" (Cheshire 2012). After Tumblr Inc. was valued at US$800 million in 2011, some trade journalists and experts started voicing doubts about this business model, which probably paved the way for the Yahoo! sale. When Karp sold tumblr to Yahoo! in 2013, he justified it by saying that Yahoo! offered tumblr "an unbelievable opportunity to shortcut a lot of the very hard things that we're about to be going through" (Lapowski 2013). Trade press, near unanimously, interpreted the "very hard things" as a need to embrace advertising, which Karp confirmed.

This focus on e-commerce continued into the early years of the ownership period we called "Yahoo! tumblr" in the Introduction. Tumblr Inc.'s employees seemed to have been persuasive enough in this framing as, by 2014, articles were touting the value of Tumblr Inc.'s consumer base. For instance, one news headline read, "Tumblr is the wealthiest social platform" (Arevalo-Downes 2014), revealing that tumblr users have a median household income of US$80,075[4], ahead of Twitter (US$79,562), Pinterest (US$78,967), and even Facebook (US$70,124). tumblr users were deemed to have "extra disposable income" and higher "average referral revenues" than the likes of Facebook users. Reportedly "over half" of tumblr users have made purchases and around 90 percent felt "inspired to buy something" based on their tumblr browsing (Arevalo-Downes 2014). Ironically, by 2017, journalists were arguing that the reason for Tumblr Inc.'s continuing difficulties with platform commerce was because its most active userbase was so young and did not yet have expendable income (Feldman 2017). At that time, however, Lee Brown, Tumblr Inc.'s head of brand partnerships, optimistically asserted that the "customer journey begins on Tumblr with prepurchase aspiration and ends on Tumblr for postpurchase celebration, making Tumblr the ultimate destination for shopping" (Arevalo-Downes 2014).

Creative advertising campaigns

In 2012, Karp reframed his initial take on advertising, saying that it was the metrics-driven web advertising, or the "hyper-hyper-targeting of little blue links" (Bercovici 2013) that Tumblr Inc. was against, and tumblr's success would instead be in ads that make people feel something for the brand. Thus, the business model was rearticulated as taking advantage of a "huge, untapped opportunity" (Walker 2012) for selling advertisers the chance to run creative campaigns. The creatives and advertisers of the time seemed to accept Karp's ideas. In a 2016 retrospective, a Fortune 100 advertising strategist is cited saying that, back then, everyone looked to tumblr "as the holy grail," meaning that those who could crack the secret of making things go viral on the platform had hit branding gold (Fiegerman 2016).

Among its earliest clients were luxury fashion retailer Bottega Veneta and exercise brand Adidas, which launched its first "official soccer Tumblr blog" ahead of the 2012 UEFA European Championship (Delo 2012a). Such advertising campaigns were either featured under tumblr's "radar" slot on the dashboard, which would feature a rotation of blogs curated by tumblr staff, or on tumblr's "spotlight" page for sports blogs, showcasing ads that run "three times wider than the teases for organic picks" to garner more user attention (Delo 2012a).

However, tumblr rationed out only 5 percent of the daily traffic for these recommended slots and charged what the trade press deemed to be fairly high rates. Later in the same year, sponsored animated GIFs were introduced. Tumblr Inc.'s rhetoric continued to focus on creative, affect-driven brand advertising over direct, data-based, point-of sales advertising. Both Karp and the trade press marked 2013 as the year where tumblr had to demonstrate that it could become a successful business.

Creatrs Network and paid ad spaces

However, by 2014 tumblr's platform commerce had fallen far behind the likes of Facebook, and, under pressure from

Verizon CEO Marissa Meyer, it eventually shifted its focus to paid ad spaces. While ads started appearing as standalone posts interspersed into the dashboard feeds (Feldman 2017), it turned out that it was not as easy "serving native ads to a blog," as it was to a "real person" (Stein 2013). The top reasons experts listed for slow ad sales were pseudonymous blogs (implying that passport name-connected identities were more lucrative for advertisers), content safety concerns (i.e., the fact that tumblr did not censor sexual content), narrow choice of advertising products (including the lack of sophisticated data mining and user segmenting), and the restructured advertising team's limited understanding of, and interest in, how tumblr worked (Feldman 2017; Whitman 2015). tumblr users, of course, had a lot of fun ridiculing tumblr's paid ads for being crass, hardsell, or tone deaf. It is not uncommon for viral tumblr posts to call out Tumblr Inc.'s in-app ads for being repetitive (depressedphoenix 2019) or for becoming dank memes resembling amateur photoshop attempts (dulect 2020a). Tumblr Inc. has also been known to post ads recommending its own tumblr app to users who are already on the platform, and rare appearances of such ads on one's dash has become known as the "infinite money, infinite energy" meme (hotboyproblems 2020a).

Perhaps as a response to tepid advertising flows, Tumblr Inc. launched its Creatrs Network in January 2015. It was branded a "formal structure" to foster collaborations between tumblr users and advertising campaigns, and started with an initial pool of three hundred users selected by the company (Gayomali 2015). Those who signed up to the Creatrs Network were promised a share of the revenue as the program developed (Toor 2016). This seemed to be an extension of Tumblr Inc.'s earlier work, where the company commissioned artists to design limited edition t-shirts for sale in its digital merchandise store, with proceeds going toward nonprofit organizations such as the Media Democracy Fund (Houston 2014). At that time, Head of Creative Strategy David Hayes said:

> We think the creative class is really the next generation that's going to come up and change the world and we think we have the largest creative class of any platform ... The idea that Tumblr will power the best advertising campaigns on Tumblr and on Facebook and on Instagram and on YouTube and on display banner campaigns and their websites, it totally makes sense to us. (Whitman 2015)

A retrospective analysis of tumblr's business model in 2015 suggests that Yahoo! and Marissa Mayer made a mistake that was common for that era, by thinking that buying an audience and inserting ads would be enough to turn a revenue (Coldeway 2019). Tumblr Inc. had fought tooth and nail for in-dashboard paid ads and hypertargeting, but it became evident that just introducing a model that might have worked elsewhere did not work well on tumblr. Attempts to remix paid advertising with more tumblresque solutions like Creatrs Network did not work either. In 2016, Yahoo! wrote off tumblr's value twice, first by US$230million and then by US$482million (Kim 2016). By the end of the year, "native," non-context-driven, nonuser-specific ads were a common occurrence in tumblr feeds. These ads were sold through Yahoo!'s Gemini and Facebook's Audience Network.

In 2019, Verizon sold tumblr to Automattic (see Chapter 1) and the CEO Matt Mullenweg commented that "right now, they're burning a lot of money" (Patel 2019). His plans, however, were opaque. He said Automattic would keep exploring advertising, but also mentioned the freemium model.

Brand commerce

The most relevant players in terms of brand commerce on tumblr are tumblr shops and digital marketing agencies, media industries attempting to leverage fandoms, and other social media platforms attempting to leverage tumblr culture as such. We will briefly describe each of these.

In the early stage of tumblr's e-commerce aspirations, a handful of digital marketing agencies that focused specifically on tumblr began to emerge. One example is digital agency Coexist Digital's development of an e-commerce platform to allow tumblr users to purchase products without having to leave the tumblog they were visiting. In-app or on-platform payment methods were supported by Stripe, a payments startup company. While the service was free to consumers, Coexist Digital and Stripe would claim around "6% cut of sales transacted through the platform" (Delo 2012b).

Early adopters of integrated e-commerce on tumblr include an Ohio- and Tennessee-based ice-cream chain (Delo 2012b), and coffee brand Nescafé (Caffyn 2016). In particular, Nescafé populated "over 50 different Tumblr pages" using tumblr-native paralanguages such as GIFs and short videos – of which ten pages offered a "buy now" button that linked to "local suppliers" for instant purchases – and reported "$200,000 in sales in the first six months" and an increase in mobile traffic by 20 percent (Caffyn 2016). Other online tumblr stores include exercise wear brand "Made by Nike" and fashion retailer "Of A Kind" (Delo 2012b). While Tumblr Inc. had actively invited more brands to participate in e-commerce on its platform, such initiatives quickly dwindled within a few years and the blogs closed down after a period of inactivity.

Television networks, too, have been trying to leverage the potential of tumblr by turning to fandoms as a "free, enthusiastic source of promotion" (Burt 2016). Yet, tumblr fandoms are not easy to commodify, as they are vocal in their demands for diversity and sensitive representation (see Chapters 4 and 5). Further, television networks observed that shows that performed well among tumblr audiences were not necessarily the most popular in terms of viewer ratings. Thus, while critics argued that television networks' attempts to "monopolize financially on fannish interests" (Burt 2016) are not going so well, others offered a more symbiotic reading. Media studies scholar Lesley Willard (2016) suggests that when media industries engage in the conventionally fannish practice of "live-giffing" where they post GIFs "in real-time via the show's official social media account," prominently "branded with the networks' logo," they both contribute to and co-opt the fandoms. The high-quality GIFs are entered into the flows of fannish gift economies, wherein they carry communal value, but as branded content they are intended to function as native advertising, carrying commercial value and co-opting the affective labor of fandom (Burt 2016).

As noted in Chapters 1 and 2, tumblr is not an easy platform to navigate. The silosociality and the sheer deluge of content are disorienting for newcomers. Savvy Facebook and YouTube users, and Buzzfeed editors profit from their capacity to curate listicles of "best of" tumblr and thus offer a "lite tumblr" experience. Facebook Pages Humans of Tumblr and Tumblr Made Me Do It, with more than 5.1 million followers (humansoftumblrcom 2020) and 2 million followers (TumblrMadeMeDoIt 2020) respectively, siphon value and earning potential from original tumblr creators and curators by redirecting this sizable viewer attention to their own platforms and posts instead. On YouTube, channels like Tumblr Reads, which features "the funniest Tumblr posts and memes daily," boast more than 102,000 subscribers and over 48 million views (Tumblr Reads 2020). Other YouTube channels also often compile tumblr posts – such as "I found the WORST of Tumblr | Tumblr deep dive" with more than 1.2 million views (STRANGE ÆONS 2018), and "The funniest conversations found on Tumblr" with more than 1.4 million views (BrainyDude 2018) – and accumulate ad revenue from the curation work. Such accounts and users are essentially parasitizing the content and labor of tumblr users by virtue of their compilation efforts, and funnel attention away from tumblr, demonstrating the curatorial value for intermediaries who can serve as "guides" to the platform. Some users have reacted by coming up with and sharing strategies to circumvent such pilfering, or to punish parasitic platforms for aggregating their content for profit. Often this takes the form of public service announcements instructing users to edit their posts to disrupt the formatting or brand-friendliness of the content, and includes crude edits with crass language, spamming edits with statements like "pay me royalties," or the spamming of dank memes (garbage-empress 2018).

Vernacular commerce

While it is common to claim that Tumblr Inc. has failed at monetizing the popularity of its platform, it is equally as common to point out that tumblr has, from its very early years helped launch creative careers, and allowed people to get book and TV deals and otherwise profit from their creativity (Fennessey 2010; Fiegerman 2016). We describe everything that individual tumblr users do to monetize or create the potential for monetization of their creative, curatorial, and community-making practices as *vernacular commerce*. These can be carried out by mainstream celebrities who use tumblr to document or promote various messages, microcelebrity and influencer users who groom their internet fame natively on the platform, and everyday users who may routinely or occasionally engage in some form of commercial activity on the platform.

Mainstream celebrities

In 2012, tumblr president John Maloney began approaching celebrities to coax their public relations teams into establishing a presence on the platform (Pollack 2012). Since then, mainstream celebrities have used tumblr in a variety of ways (see Conclusion for a discussion about whether mainstream celebrities have abandoned tumblr). For some, tumblr is a professional portfolio of their works; for example, the blog of British singer Zayn collates his latest music in the form of audio snippets, lyric videos, official music videos, and in true blue tumblr fashion, several GIFs of his music videos for easy reblogging (zayn 2020). For others, tumblr is (or used to be) a personal blog or webpage; for example, the late celebrity chef Anthony Bourdain (anthonybourdain 2020) and American actor-writer Aziz Ansari (azizisbored 2020) have posted diary entries, essays, and brief thoughts interspersed with some images and videos.

And still for some others, tumblr is a platform to cultivate parasocial relations and seed loyalty among followers; American singers Britney Spears (britneyspears 2020) and Taylor Swift (taylorswift 2020) continue to use tumblr to share personal updates about their private lives, share words of encouragement with fans, and occasionally reblog fan posts with added commentary. In particular, Swift has groomed a reputation for engaging actively and meaningfully with her fans on tumblr, such as through creating safe spaces for conversation (Coscarelli 2017), organizing "IRL house parties" exclusively for tumblr fans (Collins 2018), and financially supporting fans with donations during the COVID-19 pandemic (Tenbarge 2020). We will address such organized and networked fandoms in more detail in Chapter 4.

Toward the late-2010s, popular media articles would often collate "best of" tumblrs run by celebrities who were actively engaging with their tumblr fanbase, usually through Q&As or the "Answer Time" events run by tumblr staff, participating in threaded comments, leaving comments in fans' ask boxes, and reblogging posts by fans (Baila 2017, Norton 2015). By 2020, most celebrities seem to have migrated to Instagram and Twitter as their primary social media presence, and recaps from fans of how they used to feel more intimate remain a romanticized memory (e.g., Kenny 2017).

Microcelebrities and Influencers

tumblr-native microcelebrities and influencers are also known to use the platform to groom a loyal following, and then to leverage these audiences to branch out to entrepreneurial endeavors such as digital advertising, businesses, and book deals. Impressively, most of these success cases are teenagers, reflecting both tumblr's popularity among a niche market of young people and its vernacular (see Chapter 2), which might be easier to master for younger people. Jason Wong, a 17-year-old Asian American, started on tumblr to cope with racist bullying in high school (Reeve 2016), but after accumulating more than 1.2 million followers launched Fifthtee, an apparel brand that pledges proceeds to support animal welfare, and Wonghaus Media, a digital marketing agency (Sawchuk 2017). Likewise, Australian singer-songwriter Troye Sivan conscientiously groomed a social media following on platforms like tumblr, Twitter, and YouTube to discuss LGBTQIA+ issues as he was developing his music career (e.g., Abidin 2019). A scroll through Sivan's tumblr archives reveals a regular program of reblogs that were seeped in the tumblr vernacular and sensibility of personal testimonials, self-deprecation, niche humor, LGBT advocacy, and other social justice-oriented conversations. Sivan would also occasionally publish original posts updating followers on his career milestones, such as his first fashion show, debut on Snapchat, and music accolades (troyesivan 2015a, 2015b, 2016).

As his career developed and Sivan focused on producing professional music content rather than personal updates, he still occasionally returned to tumblr to host "asks" (see Chapter 1) – the latest of these being eighteen tumblr posts responding to fan questions in August 2018 (troyesivan 2018a, 2018b). At the time of writing, Sivan's tumblr has evolved to be more of a promotional site for his global music tour, which also advocates for LGBTQIA+ rights, with posts comprising announcements, diary entries of his experiences, and photographs with fans and volunteers at various pit stops (troyesivan 2020). Such strategies, where celebrities curate a professional stream of content related to their job in the vein of a portfolio, alongside a personal stream of content intended to give fans a peek into their lives to foster a sense of intimacy, has been studied as "anchor" and "filler" content by one of the authors (Abidin 2017).

There are also tumblr-native influencers, who have cultivated a more-or-less cult following (comprising both fans and haters) based on their personal brand, and who have leveraged this to progress from social media fame and commerce to other mainstream media and peripheral industry pursuits (see Abidin 2018). One example is sex positive tumblr blogger Laci Green, who has been open about how her Mormon upbringing stifled her sexuality, and encourages young people to pursue pleasure, body positivity, and other social justice-oriented pursuits. From tumblr and other social media, her fame and following have ushered in various opportunities, including a circuit of invited lectures at Universities (Kerkez 2015, Santos 2012), appearing as a guest expert on the prolific American talkshow TODAY (TODAY 2018), producing educational series for the likes of Planned Parenthood and MTV (Laci Green n.d.), and a book deal about sex and pleasure (Green 2018).

Social work scholar Megan Lindsay Brown and journalist Hanna Phifer (2018) have also researched instances of viral tumblr microcelebrity in social justice spaces, through their study of Hanna, better known as "Belle" on tumblr, who speaks out on victim-blaming, supports sexual assault survivors, and has built an online community to foster ethical principles among peers. In the mental health and NSFW silos that we have studied, tumblr bloggers similarly groomed popular blogs and persona through the sharing of knowledge and resources. Many do so by responding to questions for advice and guidance, weaving together their lived experience with other institutional knowledge, curating archives of pedagogical, support, and therapeutic resources (see Chapters 5, 6, and 7). Others who have expert knowledge through their studies in psychology, psychotherapy, social work, nursing, and the like offer their personal and academic knowledge to respond to users' questions. As the volume of questions and follower engagement has grown for popular blogs, some bloggers have responded to their increasing workloads by creating teams of moderators or passing on blogs to others with the time and capacity to better address their communities' needs. Others have started businesses from their tumblr beginnings. In 2013, US-based therapist John Kim started The Angry Therapist blog to archive his feelings following his divorce and his new career as a therapist (Palleschi 2013). After responding to a follower's request for advice, he slowly built up his following by offering "no bullshit" advice, and reflects that: "Without using this platform, I wouldn't have reached as many as I have in the last three years. It catches all the people that would not have sought out help because the traditional way is too expensive, and inconvenient, and for some, evasive." By 2013, Kim had established a digital therapy business and later added books, a podcast, and a coaching business to his offerings. We discuss further uses of tumblr for social justice and mental health pursuits in Chapters 5 and 7.

tumblr influencers are skilled at utilizing the discursive strategies discussed in the beginning of this chapter. One common template they use for inserting and astroturfing advertising into tumblr silos is what we call *influencer promotions*. Influencers engage in paid advertorials or hawk their own merchandise to tumblr users. In Figure 3.9, popular sex education tumblr blogger *lacigreen* announces the debut of her new book, while in Figure 3.10,[5] tumblr illustrator *shencomix* reblogs and extends his own post to promote his book after his comics went viral on the platform.

Some other instances of tumblr microcelebrities and influencers are largely pseudonymous. For example, thinspo bloggers generate popularity by publicly cataloguing the vulnerability of their weight loss through selfies (Figure 3.11) or by dispensing "inspirational quotes" throughout the silo

Figure 3.9: Artist's impression of *lacigreen*'s tumblr page, including a YouTube video in a post to promote her book, originally sighted by the authors in a blog by *lacigreen*. Art provided by River Juno.

Figure 3.10: Artist's impression of a post from *shencomix* to announce that his internet-viral comics are being turned into a book, originally sighted by the authors in a post from *shencomix*. Art provided by River Juno.

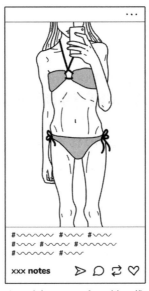

Figure 3.11: Artist's impression of the types of tumblr selfies that go viral in the thinspo blogger silo, original user anonymized. Art provided by River Juno.

to motivate other thinspo bloggers (Figure 3.12). Thinspo bloggers also build internet celebrity on tumblr through deliberate self-loathing and self-violence. They send hate letters to each other (Figure 3.13). In these instances, their fame is generated through shared aspiration toward an imagined other with the idealized body, or through aversion toward one's ruined potential in the face of thinspo failure.

For the most part, the internet celebrity of thinspo bloggers on tumblr truncates at visibility and popularity within their networks. Very few, if any, thinspo bloggers actually go on to monetize their visibility as a self-brand, apart from the rare placement of embedded ads through Google's AdSense. The rhetoric of repurposing already available content, mutual in-group policing, and focus on networked vulnerabilities does not lend thinspo bloggers well to the monetizing devices of the conventional influencer even if their follower numbers would do so.

Figure 3.12: Artist's impression of the types of "inspirational quote" posts that go viral in the thinspo silo, original user anonymized. Art provided by River Juno.

Figure 3.13: Artist's impression of the types of self-policing posts that bloggers in the thinspo silo send to each other, original user anonymized. Art provided by River Juno.

On the contrary, pseudonymous sex bloggers accumulate tumblr fame from their celebration of body positivity (see Chapter 6). tumblr sex bloggers often amass popularity first and foremost through nudity and sexuality of their content. This popularity is utilized for gain in a variety of ways, from sex work (camming) to promoting their creative work, from selling trinkets to having a wishlist.[6] Those who monetize their content adjust their posting times and frequencies to cater to the desires of the imagined audience and the logic of the attention ecology of social media, but claim to still "do their own thing" in terms of posting political views or feminist rants when they feel like it. Compared to conventional influencers, however, this monetization is very modest. Some refuse to monetize at all, but accept invites to events and interview request; others, while not rejecting monetization, purposefully post content that they know will reduce their mass-popularity in order to shape their audience:

> Katie: When I post gay boys kissing and fucking, ... I will lose followers, who followed after I posted my ass. I get it, they use tumblr to masturbate and they didn't know this wasn't a straight up porn blog. I'm ok with that. In fact, I am happy about that. I don't want these followers. (Personal interview by authors, 2018)

Finally, we have observed tumblr influencers, who have built their online fame not on their personal lives, but on a pseudonymous persona altogether. Jess Miller, an Australian teenager better known as "Pizza" to more than 700,000 followers, would post "absurdist comedy" on tumblr (Reeve 2016). By age 16, she was earning AU$10,000 a week from digital advertising (Fyfe 2016), often through commissions whenever followers clicked on the links of her reblogged posts or made a purchase. However, Pizza was briefly embroiled in a tumblr scandal for creating diet pill ads that masqueraded as tumblr posts including "fake testimonials from women talking about their weight-loss journey"; this marketing stunt earned her between AU$20,00 and AU$50,000 per week in 2014, until her blog was deleted by the platform in August 2014 for deceptive links and affiliate marketing (Fyfe 2016).

Everyday users

Although tumblr's platform logics and algorithmic organization are not completely transparent to users, specific groups of users have self-branded as tumblr marketing experts (e.g., digital marketing agencies) or volunteered advice as fellow tumblr users (e.g., on tumblr, but also forums like reddit and Quora), teaching others how to maximize engagements, boost posts, get slotted into the

Explore page, accumulate followers, and monetize tumblr attention. Such actors play with ideas of the "algorithmic imaginary" (Bucher 2012) and create "algorithmic lore" (Bishop 2020). Here, we briefly review some of the tumblr folklore around how to "hack" the platform for attention and monetization as an everyday user.

(A) *ADVERTISEMENT PLACING SERVICES AND AFFILIATE NETWORKS*

The most common of recommendations is for tumblr users to register with an advertisement placing service – such as Adsense, AdThrive, Infolinks, MadAdMedia, MediaVine, Media.net, or similar (alborden in fakelitty 2019; Hines 2014) – that earns them a small commission when followers visit their tumblog, and a small increase in commission as ads are clicked through. Another common method is to register with affiliate networks that pay users a small commission for clickthroughs and purchases, "spam hawking" blogs are also popular, with Etsy and Shopstyle Collective Amazon (fatalcharm in fakelitty 2019) among the more popular partners.

Spam hawking is a common template built on the discursive strategies described in the beginning of the chapter. It means that blogs are set up specifically to share paid/affiliate links to online stores, and blogs with high followings may at times sell dedicated post slots to advertisers as a "feature" (Figure 3.14).

(B) *START A SMALL BUSINESS*

In one of several Reddit threads seeking advice on garnering attention on tumblr, a fellow redditor responds to an Original Poster (OP) seeking to monetize their 47,000 followers that most tumblr users "want to support small businesses but they would rather buy from you, personally" (fatalcharm in fakelitty 2019), and suggests that DIY products based on tutorials on Pinterest and YouTube might fare better than simply

Figure 3.14: Artist's impression of an example of posts from blogs that curate products and aggregates links to purchase. Art provided by River Juno.

engaging in ad placements. This advice to start one's own small business on tumblr is echoed elsewhere (Aleksandra n.d.). Some everyday users who set up small businesses channel their vernacular literacy and discursive skill into another template we call *content resonance*. This means that tumblr users create and remix works for sale to multiple interested and intersectional silos. This is the most silosocially sensitive of all of the attention hacking templates we discuss here. For example, Figure 3.15 depicts a member from a K-pop group, speaking across the art tumblr, artist tumblr, K-pop tumblr, and merchandise tumblr subsilos. Such posts usually include the face of K-pop idols being superimposed

Figure 3.15: Artist's impression of a K-pop idol being depicted in a painting as fan art, originally sighted by the authors in a post from *toit*. Art provided by River Juno.

into paintings, or their likeness being painted into different genres of paintings altogether, as a way to engage with other tumblr silos. At times, tumblog owners provide opportunities for these illustrations to be sold via a variety of merchandize such as t-shirts, cushion covers, and mugs.

Other digital marketing advice blogs recommend that users stay away from pushing sales when tumblogs are still focused on growing followers, because tumblr users are primarily on the platform "to be entertained," and for its "cool and artistic" trends (Seekins 2020). While it is also possible to "purchase" reblogs, followers, and likes from service providers like SocialPromoter (Henrich in Quora 2018), such inauthentic bot actions are generally frowned upon (and forbidden by tumblr's rules as "inauthentic gestures"; see Chapter 1).

(c) Replicate posting norms within a silo

tumblr users are also advised to follow other tumblogs in the similar niche (Nichols n.d.), follow other "popular blogs" to be noticed (Seekins 2020), monitor and mimic the styles of "other successful Tumblr blogs in [their] niche" (fakelitty 2019), reblog "quality content" from within their community (Seekins 2020), and promote follower and fan contributions within the tumblr community (wikiHow Staff 2019). Such advice about selecting and staying in a niche is echoed by several digital marketing agencies, recommending users to "narrow your niche" (Seekins 2020) and to be sharp and clear in the voicing of their tumblog, including splintering from the "main" to "side" blogs in order to keep the voice coherent. This advice reiterates our book's central argument that social life and interactions on tumblr are organized into an intense silosociality (see Chapter 2).

An example of an attention hacking template that builds on silosociality is what we call *networked endorsements*. In this case the ask, comment, and reblog sections of tumblr posts may be populated or hijacked by commercial dummy or bot accounts to simulate grassroots conversation. Figure 3.16 is an ask that initially appears to be harmlessly seeking advice for improving one's Instagram account, but is then flooded with responses from various users promoting a photo-editing app. Although it is difficult to verify if these responses were sincere or indeed bot advertisers, it is observed by one of our authors during an extended period of digital ethnography that waves of such responses and shout-out posts tended to cluster around specific services, brands, or companies in a concentrated period of time. Following on from previous research on astroturfed advertising on Instagram (Leaver et al. 2020), we corroborate that this appears to be a routine method of "sentiment seeding" and grassroots advertising.

Finally, tumblr's vernacular, sensibility, and discursive strategies merge in an attention hacking template of

Figure 3.16: Artist's impression of an "ask" post being astroturfed to promote a pseudonymous photo-editing app. Art provided by River Juno.

astroturfed social justice narratives. Disparate networks of users promote products and services relating to self-care, poverty, and inclusivity, but attempt to water down the overt commercialism by integrating memes or otherwise relying on social justice rhetoric. Figure 3.17 draws on a common tumblr discourse around the struggle of students and student depression (Ask and Abidin 2018), depicting a stereotypical group of old white male professors who appear to be setting exam questions that exceed the content covered in class. To this, a tumblr user recommends a vaguely related money earning and saving app to "struggling" students. In Figure 3.18, a similar pattern of discourse occurs when a blogger uses two screengrabs from an American web TV series *Unbreakable Kimmy Schmidt* to depict a situation in which a person for whom English

Figure 3.17: Artist's impression of a call-out post focused on student struggles being astroturfed to promote a money saving/earning app. Art provided by River Juno.

is a Second Language (ESL) is struggling to understand a native English speaker. To this, a tumblr user enthusiastically chimes in to recommend a translation app. Like *networked endorsements,* the pattern and frequency of such recommendations point to a very high likelihood that these social justice narratives were carefully crafted and tailored to host pre-prepared responses that astroturfed advertising to tumblr users.

Figure 3.18: Artist's impression of call-out post focused on ESL struggles being astroturfed to promote a language learning app, originally sighted by the authors in a post from *thepotentialpolygot*. Art provided by River Juno.

Conclusion

We started this chapter with a brief description of the types of attention flows and discursive strategies used to harness attention on tumblr, then explored commercial activity on the platform. While some monetizing strategies revolving around advertisements, affiliate networks, and small businesses pioneered by "tumblr famous" users have been wildly successful, for the most part it appears that Tumblr Inc.'s multiple attempts of monetizing the platform and its userbase have failed. This was especially evident as "tumblr famous" users bled out of the platform and developed into full-fledged internet celebrity elsewhere. While attention continues to flow on tumblr, and users continue to accumulate it, it does not necessarily translate into monetization options.

Tumblr Inc. rejected paid ads for years, and even after they were introduced, the company was not overly successful in selling these slots. This has led Tumblr Inc. brands and some users to experiment with advertisements that tries to adapt the platform vernacular and users' discursive strategies, to carry commercial messages deep into silos. These strategies tend to build upon tumblr's dominant culture of self-deprecating relatability, and point to the notion of "righteous affective capitalism," wherein call-out cultures, oppression Olympics, onedownmanship, and minority celebrity are astroturfed and brandjacked to carry commercial messages.

On tumblr, there is no direct co-relation between attention, celebrity, and commerce, but, for the most part, being "famous" on tumblr – as indicated through the number of followers, notes, status, and feedback – does not guarantee monetizing potential. Further, advertising messages have to be stealthily embedded within silos through a careful learning of discursive strategies, and through the enactment of advertising templates. In other words, successful advertising messages on tumblr do not call too much attention to themselves, but are instead seamlessly woven into and accepted as part of a silo. Having discussed how attention flows and is commodified or hacked on tumblr, we extend this discussion and move to explore fandom on the platform.

4

fandom

Tumblr tags is how I figured out half the jokes / fandoms people posted to. Twitter can be kind of frustrating because if someone doesn't mention a fandom sometimes I'll never know what the art is for. What am I supposed to do? Ask???

(@balentay, July 3, 2020)

As we were putting the final touches on this book, we came across Tweets (like the above) where fans were reminiscing about tumblr, where the platform's features accommodated the efficient display of their fan creations like GIF sets, where the community's norms were ethical and utilized tumblr features for attribution and reciprocity, and where specific fandoms were easily parsed and spotted by their vernacular. While these fans seem to have migrated to Twitter, they seem to still believe that tumblr was/is the quintessential platform for fandom.

(Katrin Tiidenberg, Natalie Ann Hendry, and Crystal Abidin)

tumblr and fandom have long been considered a match made in heaven (Escribano 2016). The platform became particularly popular among fans from 2012 onwards, precipitated – at least partially – by the *en masse* deletion of NSFW fanfiction from the previously dominant fandom platform LiveJournal (Morimoto and Stein 2018). Fanfiction migrated to AO3,[1] but a void was left in terms of the more visual and social aspects of the culture, which tumblr rose to fill (Kohnen 2014).

This chapter discusses tumblr as a fan space. We paint the broad strokes of tumblr fandom in dialogue with existing research, then discuss how tumblr's silosociality shapes fandom. We then analyze practices, fan vernacular, and fan sensibilities through two empirical examples we feel are both characteristic of tumblr, yet relatively underresearched: K-pop fandom and meta-fandom, or tumblr users' fandom of tumblr.

Existing research

Fandom is a huge, visible part of tumblr, but tumblr as a platform has also been enormously impactful for the broader "participatory cultures" of fandom (Jenkins et al. 2007). The centrality of the fandom silo is evidenced in the fact that scholars increasingly sample from fan communities when studying tumblr features and affordances (e.g., Bourlai's study of tagging 2018). Many educators and instructors have integrated tumblr fan cultures into their pedagogy (Booth 2018; McCracken 2017). Yet, fandom scholars argue that the relationship between tumblr and fandom is ambiguous (see Chapter 7 on tumblr ambiguities).

On the one hand, it is argued that tumblr's features and affordances have made fandom more accessible (Morimoto 2018) and diversified fandom practices (Morimoto and Stein 2018; Stein 2018; Willard 2017). tumblr vernacular's multi-modality, for example, has been said to lower the participation barriers within the "heretofore predominantly English-language online fandoms" (Morimoto and Stein 2018). Visual content also carries different intertextual meanings in different fan communities (Hautsch 2018; Lowe 2020). It has been suggested that those tumblr affordances we called scalability and nonlinear temporality in Chapter 2 make the fandom silo chaotic, but also more diverse, increasing the visibility of previously peripheral fans and communities (Morimoto and Stein 2018), and leading to fan self-reflexivity, critique, and polyphonic discourse instead of authoritative dominance (Fathallah 2018). However, as tumblr is used by many previously isolated fandom communities and as reblogged posts are curated into new contexts and reframed, a specific different kind of conflict emerges, where fans and antifans clash (Morimoto 2018; Morimoto and Chin 2017). Fans use tumblr's unique tagging system to deal with this hostile virality and "fandom wank"[2] but also to communicate their appreciation for both canon and "fanon" (canon in fandom) and express their belonging to the fandom community (Bourlai 2018; Morimoto and Stein 2018; Neill Hoch 2018; Vásquez and Creel 2017). Tags are used to comment on posts, reinforce group behavioral norms, pre-emptively apologize for potential norm breaches to avoid conflict etc. (see Chapter 7). DUCK

Finally, tumblr's platform sensibility has created a fandom culture that centers diversity and uses fan activism and call-out culture to argue for more and better representation of queer people and people of color in fiction and on screen (Bury et al 2013; Anselmo 2018; Le Cudennec 2018; Morimoto 2018; see also "Queer Female Fandom," special issue of *Transformative Works and Cultures*, e.g.: Narai 2017; Ng and Russo 2017; Pande and Moira 2017). Compared, in particular, to the previous fan favorite platform – LiveJournal – fandom tumblr is known for its queer friendliness, racebending, and queer shipping (Morimoto 2018). As fandom tumblr has become "more and more political and critical of its consumption of media," it has incorporated a more "academic, professional lexicon, with vernacular terms like 'squick' being substituted for mental health vocabulary 'trigger'" (Winterwood, 2018). This has been linked to fandom increasingly being perceived as having a serious cultural and representational impact.

We suggest that the described ambiguities result from silosociality and that fandom is a particularly interesting case study to nuance our argument of silosociality. As argued in Chapter 2, people experience tumblr through silos that are interest-driven and sustained by the shared practices, vernacular, and sensibilities. Silos often contain subsilos, networks, and/or communities. Silos are both large and open, but can still feel like niche spaces wherein contexts remain intact. However, the case of fandom tumblr shows that what a silo feels like to its inhabitants clearly depends on whether there were previous online spaces dedicated to the interests that drive that particular silo. And if there were, what were they like? It can be argued that tumblr offered people interested in having conversations about NSFW topics (Chapter 6) or mental health (Chapter 7) a fairly unprecedented niche wherein to be with imagined like-others and have these particular, affectively intense conversations on what is, for all intents and purposes, a general-interest, popular social media platform.

Fans and fan scholars, in contrast, feel that tumblr's fandom silo made fandom less niche. It converged the pre-existing, fragmented, but super-specific fan groups that had used LiveJournal or Yahoo!Groups, and never ventured into other digital fan spaces, into a huge "panfandom community, where there's overlap between fandoms" (Morimoto 2018). Fans used to small, tight-knit communities dedicated to only one ship[3] have been argued to experience fandom tumblr as making it "impossible to have a normal conversation," because there are actually many different conversations, "and not all of them are in good faith" (Morimoto 2018.). This can lead to misinterpretation and makes it easy for "anti-fans" to harass those, whose fan practices or ships they disagree with.

Our survey of literature on tumblr and fandom finds that a vast majority of studies focus on media texts from television (e.g., *Breaking Bad* in Ruddock 2020; *Game of Thrones* in Matthews 2018; *Walking Dead* in Taylor 2018; *Sherlock* in Anselmo 2018 and Petersen 2014; *Supernatural* in Hautsch 2018; *Teen Wolf* in Willard 2017; and *Doctor Who* in DeMeo 2016), with a smaller handful focused on movies (e.g., *Marvel and Avengers* in Lowe 2020; *Marvel's Loki* in Thomas 2013), music groups (e.g., "One Direction" in Lisa 2017), or sports groups (e.g., "football" fandom in Kunert 2019). As part of an ethos to decolonize academic research, in this chapter we focus instead on K-pop tumblr fandoms. But before we get to that, and in order to better understand how such fan practices and pursuits have developed on the platform in a systematic manner, we consider how Tumblr Inc. has corporatized tumblr fandom cultures through Fandometrics.

Corporate fandom: Fandometrics

In 2015, Tumblr Inc. launched Fandometrics, to "compile a database of Tumblr's most talked-about entertainers and entertainments, and track the shifts in our users' collective conversations" (fandom n.d.). Every week, Tumblr Inc.'s content team analyzes the most frequently used tags on the platform, categorizing them and ranking the influence of different fandoms. Fandometrics also publishes yearly reports called "Year in Review" (see also Chapter 7 for mental health in "Year in Review"). For example, in the last week of June 2020, the list was topped by Avatar: The Last Airbender and Black Lives Matter, but also featured a fandom for K-pop group BTS (fandom 2020). According to the 2019 yearly review, the TV show based on Neil Gaiman and Terry Pratchett's novel *Good Omens* was the "biggest thing" on tumblr. However, it only bested the K-pop band BTS by 4.43 percent (fandom 2019a). Similarly, the most popular ship, or romantic pairing, was between the two main characters from *Good Omens* and the highest-ranking real-person ship was between two members of BTS. Tumblr Inc.'s then senior content insights and social manager Amanda Brennan said in a roundtable that anime and K-pop have both really surged as fandoms on tumblr, whereas the TV show *Supernatural* continues to exhibit staying power while other older fan favorites (e.g., *One Direction*, which was the most popular in 2013), have fallen away (Morimoto 2018).

According to Brennan, fandoms are ranked based on fan tagging – the limitations[4] of which she acknowledges – in nine categories of TV, music, videogames, celebrities, internet celebrities, anime, manga, K-pop, and ships (Morimoto 2018). We find Tumblr Inc.'s overall rhetorical alignment of Fandometrics to the power of data (fandom n.d.) quite noteworthy in the context of tumblr's otherwise metrics-agnostic stance (see Chapters 1 and 3). Communication scholars Elena Maris and Nancy Baym (2018) point out that the way Tumblr Inc. calculate the influence of fandoms does not account for sentiment, instead providing prominence to the "loudest fandoms" in a way that "encourages social jostling by online communities for relevance within fandom and wider culture."

K-pop fandom

As noted in the previous section, K-pop fandom is huge on tumblr. It has been a separate category within the Fandometrics database since 2017, with the group BTS mostly dominating in all categories. For a six-month period in 2017, #BTS was more popular than "any TV show, film, or video game" (Tmblrnorms 2018). K-pop fans, mostly known for their fierce loyalty and dedication to South Korean music, are masters of social media manipulation who use their savvy to promote their favorite musicians as well as various social causes (Abidin and Baudinette 2020). K-pop fans are known for their highly creative and dynamic fan productions and curations, but pseudonymous fans on tumblr also make the extra effort to foster feelings of affinity. K-pop fans usually call the artists "idols," the term referring to a specific type of music celebrity who has been trained in a regimental multiyear program by agencies, first founded in Japan and subsequently also practiced in South Korea and China (Gingold 2019). In this section, we analyze how tumblr vernacular is utilized for fan practices of creating digital shrines, building archives, and creating fan art, curated fanfiction, and confessions, and how the tumblr sensibility takes K-pop subsilo-specific forms through networked gatekeeping and queer normativity (see Chapters 2 and 3).

Digital shrines

Like most fandoms, K-pop networks on tumblr often create digital shrines for their favorite idols, curating "best of" posts to commemorate them. Looking specifically at the BIGBANG – one of South Korea's most successful idol groups in history – fandom on tumblr, this has included the effortful scouting of old video footage from more than twenty years earlier to create GIFs of band leader G-Dragon as a child (miggdrgn 2018), compiling GIFs featuring G-Dragon's signature moves during live concerts (sassy-dae n.d.), collating rapper T.O.P's various hairstyles across the years (choi-seunghyunie 2019a), and painstakingly curating a list of cameos by G-Dragon across videos by eight other K-pop artists and groups (ahkmunrah 2016). The K-pop fandom, in true tumblr fashion, exhibits high levels of multiple literacies.

Specific to K-pop fandoms is the notion of their idols' "duality," or the belief that K-pop idols' impeccable, suave, and fierce personas on stage are in stark contrast to their actual relaxed, goofy, and fun selves off-stage. Such juxtaposition is important for idols to remain accessible while maintaining their desirability and allure, but is more often than not ascribed to them by enthusiastic fans, who curate photos that show idols "ON" and "OFF" camera (e.g., wanted1993 n.d.; see Figure 4.1). There are also posts dedicated to tearing apart, piecing together, or closely scrutinizing idols' performances, listing minute and often inconsequential details for the most trained fandom eye to enjoy (e.g., sushihairjiyong 2018).

Some digital shrine practices are specific to particular sub-fandoms. In the case of VIPs (the fandom name for BIGBANG), the height of BIGBANG's main dancer Taeyang has long been a subject of inquiry, with fans kicking off investigative comparisons in photos, videos (soompi 2012), and

Figure 4.1: Artist's impression of fans who curate and juxtapose images of K-pop idols, to depict "duality" across their persona. Art provided by River Juno.

extensive forum threads (reddit 2020) to determine his real height. In response, VIPs on tumblr shared a witty image that was doctored to measure Taeyang's height by the number of sunglasses (showiee 2019), which has become fanon.

Screengrabs and archives

One of the most crucial and primary functions of K-pop fandom blogs is to serve as archives of social media posts from the idols themselves. This usually takes the form of screengrabs, reposted photographs, video snippets made into GIFs, or even short clips of longer videos. This practice arose out of two main necessities. First, many K-pop idols produce transient content on social media. This includes the likes of livestreaming on apps such as V LIVE and Instagram Stories, or the concerted deletion of Instagram and Twitter posts that were only intended to stay up for minutes (and sometimes even just seconds) as teasers for loyal or lucky fans. Second, many K-pop idols share exclusive content on Korean-specific, and sometimes paywalled, platforms and media (e.g., magazine scans by gnhwan 2018) that are not easily accessible to global fandoms, who rely on K-pop fandom tumblr for access.

K-pop fandom blogs often curate and archive screengrabs of posts by idols as announcements to inform other fans to "switch" platforms (e.g., julla 2018), to debrief together after having been able to witness one of the short-lived Instagram posts (e.g., minty-top 2018), to surface information that would usually be buried deep in lengthy comment threads elsewhere (e.g., ikonis 2018), or to share translated videos for non-Korean speakers (e.g., uwunnie 2019). In other instances, fans may produce GIFs of idols' documentaries (e.g., selva3bd 2019), live concerts (e.g., yooneroos 2017), television appearances (e.g., alittlepessimistic 2016), and music videos (k-popmvstills 2018) to amplify their presence into the information and visual data ecology on tumblr.

Creating fan art

Like in many other fandoms, fan art is a staple among K-pop fans on tumblr. In Chapter 3, we reviewed an example of K-pop fan art being merchandised, monetized, and sold for profit. Here, we highlight a further use of fan art. Many blogs creating original fan art tend to focus on depicting news events and milestones happenings within the fandom. These are often artist impressions of viral incidents, or those of special significance to the fandom. For example, specific to K-pop, all Korean-born males have to undergo mandatory military conscription before the age of 30. As a result, this sense of loss and grief from fans toward their idols retreating from the industry for at least two years is often commemo-rated and even romanticized in fan art.

In one example, user *yellow-sprout* posted fanart by *nonomi-hoVIP* depicting the five members of BIGBANG each enrolling for their military service in order of age (yellow-sprout n.d.; see Figure 4.2). There is great detail in each hand-drawn character, as their hairstyles and dress sense cohere with paparazzi photographs of them at the time when each of the members had left for the military. In another example, fans share images of other idol groups that have been created to be used as mobile phone wallpapers or lock-screens (minomyno 2018; see Figure 4.3), in commemoration of their first world tour. As such, fan art doubles up as "news announcements" among K-pop fandoms on tumblr, as evidenced by occasional dialogue in comments and notes threads with fans asking if any significant event has taken place to warrant an artistic tribute to a specific idol group.

Figure 4.2: Artist's impression of fan art by the VIP fandom in commemoration of BIGBANG's military conscription, originally sighted by the authors in a post from *yellow-sprout*. Art provided by River Juno.

Figure 4.3: Artist's impression of fan art collaging the faces of K-pop idols as mobile phone lockscreens/wallpaper, originally sighted by the authors in a post from *minomyno*. Art provided by River Juno.

Curatorial fan fiction

As in many fandoms, fan fiction is an important pillar of K-pop fandom on tumblr. In this silo, fan fiction primarily takes the form of text (e.g., babyrubysoho n.d.), reaction GIFs, images, and mood-boards. Since textual fan fiction has been extensively researched (see Black 2009; Jamison 2013; Klink 2017; Olin-Scheller and Wikström 2010; Parrish 2007; Tiidenberg 2019c), in this section we will focus on the other formats, which can together be categorized as curatorial fan fiction.

GIFs are often used to accompany a specific genre of fan fiction known as "reacts," where fans request, or commission, GIFs and narrations of how idols would react in specific scenarios. It is common for many of these scenarios to be romantic or sexual in nature. In one such request, an anon user had asked for BIGBANG's reactions to "You flinching during an argument." To this, fellow fan *topbap* constructed fictive prose to accompany GIFs of the idols, depicting each of the five members responding in ways that seemed to best match their public idol persona, such as "He would calmly sit you down and ask whether you always felt on edge around him or whether he ever did something to make you react like that ..." (for T.O.P) and "He would give you plenty of kisses on your head and hug you tightly for a long period of time" (for Daesung; topbap 2018). This genre of fan fiction reaction GIFs is especially popular among fans of male idol groups with many members, each of whom have been marketed by their agencies to have distinct public images (e.g., btobshypeman 2018). Returning to the idea of idol "duality" mentioned earlier in the chapter, some fans also curate reaction GIFs and captions imagining how idols would interact with them in private and public (e.g., tabithings 2018).

Another genre of fan fiction GIFs involves a narrative interwoven into a series of GIFs to paint an imaginative scenario. Some of these are close analyses of idol relationships within the group, taking on the tonality of slash fiction where fans read homoeroticism into small gestures, subtle glances, and a variety of micro-body language between idols. A common ship among VIPs on tumblr is "GTOP" (between rappers G-Dragon and T.O.P), whose fans often labor over GIFs to tease out their "domesticity" (topfied n.d.). Other instances of this draw out fans' romantic and erotic desires even more. For instance, for K-pop group WINNER, who had started in a reality TV show where they ran a daycare center, fans superimposed text with closer reads into their actions, painting them as "husband/father material" (elmosanica 2018). It is also common for fans to photoshop images of idols against carefully crafted text messages to give the impression of intimate communication. A staple in this genre is to make lock-screens of idols with superimposed text message notification bubbles displaying affection messages such as "i love you" (kpop-locks 2018; see

Figure 4.4). Many K-pop fan tumblogs are open to commissions to make "locks" or lockscreen images and wallpapers for fellow fans.

The connection between fan fiction and photoshop is best encapsulated by imaginings of idols' "private" or "actual" social media feeds, especially if they are not active on these platforms. For instance, despite the prominence of K-pop groups on Instagram, it is less common for members of veteran K-pop groups to have personal social media accounts given that they had started out in a generation that was not yet as tethered to social media. As such, this has encouraged K-pop fans on tumblr to craft mock Instagram feeds through compilations of screengrabs and

Figure 4.4: Artist's impression of fan fiction in the form of mobile phone lock-screens imagining K-pop idols sending affectionate text messages to tumblr users, originally sighted by the authors in a post from *kpop-locks*. Art provided by River Juno.

stock images, to imagine the "private" lives of these idols (e.g., arrogantcarrot 2018).

Moodboards are generally mobilized in the fan fiction genre of "concepts." This involves fans imagining idols in various scenarios, conveyed through a mixture of images and fictive prose. Some moodboards are composed entirely of screengrabs from idols' media productions and social media posts, carefully curated to match fan narratives of these idols being the tumblr user's romantic partner. For instance, a moodboard of BIGBANG rapper T.O.P's Instagram images of himself interacting with his nephew, of his movie and music appearances with a female protagonist, and of images of his home are collated to paint an impression of him as a "soft father/husband" for VIPs (soft-tabi 2018). At times, tumblr users may also place images of idols alongside stock photos to paint an ideal date scenario, such as the "Beach date with Bobby moodboard" that features iKON rapper Bobby in surfwear on the beach in a grid of stock photos showing waves, sand, and turtles (skyfoxx186 2018). Among K-pop tumblr fandoms, it is also common for users to commission prominent fans and artists to design fan fictive moodboards for them, such as in the case of user *madelinelist's* "First dates with Choi Seung-hyun" moodboard personalized for fellow fan *consumedbykpop* (madelinelist 2018).

At times, specific items take on a sacred or symbolic meaning within fandoms and are used frequently in moodboards. For VIPs, flower beds, paths, and gardens became a sacred symbol after the band released the song "Flower Road" in March 2018 as a farewell gift, when the group went on hiatus to serve their mandatory military service. Two specific lyrical lines in the song read:

> this is not the end of us
> I hope we'll meet again when the flowers are blooming.
> if you want to leave, I understand
> I'll scatter flowers on the road you'll walk on.

This sense of longing, the plea for fans to wait for them, and the hopeful pining for a future together is canon among male idol groups, who run the risk of failing to reignite their careers after the two-year military service hiatus because of the competitive nature of the industry. As such, many of the moodboards constructed by VIPs on tumblr often feature collages of flowers (seoftly 2019a) or imagine the BIGBANG idols (and their fans) frolicking in gardens together (flower-tabi 2019; seoftly 2019b), until the band reunites and returns to the industry after the completion of their military service.

Confessions

K-pop confessions are another staple among tumblr fandoms, usually comprising aggregate tumblogs in which users can submit confessions to post within a community. As such, these confession blogs collaboratively curate "(trans)personal/ (trans)media archive" that "calibrate and continuously stylize" communal discourse (Munteanu 2017: 146–8) and at the same time serve as affinity building exercises, contributing to shared identities and identifications (see Chapter 2). There has been a long legacy of such fandom confession blogs since the early-2010s, although many have since been abandoned despite an intense period of activity over several years (e.g., confessyourkpop n.d.). Such submissions usually comprise images and a short prose (e.g., kpop-confessions n.d.), although each K-pop confession community has its own set of specific rules.

Some niche confession blogs disallow "dirty fantasy confessions" (e.g., mykpopconfession n.d), while others welcome sexually explicit conversations. These invite fans to include their "wild fantas[ies]" (e.g., kpopsexconfession-blog-blog n.d.) and "think sexually about people [they] are attracted to" (e.g., its-dirty-kpop-confessions n.d.), or focus on male-male ships (e.g., 1kookieyeolssecondblog1 n.d.). There are also confession blogs focused on specific K-pop agencies (e.g., ygconfessions n.d.), and specific language speakers (e.g., confessyourkpopsin-blog n.d.). Many confessions veer on the negative side, at times bordering on hate comments, so as a response, there are also niche blogs focused only on "positive" confessions (e.g., positivekpopconfessions-blog n.d.).

Social justice within K-pop fandoms

As argued in Chapter 2, a commitment to social justice is part of tumblr's broader shared sensibility, and K-pop fandoms on tumblr also draw on this in their subsilo-specific practices. In particular, the discursive strategy of queer normativity (see Chapters 3 and 5) is used. K-pop fandoms are fond of praising and amplifying content of idols who appear to be LGBTQIA+ friendly. In some instances, this takes the form of curating symbolism and imagery from across their music video and live concert productions (kelofthesea 2019), while, in others, this takes the form of careful compilations of idols' speeches, referents, and subtle hints in various interviews and speaking engagements (agustdboyfriend 2019).

tumblr K-pop fandom's LGBTQIA+ visibility is especially pertinent given that in South Korea same-sex marriage is still illegal (Denyer and Kim 2020), that widespread homophobia was exacerbated during the COVID-19 pandemic (Klasto and Simpson 2020; Thoreson 2020), and that LGBTQIA+ celebrities still face harsh sanctions and risks in the industry (Hollingsworth 2020). In 2018, singer Go Tae-seob, better known by his stage name Holland, came out as the first gay idol in South Korea, much to the disdain of his label, which he had to quit (Hollingsworth 2020). On K-pop tumblr, he is celebrated as a gay icon – much like *troyesivan*, as we saw in Chapter 3 – and GIFs of scenes from his music video that normalize same-sex affection are often circulated by fans (seungcheolsboyfriend 2018, underrated-idols 2018). However, social justice in the K-pop fandom can be ambiguous. In addition to the above-described LGBTQIA+

visibility and ally-practices, the fandom has also been seen to make light of suicide (baekhyuns-high-notes 2019), and been observed for their insensitive and inappropriate spamming of fan cams on Twitter (fuckheadsawhore 2019).

Community making and networked gatekeeping

Many of the K-pop fandom blogs and networks of blogs are run by small groups. It is common to see such groups initiate recruitment drives calling for more help or seeking more moderators. While there are dozens of such calls across the thousands of K-pop fandoms each month, we will consider two examples of such posts to provide insight into the role of fandom moderators. One K-pop fandom network known as *iKON-OFFICIAL* called for "3–5 moderators" in February 2019 in lieu of "internal changes" within their organization. The main goal of the network's expansion was to "improve [their] ability to provide better and faster updates," and to "work harder, just like [their] boys, and show iKON [their] support through a fanbase that they can be proud of" (ikon-official 2019). Similar to many other K-pop fandoms on other platforms, on tumblr, time is of the essence to establish one's fandom at the forefront of the silo. Fan networks that have the ability to debut photographs and news updates, post translations and subtitles, and mobilize their network to instigate viral posts in the quickest time possible tend to groom a reputation for being a "serious" fandom.

However, other K-pop fandoms seem to require more stringent and sacrificial displays of membership. For instance, a call from *iKON GLOBAL* in January 2018 called for a moderator to "post fantaken pictures/fancams & iKON related updates on a daily basis" as well as translators (Korean to English, Japanese to English, Chinese to English) who were to serve "full time" to translate articles, info, news, etc. (ikon-global 2018). This fanbase usually prides itself in providing "the latest news and media about iKON" and also produces its "own English subtitled videos" (ikon-global n.d.). Prospective applicants were expected to have the qualities of being: "team-player," "dedicated," "responsible," "friendly," "organized," "trustworthy," and "active on Twitter" (ikon-global 2018). More specific requirements from the tumblr fandom network state: "We are looking for people who can be with us on a daily basis. Someone who can be active at least 3–4 hours a day. We want to improve our ability to provide better and faster updates." They had also indicated a preference for "previous admin experience" on various social media, and for candidates to be online from "4pm to 12am Korea Time" (ikon-global 2018), indicating a glimpse of the extent of time, dedication, and labor that these K-pop fandoms pour into their tumblr networks, often amounting to a full time "job" (mcltifandcm 2018).

K-pop tumblr fandoms also play an important role in sustaining the sense of affinity of the fandom through several activities. One popular example, continued from the iKON fandom above, is the card exchange program. Most K-pop album releases by the top groups include collectible items such as limited-edition posters, stickers, keychains, and photocards with the actual CD. Photocards are exclusive items that are Easter eggs,[5] usually featuring just one idol per card per album purchase. As such, this encourages fans who wish to collect cards of their favorite member in the group to purchase multiple albums to increase their odds. Such cards have become a common trading commodity, and the K-pop fandoms on tumblr facilitate such card exchanges on an international scale. In a variant of this, some K-pop fandoms may also facilitate small gift and card exchanges during festive periods such as Christmas, to "promote friendship and winter greeting globally" with fellow fans (konycardexchange 2018).

Within prominent K-pop fandoms tumblr's social justice orientation is also enacted through gatekeeping that excludes fans who have broken community ethics. It is not uncommon for fandom blogs to report (e.g., fy-winner 2018), or even publicly name and shame (see also Chapter 5), fans for poor behavior, especially if they are "*sasaeng*" – an obsessive fan who is usually involved in stalking or harassment (e.g., concernedfansofgdragon 2018; sungri-seyo 2018). However, the positive flip-side of such in-silo self-governance is that it is also common for fans to help each other seek out "lost" friends and mutuals, especially if the latter might have changed their URL/handle or deactivated their tumblog (choi-seunghyunie 2019b). Above all, the silosociality of tumblr is underscored when fans retreat away from other social media to tumblr during various scandals – a frequent occurrence in the K-pop industry. As user *choi-seunghyunie* (2019c) notes during the time of one particular scandal:

> It's still extremely hard being a VIP [fandom name for BIGBANG] and enjoying BIGBANG. Tumblr is really the only place right now I can be as open as I am with my fandom. I really don't want to have to keep going through this for the rest of the time I'm in the fandom. This is hell and I feel so alone anymore. I can't enjoy anything.

Fandom of tumblr, or, "Just tumblr things"

Our second example of fandom on tumblr is what we call tumblr meta-fandom. Unlike most of the studies on tumblr fandoms and even the case study of K-pop fandoms above, which primarily congregate around content from the mainstream media, tumblr meta-fandom is focused almost entirely on tumblr as a culture and community. In essence, this is the fandom of tumblr's silosociality. These fan tributes are often parsed in languages of love, hate, nostalgia, longing, anxiety, and an assortment of feelings toward tumblr (see Conclusion). In this section, we review some of the longstanding meta-fandom memes on tumblr that have emerged as a genre of "just tumblr things" (see Chapter 7).

Fandom of tumblr feels

A common discourse in meta-tumblr fandoms is a sense of undying loyalty to the platform despite all its disappointments (see also the discussion of "beautiful hellsite" in the Conclusion). Sentiments in this vein are exemplified in the following ambivalent text post memes:

> "just to be clear, I'm staying here as long as this site functions. I have o intentions of deleting this blog, I will go down with this ship if only to see exactly how bad it gets." (thankyousirmayihaveanother 2018)

> "If you hate tumblr so much why don't you just delete???"
> "I have to die in this strange country. Just like you." (ourexes 2018)

> "one day I will escape from this website." (damsandwich 2020)

There are also users who express their love–hate relationship with tumblr by commenting on specific failures or faults of the platform or its users, such as those who repost art without permissions or credit (marklightgreatsword 2020), those who like posts without reblogging and thus starve posters of exposure and appreciation (queentianas 2019), the unwieldy format of tumblr mobile (cleanie 2018), and the fact that frequent changes of icons and tumblr handles/ URLs made it difficult for users to identify each other and continue long-term relationships on the platform (bovidae n.d.). Yet, the overall tonality in the meta-tumblr fandom still appreciates its anonymity (hypeswap 2019; thothoes 2019), the variety of its genres and silos (mothric-bry 2017), and celebrates a communal schadenfreude as exemplified in an animated GIF of a glitter ribbon badge that says: "I contribute daily to the downfall of tumblr" (dulect 2019).

Fandom of tumblr folklore

tumblr thread collaborations are a rare, but very tumblr-specific phenomenon that is treasured by fans of tumblr. We argue that these are a form of fandom for tumblr folklore, combining love for tumblr vernacular (Chapter 2) and attention hacking discourses (Chapter 3), love for tumblr's reblog function (Chapter 1), and appreciation of its more poignant examples (which are often published on other sites and platforms, fueling the public imaginaries of what tumblr and tumblr humor is). The thread collaborations usually take on one of three forms.

In the first form, users who reblog posts with comments extend and add to the commentary in the post, at times taking the original post to surprising new directions that keep readers in suspense. In one example of a thread, users compared various Star Wars characters to confectionary, with, for instance, young Anakin Skywalker being an "Untoasted slice of white bread," Darth Vader being a bread toaster, and Rey being a cinnamon roll (dulect 2020b). After more than fifteen pictorial contributions and more textual interjections by various users each expressing that the previous pictorial contribution was the punchline, the latest integrations of this months-old dialogue arrived in the form of baby Yoda being compared to a petit and cute green macaron (dulect 2020b; see Figure 4.5).

In the second form, these long collaborative threads also take on a gamified nature as users attempt to out-do each other through wit, humor, and sass. Versions of this occur when users intentionally deteriorate the quality of a post through ironically "shitposting" (thebootydiaries 2020) or through introducing more incorrect facts and intentionally reproducing errors as a form of trolling (just-shower-thoughts n.d.). There are also rare occasions where tumblr thread collaborations that start off as nonsensical and whimsical inside jokes end up unwittingly replicating great philosophy works in the register of tumblr vernacular (e.g., airborn-eranger63 2020). As an astute user points out, the suspense

Figure 4.5: Artist's impression of the tumblr folklore meta-fandom battling out their wits in Star Wars-pastry metaphors, originally sighted by the authors in a post from *dulcet*. Art provided by River Juno.

of such threads emerges as the discourse unfolds with various users chiming in: "the most exciting thing about tumblr is when you're reading an issue post and you have to guess if you're supposed to agree with it or not before getting to the last comment" (chromolume 2019).

A variant of this involves users "hunting" down proper attributions to viral posts and reblogging them with appropriate captions and links (e.g., mehreenqudosi 2020). A rarer version of such "found" posts are when the original person in the viral post chances upon the thread and "comes out" or "outs" themselves as the original poster. This sometimes happens several years later, so a young adult is looking back upon a viral occasion as a child (e.g., transgender-neurotica 2020).

Finally, in the third form, there are instances where tumblr thread collaborations evolve into their own brand of niche tumblr humor through seemingly pointless reblogs. This includes reblogs of the same comment by the same user on a regular basis, as if invoking a human bot (e.g., rslashrats 2020), and reposting circular conversations that are incoherent or nonsensical (slimetony 2020).

A subset of tumblr folklore fandom is what we call meta-dash magic, another genre of highly tumblr-specific humor, wherein the sequential organization of posts on one's dash coincidentally dialogue with each other by way of a sharp juxtaposition/contradiction of content or unexpectedly smooth continuity. Such happenstance is often gleefully parsed by tumblr users as almost an example of tumblr, or at least their tumblr dashboard, having agency. Screengrabs are typically accompanied with expressions such as "my dash did a thing." This includes the likes of two people making the same facial expressions in sequential posts (e.g., viniumsab-bathi 2014; see Figure 4.6), or sequential posts having the same visual framing (e.g., avecesfui 2020).

Figure 4.6: Artist's impression of an example of tumblr dash magic. Art provided by River Juno.

Fandom of tumblr's features and functions

Enthusiasts in the meta-fandom of tumblr often commemorate inside jokes about the platform's various features and functions. Usernames, or tumblr handles, are prime real estate, and can often be the shortest punchline in tumblr jokes. tumblr's default grammar under notifications takes the form of "[username] liked your post/photo" or "username reblogged your post/photo." Toying with this template, users with quirky handles sometimes craft witty tumblr jokes and pick-up lines. For instance, in this viral post of user *could-i-have-sex-with-you-if-i* engaging with user *fasterfood*'s photos, the latter screengrabbed two notifications and responded to them (fasterfood 2020; see Figure 4.7).

Figure 4.7: Artist's impression of tumblr meta-fandoms constructing inside jokes with feature of usernames, originally sighted by the authors in a post from *could-i-have-sex-with-you-if-i*. Art provided by River Juno.

In another collaborative tumblr thread, a user posited the scenario, "what if one day, for 24 hours, everyone on tumblr turned into whatever their url is" (ruinedchildhood 2020), which solicited a repertoire of witty responses from users with quirky handles, such as:

xsillynoodleoodlex: "Bold of you to assume I'm not a noodle"
wowdeathwouldbenice: "Huh."
thatɪweirdkid68: "i already am that weird kid"
bitch-in-a-galaxy: "i'd stay the same"
thegreenpea: "Gonna get eaten out"

In a sense, users in the meta-fandom tumblr may feel compelled to live up to the name or reputation of their usernames (e.g., realbarbiex 2014), which are calling cards for their displays of wit when engaging in tumblr threads.

As noted earlier in the book (see Chapters 1 and 2), reblogging is perhaps the most iconic feature of tumblr. Here, fans of tumblr often push to reblog content as their main agenda. tumblr adages such as "reblog till I die" or "reblog or no blog" are (un)ironically taken as statements of a life ethos, which also appears in a genre of tumblr reblog jokes, many of which underscore the loyalty of meta-fans who have stayed on with the platform even after the NSFW fiasco (see Chapter 1) saw a massive dip in membership: "tumblr is dead but also if i dont reblog pointless images ill die" (futbolwag 2020); "Reblog if you"re dead" (tychography 2020).

Another genre of meta-tumblr jokes are when users share screengrabs of their overwhelming "inbox stats" (roswell-newton-vargars 2020) or talk about the lack of activity in their inbox (vetoing 2020). As indicated in Chapter 1, "notes" on tumblr posts are an assortment of likes, reblogs, and comments, none of which are differentiated. Without a tumblr feature to signify intention or emotionality (like reddit's upvote and downvote, or Facebook's assortment of emoji reactions), the number of notes on a post does not always denote its popularity or acceptance within a silo, especially as positive and negative feedback is meshed together. As such, meta-fans of tumblr sometimes joke about constructing arbitrary yardsticks to assess the quality of a post (christian-stepmoms 2020):

> 0–4 notes – your post sucks
> 5–29,999 notes – your post is good
> 30,000+ notes – your post sucks

Fandom of broken tumblr

There are also subsets of tumblr users who exercise their meta-fandom of the platform by finding humor and unexpected content through its bad interface, features, and design, or its failures in corporate commerce (see Chapter 3). For instance, humor comes in the form of frustrated reaction GIFs for when a dash refreshes and causes users to lose sight of content they were interested in (colourofoctober 2015), when the tumblr mobile interface fails to render images properly (goodraandyy 2020), or when tumblr does not have adequate features for users to bookmark and save posts thereby resulting in millions of "liked" posts that are unsearchable (cakejam 2014). As commented on by digital creative Allegra Rosenberg (2020), "there's a whole genre of Tumblr posts that just screenshot and mock the bizarre hosted ads that spawn on the dashboard like mutated fish in a radioactively-poisoned river."

At times, this inadvertent humor occurs when tumblr and tumblr posts fail to load (realmckitten 2019), thus altering the narrative and intention of the original post altogether (e.g., hotboyproblems 2020b). For instance, one post reads "20 minutes into tumblr mobile he gives you this look," followed by a blank image which the tumblr platform has failed to parse or load (slow-riot 2015). When read in the context of tumblr's vernacular of affective personal testimonials (see Chapter 2) and discursive strategy of self-deprecation (see Chapter 3), this gives the impression that tumblr users are lonely and struggle to secure romantic partners. As such, making fun of broken tumblr becomes an act of identification with the broken tumblr and links back to the common imaginary of tumblr as a space for weird people (see Introduction) and a reiteration that "we're all kind of broken" (see Chapter 7).

Tumblr Inc.'s increasing censorship of content has also resulted in some unexpected humor. At times, sequential images are removed and substituted with a "Community guidelines" poster, leaving only one or two original images accessible for viewing, which without the surrounding context appears as a grim assessment of what remains of the platform's vibrant culture (e.g., acidwaste 2020). In a variant of this, subsequent posts in long tumblr thread collaborations are censored and replaced with a notice that states, "This content has been removed for violating Tumblr's Community Guidelines" (hotboyproblems 2020c), thus giving the impression that the gamified one-upmanship in the thread had exceeded tumblr's yardstick of allowable public morality.

Fandom of weird mutuals

Another form of meta-fandom on tumblr is directed toward one's mutual. Similar to the love–hate rhetoric expressed about tumblr as a whole, this meta-fannish meme is expressed as a relationship torn between kinship and avoidance. One's mutuals (the tumblr users who follow one another's blogs; see Chapter 1) are described as disturbingly weird, but in a "right" enough way so that it is almost imperative to read or consume their weirdness (see Introduction). "I feel like I can legitimately sue half of you for the things you make me read" (oldnapkinned 2019).

Other posts demonstrate the bizarre sense of kinship that users feel toward mutuals. These memes highlight the importance of a resonating sense of humor and the desire to be the one who offers attention (likes, reblogs) to mutuals: "when you tag something #FSLDMSLNDSSDLKFD and your mutual reblogs it like #text post and you start questioning if it was really that funny in the first place" (bodyglitter 2020); "*unlikes post so I can like it from u" (burgrs 2020).

The ambivalent sense of familiarity at a distance that tumblr and its silosociality affords is memefied too (see Chapter 7 for a discussion of the importance of the nuanced sense of closeness and distance in the mental health silo):

> "being mutuals is so ... intimate ... like u follow me but i also follow u? this is so forward i'm blushing ..." (mogie 2019)

> "If we're mutuals and I ever awkwardly reply to a post yes that is me trying to communicate with you and I'm very sorry" (blurberrys 2015)

> "*doesnt talk to tumblr friends for 6 months*
> *thinks about them and hopes they are okey dokie*" (prince-vegeta 2016)

The meta-fandom of tumblr mutuals is linked to the contested relationship tumblr users seem to have with identifying themselves or being identified as a tumblr user. Memetic content about the mutual, half-joking cringe of identifying (each other) as tumblr users "in the wild," offline, or among non-tumblr users is circulated on the platform. Users have half-jokingly refused to admit that they are tumblr users even when caught "red-handed" in the act (shewillfeatdrake 2015), advise that it is "never safe to use tumblr beside your parents" (suspend 2013), and muse about developing "secret codes" to identity each other without the knowledge of others in public (aru 2020). In general, the consensus among tumblr meta-fans is that there are emic and etic perceptions of tumblr, where outsiders are completely incapable of understanding the platform, its strengths and its weaknesses (valucard 2020).

Fandom of tumblr nostalgia

At times, tumblr users fan specific periods of tumblr history, compiling posts pining for or waxing nostalgic about a tumblr "of the past" (see Conclusion). These include reviews of top tumblr memes across the decade (e.g., gayarsonist 2020), throwbacks to tumblr memes in specific years (e.g., baelor 2020; mothurs 2017; phantomrose96 2018), and even predictive "throwback" posts for future years (e.g., ommanyte 2019). Users also reminisce on *passé* or expired tumblr norms and incidents, such as the old "create post" page (kittyzumi 2020), toying with htmls to construct personalized tumblr themes (meanplastic n.d.), hitting post limits (sexhaver 2019), following "dash drama" before "reblog with comments" was redesigned into the more readable format (q-shinji 2019), and the times where the tumblr interface crashed (trillow 2020). There are also inside jokes among tumblr veterans about how being 18 and above pits them as the "Adult" on the platform with the duty to "protect the young ones" (toopsy 2020), or that the "tumblr old" feel marginalized by younger users (mjalti 2016, quandrinips 2020).

Conclusion

In this chapter we discussed the tumblr silo that the platform is perhaps most known for: fandom. tumblr has long been a space for fan cultures and fannish hyperfixations, something that Tumblr Inc. seemed to have largely publicly ignored until the 2015 launch of the Fandometrics initiative. Fandometrics offers a partial understanding of what tumblr users discuss in their tagged conversations, but understanding tumblr as a fan space requires deep dives into specific subsilos. Much of this deep diving scholarship on tumblr fandoms has thus far focused on text-based creations, and on Anglo-centric media productions of mostly TV shows (and a handful on movies and music groups). Some of these treatments and discussions of tumblr fandoms seem to relegate the platform to being a mere placeholder for fannish texts, especially when studied in tandem with fan fiction networks like AO3.

While we build on this rich scholarship in this chapter, the original contribution to understanding the tumblr fandom silo in this book is to focus on systemic practices that permeate across most tumblr fandoms. We do this by surveying K-pop fandoms on tumblr and their assortment of subsilo practices, many of which shift away from text-based engagements to visual media-rich forms including images and GIFs in the shape of screengrabs, mood boards, reaction GIFs, fan art, and the like. Finally, to situate tumblr as a platform more centrally in studies of tumblr fandom and to illustrate our conceptual framework of silosociality, we took a meta dive into the world of fans of tumblr, or what we called the "meta-tumblr fandom," understanding how users were creative and witty with tumblr's various histories, contexts, features, functions, affordances, and even glitches to demonstrate their love, loyalty, and longing for the platform.

5

social justice

Interviewer: How would you describe your tumblr?

Charlie: Um ... I think it's just some things that ... I'll find things that are, um important to me such as, I don't know, it could be like a TV show that I really like or it could be issues that have arose, if that's a word?

Interviewer: It is.

Charlie: Yeah. [*laughs*] Things that ... things that I think other people should see, just because they're important, or you know, I think should be important.

(14-year-old Charlie: personal interview by authors, 2015)

Social justice and activism are undoubtedly very important to many communities, subcultures, and multiple silos on tumblr – a point we make throughout this book. This ethos toward social justice is reflected in the platform's public image; tumblr is framed as the exemplar of liberal online culture and a place for the "ultra-sensitive" that is "equally subcultural and radical" as 4chan and Reddit (Nagle 2017: 51). We think social justice deserves a separate chapter not because there is a single, coherent social justice silo, but rather because social justice underpins tumblr's shared sensibility, thus leading to most silos being explicitly concerned with social justice. We start with a brief discussion on social justice and activism in digital spaces, then explore how tumblr's governance and practices drive its social justice sensibility. We analyze the pedagogical practices oriented toward learning about social justice and contemplate the figure of the "social justice warrior" (SJW) as a useful opening to understand the complicated and ambivalent relationship of tumblr to social justice.

We end the chapter exploring queer tumblr as an exemplar of a social justice silo and attend to both the joys and frustrations of silosociality.

Our discussion relies on media and communication studies scholars Adrienne Massanari and Shira Chess's (2018: 527–8) definition of "social justice" as a term that has "long been used by feminists, antiracist activists, and other progressives interested in ensuring both economic justice and recognition for marginalized identities so that, '... assimilation to majority or dominant cultural norms is no longer the price of equal respect' (Fraser 1999: 25)." Social justice on tumblr is connected to issues related to racism, feminism, sexual and gender diversity, body politics, ableism, and, importantly, the intersectionality of these. Yet, given tumblr's social justice lean in the public imaginary, it incurs the curious and wrathful attention of other (anti-)interest groups, complicating the politics on the platform. Given this complexity, we offer an ambivalent reading of social justice on tumblr.

Digital activism and social justice

Digital technologies have expanded and complicated how people engage in social justice, politics, and activist knowledge-sharing, organizing, and activity. Yet "doing" politics online is devalued as a lesser form of engagement and action. In particular, young people's supposed disengagement, limited political awareness, care, and action are framed as a worldwide problem. Youth are often disillusioned with traditional, institutional forms of political engagement such as voting, lobbying, and membership in organizations, but increasingly "practice participation" in online and digital spaces (Tiidenberg and Allaste 2016). We concur with other scholars who stress that digital cultures and practices have the potential for political change – through awareness-building, skills development, organization, and protest – in nontraditional, often informal forms (Burton 2019). Recent work emphasizes that digital practices *do* matter, and can be political, even if not all of them lead to overtly political outcomes. Importantly, informal or (sub)cultural digital practices of civic and political participation are not exclusive to any one political party or position. For example, meme culture is as crucial for the success of spreading alt-right views as it is important for the dissemination of liberal critiques or progressive ideas (DeCook 2018; Frazer and Carlson 2017; Highfield 2016; Milner 2016).

In Chapter 2, we argued that tumblr is often attributed an important role in social justice and activism. The platform's "convergence of popular culture, socially critical discourse, and peer education" (McCracken 2017: 151) has birthed an imaginary of tumblr activism and a perception of a social justice tumblr. In 2014, the *New York Times* declared that millennials had entered the "age of tumblr activism," suggesting that on tumblr supposedly apathetic youth finally found inspiration to work toward social justice, "just hidden from the eyes of their elders" (Safronova 2014). In this piece, activism researcher Philip Howard explained that "Tumblr is kind of like a gateway drug for activism ... Once you connect to other people who feel strongly about race or crime or gay marriage, you stay engaged on that one issue area."

Tumblr Inc.'s social justice

Tumblr's social justice sensibility emerges not only from users' practices (we discuss this later), but also Tumblr Inc.'s corporate commitment to social justice. This is illustrated, in part, by platform-wide campaigns such as Action on Tumblr, Art Action Day, and Post It Forward (see Chapter 7), as well as collaborations with other social, political, and cultural organizations and movements worldwide[1] (see also Calhoun 2020 in relation to everyday practices of Black Tumblr; Chapter 6 in relation to BlackOutDay;[2] and Chapters 1 and 3 for PSAs regarding eating disorders). In 2015, tumblr launched "Answer Time" (#answertime; staff 2015), which, akin to Reddit's "Ask

Me Anything" model, allows users to ask questions of celebrities, creatives, and artists, as well as representatives from not-for-profit and activist organizations (Opam 2015). Cecile Richards, president of Planned Parenthood, was among the first Answer Time respondents and, at the time of writing, London physician, Dr Rita Issa was answering tumblr users' COVID-19-related questions. Alongside related #answertime posts, #issuetime posts cover topics such as prison abolition, net neutrality, reproductive rights, Black History Month, Trans Day of Remembrance, voting rights, and immigration.

Early in 2020, tumblr launched the #Issues2020 campaign to build users' civic engagement, stressing that "It's not too late to make a change ... the power is in your hands" (action 2020). Even though the blog post introducing #Issues2020 mentioned elections around the globe, some of the responses (see Figure 5.1) challenge tumblr's presumed US-centrism and politically left bias. Other comments ranged from

#dumblr

#this social network is a mess but I FUCKING LOVE TUMBLR

#there are more pressing matters in europe than voter suppression

Soooo, y'all finally gave up on hiding political bias, huh

Obvious political bias, much?

Меж тем по всем измеримым показателям мы живём в лучшем мире, чем все наши предки, каких ни возьми. (Translation: Meanwhile, by all measurable indicators, we live in a better world than all our ancestors, whatever you take.)

Tumblr: Let's talk about global issues! Also Tumblr: Most are issues from USA but u guys get it.

Vous maniez l'ironie avec brio. A ma connaissance, personne n'a fait mieux. (Translation: You master irony. To my knowledge, nobody's done it better.)

#tumblr is dense as shit I swear

#tumblr be like the world is like america but in different languages

Figure 5.1: A selection of responses to the tumblr staff's blog post on January 27, 2020, announcing their #Issues2020 campaign, including comments and hashtags added when users reblogged the post. Collated by authors.

enthusiastic praise to brandjacking the post to promote unrelated products (see Chapter 3).

Although social justice is a shared sensibility on tumblr, there are limits to its scope and influence. tumblr staff are not oblivious to this. Speaking to *Mashable* in 2016, social impact and public policy manager, Victoria McCullough, worried about the risk of tumblr's silos and communities becoming echo chambers not in dialogue with each other (Petronzio, 2016). Likewise, user reactions to the NSFW ban (see Chapters 1, 2, and 6) stressed that the platform was developing a Nazi, not nipple, problem, one the platform might also be slowly responding to. The most recent updates to tumblr's Community Guidelines acknowledge such hate speech. A staff blog post shares:

> You are why Tumblr feels like a home for so many. You care about this place, and you let us know when something doesn't feel right. Many of you have called on us to further reevaluate how we deal with hate speech, particularly hate speech from Nazis or other white supremacist groups ... so we're changing how we deal with them. ... We are, and will always remain, steadfast believers in free speech. Tumblr is a place where you can be yourself and express your opinions. Hate speech is not conducive to that. (staff 2020b)

The post illustrates tumblr's apparent struggle to consolidate its two conflicting commitments: to social justice and safe spaces, on the one hand, and to free speech, on another. Unlike many of its peers (e.g., Facebook), tumblr seems to be choosing justice, but this commitment should be taken with a grain of salt as corporate demands complicate tumblr's capacity to function as a safe space for social justice and respond to the less favorable qualities of silosociality. The NSFW ban we discussed in Chapter 1 demonstrates this clearly.

Practices for social justice

We now turn to *how* tumblr produces a social justice sensibility, returning to some of the ideas first offered in Chapter 2.

Presuming that most readers agree that social justice, in and of itself, is a good thing, it is important to note that the shared social justice sensibility is not uniform, nor does it always generate outcomes experienced to be just by all tumblr users. The shared sensibility should be thought of as a dominant way of sense making and moral value assigning, which in tumblr's case is indeed preoccupied with social justice, but can lead to harassment or bullying in the name of maintaining safe spaces or attending what is "problematic," depending on how one defines social justice.

Different silos and networks may embrace different rhetoric and language that produce *feelings* of a boundary, which intensify the political position within a silo and stress tumblr's politically charged character. This also contributes to how social justice sensibilities appear in different subcultures and communities as political, or how social justice language becomes siloed within shared interest-based groups. We first explore the "safer" spaces for social justice and the pedagogical social justice practices that tumblr is known for, then move to discuss virtue signaling, call-out culture, and dogpiling, most often linked to the figure of a Social Justice Warrior.

Safer spaces

Young people in our and others' research stress that tumblr was where they developed a social justice sensibility (see Chapter 2) and a vocabulary for identity politics and discrimination. tumblr was a "saviour" for Australian writer Jonno Revanche while growing up. Writing for the *Guardian* newspaper, Revanche (2016) shares feeling uncertain about their gender and sexual identities:

> witnessing other young people navigate those same issues in an open, honest way was incredibly validating for me. They proved that there could be more layers to those things than the stereotypes I saw portrayed in the culture at large. And

these weren't forced appeals to the youth like in LGBTQI-targeted youth services and mental health services (which clearly weren't made by young queer people) – they felt accessible, kaleidoscopic even, and I began sharing my own stories, feelings and experiences in response.

Likewise, writing about the experiences of queer youth of color on tumblr, Cho (2018a: 3184) asks:

> Where do you go when the world is tilted against you? How do you express yourself when the act of expressing – speech, desire, the smallest hand gesture – is itself a grave bodily liability policed out of the corner of a stranger's eye, by hostile peers, or even by the actual police?

As a safe space, or rather a *safer space* (see Chapters 2 and 6; Sharp and Shannon 2020; Vivienne 2019) for users facing everyday discrimination, marginalization, and violence, tumblr is where they go when the world is tilted against them. For some, tumblr has become an essential platform for sharing experiences, learning and debating ideas, and motivating action on social justice, activism, political issues, and identity. The platform allows users to find, define, and redefine their sense of self and identity, build affinity, and create and share resources (Dame 2016; Fink and Miller 2014; Oakley 2016; Renninger 2014). However, the value of tumblr as a safe or productive space is not static; users may embrace learning about issues and building skills to participate in personal and social change, but later find the same silo that made it possible to feel overwhelming or even "toxic."

Pedagogy for social change

As highlighted already in the Introduction, the participatory culture of tumblr is pedagogical. Pedagogy means teaching and learning, knowledge creation, and the practices and forms in which education happens. This is particularly true for social justice discourse. Creating, curating, and circulating resources for social justice and making and maintaining communities that function as safe spaces take on a distinctly pedagogical bent on tumblr. Learning on tumblr is different from learning in formal education settings like schools or from websites that organize information coherently under headings or key words (McCracken 2017). Typically, tumblr hosts information that is ignored in school curricula or in mainstream press or reframes curricula topics in more accessible ways. A popular tumblr post illustrates this: "Tumblr has taught me more about feminism, women rights, rape culture, slut shaming, etc, more than school ever had. And there is something wrong with that" (a deactivated 2013 tumblog post, 702,000 notes).

In Chapters 1 and 2, we highlighted tumblr's key affordances and its shared platform vernacular. These play an important role in how social justice is pedagogical. For example, reblogging allows users to curate archives and share information new or important, to them, for others to see. Reblogging, as we will go on to show, stands out as an informative, community-building practice rather than a mere gesture of political posturing or clicktivism. Pseudonymity and the ability to toggle between multiple blogs, but also the high interactivity, yet low reactivity, sponsored by tumblr's messaging and commenting systems decreases users' vulnerability, allowing young people to experiment with sharing political opinions.

tumblr's multimodal, remix-driven, and personal testimonial-based vernacular that foregrounds personal experiences underpin many users' motivations for social change, because it allows them to experience personal change (see Calhoun 2020; Mahmud 2020). Journalist Emma Sarappo wrote a 2018 story on how tumblr taught social justice to Generation Z, describing the slow process of learning to listen to other people's personal experiences. One interviewee, a white gay man, said that "prior to Tumblr, I was a Republican asshole." He described having joined tumblr "because of the memes," but realized that meme accounts frequently reblogged "some very new and liberal ideas" that he hadn't considered (Sarappo 2018). In particular, this man felt challenged about tumblr content regarding race, racism, and his own white privilege, and he was upset to the point where he would write "lengthy posts about how reverse racism is real." However, after "getting minor backlash for those posts" the interviewed man said he opened his mind to new perspectives, primarily because other people on the platform were sharing personal experiences and doing so in a very sincere way. Another of Sarappo's interviewees encapsulates the importance of the vernacular for social change: "tumblr had something that no other social media platform has really been able to replicate, which is the ability to get to know people in an environment that's sincere and earnest ... people fucking bared their souls on Tumblr." As Sarappo (2018) summarizes it, young adults on tumblr honestly and openly post "about how sexism or transphobia impacted their offline lives, or about how good it felt to see characters who looked, sounded, or acted like them as heroes in their favorite media." Similarly, Tom Ewing (2014) of the pop culture site Freaky Trigger has written: "What looks to dim outsiders as some kind of obsession with 'social justice' often just springs from people talking about themselves, their lives and the shit that happens to them."

Social justice on tumblr is about learning and teaching what aligns most with what scholars call social learning or critical pedagogy, a democratic learning process through communication and conversation with others (Freire 2018; Sharp and Shannon 2020). Some resources on tumblr do resemble traditional learning material (e.g., lists of statistics or histories), for example where users create educational materials, bringing academic vocabulary into discussions of TV shows, films, sexuality, or mental health (see Winterwood 2018; Chapter 4). Yet most social justice related learning on tumblr happens as networked peer learning (see Chapter 3 on "adulting"), via watching and listening to what other people do (Fox and Ralston 2016), or through the "process of cultural translation and connecting networks" (Ito et al. 2018: 3). As one example, in Julian Burton's (2017: 185) exploration of youth fandom communities on tumblr, a 14-year-old user *forestofgay* (a pseudonym) reflected: "[tumblr]'s helped me understand so much about current events, and develop my own political opinions different to those of my parents ... helped me to think about not just believing what I'm told (by adults, the media, or even other tumblr users)."

tumblr creates an enormous curated resource for social justice. In one of our research projects, tumblr was described as an important source that challenged representations in mainstream news media and offered different perspectives on the world through art, images, and visual content. Our research participant, 16-year-old Lana, reflected:

> Occasionally I watch the news on TV but a lot of how I find out about what's going on [is via tumblr]. It's almost like a less biased view on world topics, because I feel like the news is really ... it's really political, the news. They say it is free of, like politics and stuff, but it's not and it's definitely from an Australian perspective ... You see all these people portrayed as just horrible people and we shouldn't help them, they're totally different to us, all this, nonsense. And then you go on places like tumblr and you see the same issue but you get to find out about more perspectives ... and instead of just sitting on the couch and watching something and sort of mindlessly taking it in ... When I see something ... [about social change on tumblr] I want to know who did it and I want to know how ... what it was inspired by ... what their background is and all that sort of stuff. (Personal interview by authors, 2016)

But the multimodality and interactivity that tumblr affords also shape tumblr as an educational space. Users like Lana, who might not feel comfortable sharing their own personal experiences or feel they do not have personal experiences of systemic injustice, still curate visual and playful resources that create narratives of political and social issues they find personally relevant. "Aesthetics teach us by changing how we feel" (Hickey-Moody 2013: 79), which makes tumblr curation a type of affective pedagogy.[3] Visual images and aesthetically pleasing artwork provoke Lana's curiosity, because they connect emotionally and counter dominant discourses about politics, inspiring her personal expression about what is important. A photograph from her blog illustrates this, showing the outside wall of a building spray painted with the words "I DON'T BELIEVE IN GLOBAL WARMING," partly covered by a seemingly rising level of water, emphasizing the absurdity of disbelief in climate change in the face of physical evidence.

tumblr users selectively choose if and when they discuss justice and politics on tumblr based on what they feel is missing in conversations and posts. Burton's (2017) research participants articulated this as underrepresented or "important" topics that needed "signal boosting." One respondent, *wyvern-bodyguard* explained that "important" content includes "mostly social justice posts or anything with a more serious message that I think should be addressed" (Burton 2017: 154). Similarly, as 14-year-old Charlie described in the vignette opening this chapter, their tumblr is a space to collect "things that are important to me ... things that I think other people should see because they are important." Reblogging "important" posts or tagging posts with #important entered them into the collectively curated pedagogical streams, instead of explicitly engaging in contentious social commentary or political debate. This, Burton argues, allows users to "normalize their positions by pulling them out of the realm of controversial ideology and into that of information, thus figuring contrary views as somehow radical or simply uninformed" (2017: 183).[4] While this can be less antagonistic and less aggressive than social justice work that is experienced and framed as debate, it also runs the risk, as one of Burton's respondents described it, of "going after specific people who are seen as doing something wrong" (2017: 184). Thus tumblr's form of political debate as *education*, rather than *conflict*, aligns to the call out cultures we will describe shortly, and potentially makes challenging ideas dominant within a particular silo at a particular time quite difficult.

Finally, it is important to note that social justice-oriented learning, like the earlier circulation of feminist and women of color consciousness-raising material through social networks, normalize the "transformation of intellectual production from paid labor into unpaid 'content creation'" (Adair and Nakamura 2017: 263).[5] Such pedagogical work is rarely remunerated or even acknowledged; it becomes invisible, "allowing it to be easily extracted for free and compounding material inequalities between media owners and media users" (2017: 263). Social justice work on tumblr becomes another example of the invisible labor of, predominantly, marginalized users and communities.

Social justice warriors

tumblr's ambivalent relationship with social justice is perhaps most keenly illustrated through the figure of the "social justice warrior." Listing the "10 people you will meet on tumblr," in her article for *Thought Catalog*, Gaby Dunn (2013) writes that these zealous tumblr social justice activists are:

> the loudest in the Tumblr game. They are everywhere, ready to reblog a post that uses the word "crazy" in an ableist way and scold the person doing it. You run the gamut of social justice people on Tumblr – often, they're just kindly pointing out stuff you may not know (fair enough), but sometimes they're reeeeeal intense and should just be left to their own corner of the internet. If you f—k up, trust me, they'll find you.

Trying to uncover the amorphous practice and history of the contested figure and term of "social justice warrior" – SJW in its common and decontextualized abbreviation – is challenging. Massanari and Chess (2018) point to two simultaneous meanings of social justice warrior, depending on how and where the term circulates. In the first meaning, it is potentially empowering, evoking a strong warrior for global social change. Indeed, some tumblr users embrace the term and proudly label their blogs and tag posts with SJW. In the second, SJW is a pejorative take on a cartoonish, caricature figure of someone who is overly offended and "overly invested in identity politics and political correctness" (2018: 526). This take characterizes SJWs to only post about – not act on – social justice issues while hiding behind their pseudonymous blogs, an insincere activist version of the keyboard warrior.[6]

While the history of SJWs is opaque, they reached public mainstream visibility following Gamergate in 2014, where anti-SJW attention toward ethics and games journalism masked a backlash against gendered and progressive influences in gaming, and led to coordinated and persistent harassment and violence targeting women in gaming (Brock 2015; Chess and Shaw 2015; Massanari 2017; Massanari and Chess 2018). SJWs became a target "for a loose coalition of frustrated geeks, misogynists, alt-righters, and trolls," which allowed them to "coalesce around a common idea – that popular culture was "overly concerned" with a particular kind of identity politics" (Massanari and Chess 2018: 527). The long list of criticisms by bloggers, alt-righters, anti-tumblr redditors, trolls, and even some tumblr users directed at SJWs (and other associated figures like "snowflakes,"[7] "keyboard warriors," "feminazis," or "tumblr feminists") disparage the sincerity, logic, or motivation of SJWs' concerns, attention, and actions.

Yet, tumblr users are highly reflexive about the limits and problems surrounding SJWs and social justice tumblr. Internet meme archive site, Know Your Meme, points to critical and satirical engagement with SJW themes on tumblr prior to #Gamergate, documenting the tumblr blogs "Fuck No Tumblr SJW" (fucknotumblrsjw 2020) and "Social Justice Warriors of OKCupid" (sjwsofokc 2020) as early as 2011.

Reflecting on claims made by trolls who hacked tumblr's interface in 2012 to protest its complacent politics,[8] radio producer and playwright Bim Adewunmi (2012) acknowledged the complexity of tumblr and social justice:

> Here, the hackers' comments came uncomfortably close to a lot of Tumblr users' excesses. It is sometimes a deeply silly place, keen on self-congratulation. It is also largely decadent ... made of millions of fallible human beings, it's not always terribly original or profound. ... Tumblr is where I go to laugh, but it [is] also a fantastic place to learn: this is where I first read about Trayvon Martin, for example. It often hosts some of the most eloquent and nuanced conversations about society, from gender to race to equality and social justice.

This take reiterates what our research has discovered repeatedly: tumblr users may often be sincere in drawing on social justice language and concepts, but they also employ the term ironically as an inside joke or as a critique of click-activists' inaction. Only being embedded in a particular silo allows one to differentiate between the two. Whether or not SJWs are a real or coherent identity or group is beside the point; they become a shared antagonist figure that brings together diverse, broadly rightwing critics in their collective derision of the inauthenticity of a perceived SJW (Phelan 2019), alongside liberal activists who are critical of digital practices to make effective social change.

Virtue signaling, clicktivism, and brandjacking

Critique of SJWs emphasizes their actions as insincere "virtue signaling," the practice of conspicuously doing something "good" to show other people your moral values in order to gain social approval or praise, a self-interested desire for moral superiority (Phelan 2019: 45). They are framed as online-only activists who would prefer to *look* good rather than *do* good. This critique frequently aligns with accusations of "slacktivism" or "clicktivism," pejorative terms that refer to highly performative online practices as a form of political engagement that arguably have little impact overall. This may hold true if we accept traditional political action as the only legitimate form of political engagement. As Cho (2018b: 191) writes in relation to #BlackOutDay's selfie-based tumblr activism championing people of color (see Chapter 6), these practices may be "lacking conventional badges of political significance, centered around the most mundane and self-serving act of digital participation," however we should rather "disentangle affirmation in this sense from its connotation as a superficial platitude and understand that, on a register of visual, collective interference, it can be joyous, disruptive, and militant" (2018b: 199).

Specific anti-SJW practices on tumblr include hashtag jacking. Hashtag jacking is a form of brandjacking (see Chapter 3) – a set of "behaviours wherein consumers or customers appropriate, takeover, spam, or spoil a brand's original message or campaign by way of user-generated content" (Abidin forthcoming). In the case of anti-SJW practices on tumblr, "a hashtag ... becomes commandeered by others in the community and is then instead used to mock, satirize, or negatively critique the original hashtag sponsor" (Gilkerson and Berg 2018: 141). On tumblr this might involve deliberately hashtagging a critique of SJWs with the #sjw tag, or creating parody blogs that mock new gender and sexuality vocabulary. In our research, we found blogs and posts questioning "transgender radicalism" tagged with #trans and #pride, and blogs mocking discussions of white privilege using trigger warnings. These examples intentionally employ the language of social justice bloggers and redirect attention to their own critique, ridicule, or harassment. Ironically, understanding such trolling techniques as "satirical trolling" further highlight tumblr's silosociality, where even trolling tumblr users requires a deep knowledge of the right vernacular (Fichman and Dainas 2019).

Call out cultures and dogpiling

Anti-SJW discourse portrays SJW attitudes and actions as pointless and unconstructive, preferring to adopt a fascist orthodoxy that aligns to a politically correct (PC) culture that offers no meaningful contribution. In this light, SJWs are supposedly more interested in policing speech than changing the world. For example, YouTube "conscious" comedian (and later, COVID-19 denier) JP parodies SJWs outlining the steps to serving social justice: "I tell you what you should think while also getting the point across that you're a terrible person!" (AwakenWithJP, 2018).

Broadly, we can describe practices on tumblr that focus on demonstrating the "The Right Way To Be" or "correct" language or values through the notion of "call-out culture." A practice that directs attention to a person's moral aberration, call-out culture "publicly name[s] instances or patterns of oppressive behaviour and language use" (Ahmad 2015). As anthropologist and ethnographer Crystal Abidin (forthcoming) writes:

> By relying on their personal network of followers, viewers, fans, and even haters to audience and (hopefully) circulate their calls for social justice, users who partake in call-out cultures generate a slow thrust by spreading their politics and ethos through streams of social media "shares" dispersed across communities of users unknown to them.

Calling out problematic situations and behaviors is, like the notion of the SJW itself, contradictory. Call-out culture is portrayed as negative in the anti-SJW discourse, while, among tumblr users committed to social justice, calling out unjustness is a central, if thankless task. Digital media scholar Lisa Nakamura (2015: 106) highlights that much of this labor is "often-stigmatized and dangerous [and] performed by women of color, queer and trans people, and racial minorities." As such, the consequences of calling out, protesting, and educating others on platforms like tumblr are likely to be "rewarded differently and under different conditions" (2015: 107). tumblr users tend to nuance calling out. Olly, a transgender participant in one of our studies, reflected that:

> I've found a lot of sexual spaces, online and off, that are supposed to be safe – to actually be pretty intensely judgmental and policing – there's a whole lot of "This Is The Right Way To ... (fill in the blank)." Something I have noticed on tumblr and not on other sites (I'm thinking specifically of LiveJournal, here) is that there are relatively few instances of a group with a particular perspective or way of doing things sort of dogpiling someone who broke the rules. Groupthink seems to be frowned on. Plenty of individual call-outs, and there's room for those, which I dig, but not the YOU SAID THAT THING WRONG WE'RE ALL GUNNING FOR YOU NOW thing. (Personal interview by authors, 2012)

Dogpiling is a practice whereby someone encourages other users to respond en masse to something that is perceived as wrong, often leading up to collective harassment. Olly differentiates between individual call-outs and "dogpiling," arguing that he has experienced less of the latter on tumblr compared to other spaces.

Yet, in 2015, a 20-year-old user attempted suicide following dogpiling on tumblr. Writing for *Vice*'s technology site *Motherboard*, Clinton Nguyen (2015) describes how the user, *Zamiio70*, was labeled "problematic" for their drawings reimagining *Steven Universe*'s[9] non-normative characters in more stereotypical ways (drawing fat characters as skinny or whitewashing people of color). What some tumblr users perceived, and even later justified, as reasonable call-outs was described by tumblr user *midopyon* as a "[social justice warrior] circlejerk where you get to choose who stays and who is a racist ableist cis scum that deserves to be harassed to death" (Nguyen 2015).

Queer silosociality

On tumblr, users not only curate collective pedagogical and political resources through their posts and reblogs, they also produce new ways of understanding and expressing who they are. In this section, we focus on one specific social justice-related tumblr silo that illustrates both the love and the frustration of tumblr's silosociality; we also explore LGBTIQA+, gender diverse, and queer communities on tumblr. We draw on an in-depth case study with young women engaged with an Australian mental health service and on an extended ethnography with NSFW bloggers on tumblr; we also engage with work from other tumblr scholars. We explore what tumblr's silosociality produces for gender and sexually diverse individuals, referring here to queer, gay, lesbian, bisexual, asexual, pansexual, transgender, nonbinary, and intersex identifications.

The various gender and sexuality diverse communities and networks within the queer silo on tumblr are fitting as a "counterpublic" (Renninger 2014) "constituted through a conflictual relation to the dominant public" (Warner 2002: 85). tumblr's silosociality therefore allows and encourages users to explore their sexuality and gender removed from mainstream, heteronormative cultures and societies. Some have even argued that tumblr's features, affordances, and vernacular facilitate queer normativity (see Chapter 3) and queer and trans production (Fink and Miller 2014), justifying tumblr as a "trans technology," at least prior to the NSFW ban (Haimson et al. 2019: 10). However, while tumblr users may speak of "queer tumblr," of tumblr's "queer community," or even of tumblr as a "queer utopia" (Cavalcante 2019: 1720), the felt and affective experiences of connection within the silo may not be stable or enduring. In later chapters we highlight how curatorial and community-making tumblr practices enable users to accept their bodies, kinks, and desires (Chapter 6) or to make visible their emotional struggles (Chapter 7).

But here we pay close attention to the affective – productive as well as potentially ambivalent, overwhelming, or toxic – practices of identification.

Researchers have found over and again that tumblr counters dominant hegemonic heterosexual publics by enabling queer connection, belonging, and recognition (Oakley 2016; Vivienne 2016; Warner 2002), which make it "a crucial resource for connecting to and learning from queer and gender-diverse peers" (Byron et al. 2019: 2245). Platforms like tumblr provide "opportunities to mobilize, break down isolation and construct an alternative and liberating narrative" (Hanckel and Morris 2014: 886) through collective representations and practices that support recognition and inclusion (Fox and Ralston 2016). Users learn about sexual and gender diversity on tumblr through its queer normativity (see Chapter 3) and identify with and recognize themselves in others' shared experiences.

As one respondent, 19-year-old Charlie, explained in Byron et al.'s "Scrolling Beyond Binaries" project:

> Knowing there were other people who were this sexuality, or they were also transgender, that was a really big thing for me to able to see – that there were other people that were also figuring themselves out sexuality wise. That was a nice thing for 15-year-old me to find out about. (2019: 2245)

Likewise, media scholar Andre Cavalcante (2019: 1720) understands tumblr, compared to other platforms, as "the queer standard-bearer." One participant in Cavalcante's fieldwork with American LGBTQ youth stated: "There's this joke about Tumblr that everyone is queer, or at least some sort of 'social justice warrior.' And it's kind of true" (2019: 1720). The value of queer tumblr is that it "sustains LGBTQ users' sense of self, encourages them to talk back, and alters what they expect from the people and institutions they encounter in everyday life" (2019: 1727).

In our research, 14-year-old Mara shared an image from her blog, of two girls in "hipster" outfits and bright colored hair kissing. Mara reblogged mostly visual content from other tumblr blogs, including photographs, animated GIFs, and videos related to gender and sexuality issues, animals, funny content, social change posts, poetry, and "pictures that are cool." Central to her blog was the visibility of LGBTIQA+ and queer themes as "I haven't had really that much experience with a community like that, outside of social media."

> Mara: I didn't really know before I started dying my hair, that it was a big deal and a lot of people can't express themselves that way or other ways ...
>
> Interviewer: What kind of pressures would make it difficult for some people to express themselves?
>
> Mara: Well maybe religious, or their schools or education. But you know even their family or being part of the LGBT community. That could be kind of a bit of pressure too. That's another thing with identity, identity is really complex, people are like "Oh, but this is so important, you must get it right!" But being part of that community [on tumblr], being gay or whatever, that might be hard as well you know. Some people have a real issue with how other people express themselves.
>
> Interviewer: Is that a community that you identify with?
>
> Mara: Yes!
>
> Interviewer: It is a very complex picture then, for something you said is just two people kissing.
>
> Mara: But also, I was like this is really cute! And if I may say so myself, goals! [laughs]
>
> Interviewer: [laughs] Goals!
>
> (Personal interview by authors, 2016)

Mara was proud of her knowledge of LGBTIQA+ and "queer communities" – her words – on tumblr. Finding relatable "goals," Mara embraced new language and curated a potential future self that she could not see reflected or share elsewhere in her school or community. However, in the conversation about the image, it also became apparent that while tumblr was a place to learn, belong, and build a sense of self, it could also be a complicated place with its own pressures. We now explore the benefits and complications of queer silosociality in more detail.

Queer identity curation

Queer silosociality on tumblr enables identity curation, meaning that queer, gender-diverse, and sexuality-diverse users find themselves able to negotiate the risks of self-presentation and visibility and curate how they want to be seen and what they identify with (Hanckel et al. 2019). Writing about nonbinary people's experiences, Sharp and Shannon (2020: 139) posit "identity curation" to center how

> non-binary people synthesize the representations they put forward in social worlds, and simultaneously use to (re) form their identities. "Curation" may connote a considered particularity to the kinds of embodiments one chooses to perform, however the term also recognizes the embedded autonomy of living a queer life. By piecing together various forms of symbolism, communication and information, queers construct identities and embodiments that are representative of their most desired self.

tumblr allows identity curation where the "visual, textual and auditory representations of non-binary people can be tried out/tried on" (2020: 140). Users can modulate their identity performances (Duguay 2017), curate their real and imagined lifestreams, and produce narrative archives and be known "on one's own terms" (Wargo 2017b: 576).

However, this ability to curate and modulate identity performances can also create what Cavalcante (2019: 1717) has deemed a queer "vortex," one "defined by short periods of intense social interactions that do not sustain over time." Building and experiencing tumblr as a safe space for multiple, dynamic, and affectively authentic identity performances can tip over into "an almost totalizing" pull of attention that is unsustainable and becomes experienced by users as "too much." In Byron et al.'s (2019) study, users highlighted a similar ambivalence, describing both the joy and the discomfort of belonging to queer tumblr spaces, leading the researchers to question the usefulness of the language of community, a point we extend in the next section.

Overwhelming connection

Just as we noted in Chapter 2, tumblr is not a utopia. Engagement with and in tumblr's often disorienting dashboards and blogs may require sophisticated literacies to make sense of a playful "terrain of affinities speaking at a thousand miles a minute" (Cho 2015b: 44). For young people who find themselves with limited queer cultural (and economic) capital, this can be a challenge (Kanai 2019). Creative and emerging queer connections and recognition may not always be useful, productive, or even desired by all users, all of the time. For Revanche (2019), writing after their 2016 piece cited earlier in the chapter, tumblr's transformative power gradually crumbled as the platform lost some of the clarity with which it existed in public consciousness:

> A more analytical person might pin it down to changes made to the website in order to make it more sellable, as its creators thought about putting it on the market. However, in the process the things that made it unique, the aspects that separated it enough from Facebook, began to be lost.

Ambivalence toward participation in queer tumblr – its silosociality, emergent and dynamic vernacular, and shared practices – demonstrates the effects of tumblr's economic moves over time as well as some of the consequences of intense silosociality. The intensities of silosociality produce *both* a queer utopia (Cavalacante 2019) *and* an "atmosphere of negativity" (Byron et al. 2019: 2553), followed by an almost mandatory "cooling-off stage" (Cavalacante 2019). Making meaning from digital vernacular is a community-making process, although not always, for everyone and for the same people in a sustainable, unchanging manner. Even as our research participant Mara described what tumblr offered her, she found the platform "overwhelming" and "intense." She explained that working out who you are means that: "There's also a lot of pressure from the LGBT community, because there are so many different things and so many different labels ... I don't know if it's just teenagers, but ... especially I'd say at my age ... it's like a really big deal." This is complicated, she reasoned, while laughing: "There are all these people who are like 'Oh yeah there's a new sexuality, there's this, there's this! There's that!' I'm like 'Oh God, there's a new thing that I could be, and I don't even, I don't even know about it!'" (personal interview by authors, 2016).

Mara takes pride in her identity and regularly reblogs "LGBT community kind of stuff" even though it requires significant energy and motivation to manage feelings of being overwhelmed. Like Mara, respondents in Byron et al.'s project described tumblr to be both a crucial resource, yet at times, uncomfortable or exhausting (2019: 2550). They write that their research participants sometimes felt they had to "leave Tumblr, modify their use, or come to accept that Tumblr is an uncomfortable space." Of course, different users react differently to the utopian and vortex-like characteristics of the queer silo. While some might be overwhelmed, even paralyzed by the multiplicity of identity and sexuality labels, others might interpret the multitude as informative in and of itself. One of Byron et al.'s respondents, 20-year-old Casey, commented:

> I've learned a lot from Tumblr about sexualities. There's tons of argument – or used to be – between bisexuality and pansexuality. Some people are like, "They're the same." Some people thought that bisexuality was inherently transphobic because it's two genders ... But after Tumblr, I'm like, "words don't mean a thing." (2019: 2550)

The experience of being overwhelmed is not linked only to queer and gender-diverse identification. Our participant Mara also highlighted that she sometimes struggled to identify and interpret the US-centric and middle-class ironic queer cultural references and representations that remixed unfamiliar TV shows and films, internet celebrities, musical performers, and other cultural objects. It was difficult for her to keep up with a constant flow of new or changing representations of not only new gender or sexuality taxonomies, but queer culture in general: "[laughs] Because you see all these things that you don't know about yet, and you're like, God, there are more things to think about! Damn!" (personal interview by authors, 2016).

tumblr is a space for queer taste displays par excellence. It affords incoherence and unintelligibility, making it a perfect place for playful or ironic queer expressions that escape simple interpretation without compromising users' privacy or visibility. Yet, as evident in Mara's experience, it can also be confusing, perhaps even marginalizing. Cho's (2015b) reading of media scholar Henry Jenkins et al.'s (2007) work about participatory cultures is useful here. Cho notes that they outline that any participation gaps "may in fact be a class-based osmosis of a set of intuited or felt sensibilities, a sort of soft skill set that is not taught in school but rather absorbed by carefully crafted environmental surroundings and that were sensed and learned at the furthest end of deliberate consciousness" (2015b: 77). The affective work of social class, taste, and cultural capital shape tumblr as a silo that values particular classed, gendered, and sexualized experiences.

Emerging taxonomies

Despite being a source of potential confusion and overwhelm, queer tumblr's language developing, taxonomy making, and world building role has to be acknowledged. New language and words are a powerful resource for making sense of one's experiences (Robards et al. 2020), and cultural studies scholar Rob Cover (2018) identifies tumblr as a key site for creative and emerging taxonomy to articulate sexual and gender diversity. Complex language makes diverse experiences and identities recognizable (Oakley 2016) and allows for more nuanced, deeply felt, inclusive, and relational ways to describe desires and feelings. Yet, it also carries a risk of micro-minoritization, surveillance, and exclusion (Cover 2018). The iterative debates about sexuality or gender identification on tumblr resist closure: "questions are always open for debate because they remain persistently visible, shareable, and spreadable" (Dame 2016: 34). Returning to Mara, she reflects that she delayed identification: "I just calm myself down, like reassure myself like I don't have to ... be like anything now ... especially because I'm still a teenager, it's not a big deal" (personal interview by authors, 2016).

Whether or not Mara will later go on to embrace or dismiss this tumblr-based work to identify her sexuality, it is a form of what anthropologist Mary L. Gray (2007: 51) has called "queer identity work ... that at once chips away at and stabilizes coherent gay and lesbian identity categories."

Conclusion

While there is a shared sensibility of social justice on tumblr, users in specific social justice-oriented silos experience an ambivalent relationship to it. In this chapter, we explored how tumblr is a politically charged platform that has crucially shaped the political awareness and engagement of its users, particularly young people, through its history. User practices center personal stories about their lives and this makes tumblr a pedagogical space for addressing and making sense of social and political challenges. Queer tumblr, as one silo related to social justice, enables gender and sexuality diversity, and gives young people a way of recognizing and expressing their personal narratives within a collective of "like-others." It also produces an intense space for users to make sense of their lives and identities.

While we understand and accept the relevance of the broad imaginary of tumblr as a left-leaning social justice space and one that is celebratory or affirming for its queer- and gender-diverse users, we resist the generalization and simplification these imaginaries may invite. Just as tumblr empowers self-care and recognition, so too does disconnecting from the platform. In the next chapter we extend our discussion of sexuality on the platform and explore the NSFW silo and communities.

6

NSFW

Marilyn: I think our tumblrs sort of set up this openness with others.

Interviewer: With others who are on tumblr, or generally others, or just others that have specific types of tumblrs?

Marilyn: Others who have sex Tumblrs. Like the NSFW tumblrs. Or intellectual blogs. Hm ... I dunno.

Luna: It's not just about the sex, is it?

William: One of the things that happened for me with NSFW tumblr was that I, uh, matured? Originally for me it was all about sex. I guess at one point in time I was more comfortable letting people see my penis than I was letting them know how I lived my life.

Dan: This sounds odd, but over the past 18 months with tumblr I've "refined" who I am on tumblr AND in RL.

William: And sexuality is still a pervasive influence ... but it's much more complex. And it has to do with this openness of NSFW tumblrverse.

Luna: It seems to me that NSFW on tumblr kind of weeds out the narrow-minded ones.

Marilyn: I've learned so much from some of the pornblrs I follow. Relationships, literature, politics, BDSM, Australia ... I could go on.

Interviewer: If it's so diverse, then do the NSFW tumblogs have anything in common? Does anything unite all these blogs and people?

Marilyn: We're people who are willing to be "open."

Dan: What unites us is the willingness to converse with people about things we can't talk about in public (at work, at home) and be true to ourselves.

> (Group interview by authors with NSFW tumblr users, November 2012)

For more than a decade NSFW[1] content and cultures flourished on tumblr. It was an ecosystem of diary-like sex blogs, carefully curated galleries of sexual visuals, collections of literotica (erotic literature), blogs that were not about sex, but occasionally sexually explicit for activist, self-reflexive, or humorous purposes, repositories of porn GIFs and, on the fringes, a growing rot of porn bots. tumblr was known and accepted – both on and off the platform, both in and outside the NSFW silo – as a space that was profoundly relaxed about sexually explicit content. As a result, NSFW content spread far and wide, and people who spent a lot of time on the platform in the mid-2010s credit it with their sexual awakening to this day (Barrett-Ibarria 2018; Greenwood 2020). Those who took part in the NSFW-silo have, for years, told researchers that their experiences were deeply meaningful far beyond horny browsing or attention seeking. NSFW tumblr allowed them to appreciate their own and other people's bodies; to express, learn about, and accept their own and other people's sexualities; to diversify their desires and worldviews; to build and belong to intersectional communities; and to push back against hegemonic representations (see Byron 2019; Byron et al. 2019; Cho 2015b; Engelberg and Needham 2019; Haimson et al. 2019; Hart 2018a, 2018b; Mondin 2017; Paramanathan 2019; Tiidenberg 2014b, 2017, 2019b; Tiidenberg and Gomez Cruz 2015; Tiidenberg and van der Nagel 2020; Zamanian 2014). NSFW, thus, was threaded into the very fabric of the platform just like fandom and social justice are.

To illustrate the nuance and richness within the NSFW silo, this chapter explores the life of a specific community and focuses primarily on the golden, pre-NSFW ban years (see Chapter 1). The pseudonymous, fairly tight-knit community of internationally situated, but anglophone, bloggers created original visual and textual sexual content and curated each other's and web-sourced content to give it new meaning, or to incorporate it into personal narratives of pleasure, desire, politics, and identity. The bloggers we studied as part of this community were 21–60 years old at the beginning of fieldwork in 2011 and most, but not all of them, were White. Their sexuality, gender, and sexual lifestyle identifications varied (cis, nonbinary, trans, straight, gay, bi, queer, vanilla, kinky, non-monogamous, monogamous). We call them a community because they shared activities, identities, and a sense of space, offered social support to one another and built close relationships (Baym 2015, Tiidenberg and van der Nagel 2020). But also because they articulated their experience as a community. "It's a space where a common language, perspective, and a set of rules exist, founded primarily on respect and consideration," one participant said when describing the community, while another remarked that "there is very little judgment, people often reach out without hesitation and can be super helpful."

In this chapter we discuss how the community became a safe space that allowed sexual exploration, encouraged body-positivity, and helped users to find an agential voice and use it for both activism and self-care. In the empirical reality these are, of course, entangled. Trans* selfies (Haimson et al. 2019), for example, often function as documentations of transition, gestures that seek support, statements intended to purpose-fully diversify visual discourse, *and* as self-(re)presentations intended to be sexually or aesthetically appealing (see Chapter 5). Further, people's experiences of what NSFW tumblr afforded transformed over time. Something that started out as fun could become educational, empathy fostering, tolerance generating, and, finally, agency building (see Conclusion). For the purpose of analytical clarity, we have organized this chapter in five sections. We start with an exploration of how this NSFW community came together and how it functioned. We then move to how partaking in the community allowed its members to accept their own and other people's bodies and sexualities. Then, we discuss how all of this gave some people a stronger sense of agency to the point where they started advocating for social justice. We then describe some of the issues and conflict within the community and the NSFW silo. Finally, we pan out to a discussion on why we call it the NSFW silo, rather than, for example, a porn silo or a sex silo.

NSFW community as a safe space

For most of our research participants tumblr was the first place where they found information and discussions on pleasure and sex that were not judgmental. Participants habitually attributed a specialness to tumblr that allowed them to have validating and generative experiences. Bloggers struggled to break down this specialness, but, when asked, usually named the affordance of pseudonymity and the rules that allowed NSFW content, but also hinted at the importance of the shared vernacular and sensibility by saying that the "overshary and raw" blogging style tends to "accelerate intimacy." All together this led to NSFW tumblr being experienced as "open" and "flexible." Eric, one of our research participants, offered the following analysis:

> tumblr is more flexible. It doesn't confine things. Like, no one is going to be sharing erotica on Twitter, or have a stream of explicit images on their Facebook. Other than Fetlife (which I would wager is much, much smaller than the similar demographic on tumblr), there's nowhere you could post a story, an explicit photo of yourself, easily share a photo of another person you follow, etc. ... So it's much less confining to post a variety of content on tumblr and it's also much easier to be sexually explicit because you have more anonymity and less chance of running into your IRL friends. There isn't another platform that's very accommodating for sharing the wide variety of sexual content you find on many tumblrs. Let alone interacting around it. FB and Instagram ban sexual content. So first and foremost, there isn't another platform that resembles tumblr without a whole lot more regulation. (Personal interview by authors, 2016)

Many of our participants had worried, prior to finding NSFW tumblr, that their preferences, practices, or fantasies somehow deviated from what they presumed to be the norm. On tumblr, they felt assured that there were other people – nice, friendly, fascinating people – who were interested in the same things. One of our participants, Nadine, confessed:

> When I was a kid, I figured out what I wanted in terms of, like, not only on a sexual level, but I had a very vague inclination that I didn't want to be monogamous and that I had sort of these kinky things going on, and I, like, really couldn't find anyone to relate to for a really long time. And I didn't know how to talk about it. I actually went to my mother, which was a really stupid idea, and tried to talk to her about it. She got very defensive, and very upset, and very disturbed by it, and just for years I didn't talk about it. I was actually proud of myself when I spent a week not thinking about it and I don't know ... on tumblr it's just nice to see that there's so many other people and they're not, like, judging you, for the most part. I've been surprised to see that people have had similar experiences, because I've felt like, I must be the only person who is that disgusting, and then to figure out that it is actually not that disgusting, and actually a lot more common than I was giving myself credit for. It sort of validates that I'm not, like, a weirdo. (Personal interview by authors, 2012)

Silosociality, as described in Chapter 2, functions through intensities of affect and affinity, which stick particularly strongly to those interests that people presume they would be marginalized about in other online and offline social spaces. NSFW tumblr offered exactly that – a space to express usually suppressed aspects of one's self. In this context, it is unsurprising that our participants described their NSFW tumblr community as a "tribe," a secret part of the house behind a hidden door, a crowded bar created solely for the purposes of therapy, even a VFW hall.[2] Whichever metaphor they chose, validation and affinity were almost always mentioned. The bloggers we studied felt that on their blogs and in the shared conversations between them, they could talk openly about personal sexual experiences and desires, which reduced the shame they felt, destigmatized specific sexual acts or preferences, and challenged assumptions about who has or desires what kinds of sex (Tiidenberg and van der Nagel 2020). By definition, this is what safe spaces afford (Muise 2011; Wood 2008). But what made NSFW tumblr a safe space? Was it just the spark of the potentially stigmatizable shared interest?

We argue that the experience of safety emerged from and was maintained by what philosopher Paul B. de Laat (2008) has called *trust responsiveness*. In simple terms, it means that people assume others can be trusted to accept what they post, or if they do not, to move on without judgment, scorn, trolling, or abuse. If these assumptions are repeatedly justified, trust responsiveness is maintained and contributes toward trust and intimacies between strangers. Look at how Jenna described the tacit rules of the community:

> [A]s a general rule you don't ... sort of ... you don't make negative comments that are going to hurt somebody's um ... confidence about, like their body or ... especially their body, because I think as a society we're very, very hard on that. There's definitely some underlying rule, I'm not totally sure what it is, I feel like it's sort of just "treat others the way you want to be treated." I feel that's a rule, but it's also a rule offline that should be followed, but I feel it is followed much more on tumblr. (Personal interview by authors, 2012)

One of the prevalent shared practices in the community was taking and sharing sexy selfies – images of bodies[3] in various stages of undress. These sexy selfie practices are a perfect case study to demonstrate the trust responsiveness in action. Because of the cultural status of public nudity and the gendered double standards historically attached to it, posting sexy selfies on technically public blogs opened tumblr users up to potential stigmatization and scorn. Widely publicized cases of revenge porn, leaked images, and sexting scandals have taught us that people (especially women) posting their naked bodies are at risk of being judged or harassed on grounds of lacking morals (e.g., slut shaming, threats to professional image) or because of their appearances (e.g., body shaming). In this community, however, people repeatedly experienced no abuse concerning either of these vulnerabilities (this is not always the case across tumblr; in Chapter 7 we talk about people reducing disclosure to avoid vulnerability). Instead, study participants felt accepted and appreciated, registered this with surprise, and committed to consciously contributing to such support being available to both themselves and others. They did so through practices of *voluntary vulnerability* and *paying it forward* (Tiidenberg and Whelan 2019), which we consider to be NSFW silo-specific expressions of tumblr's platform sensibility (see Chapter 2). Peter's experiences illustrate this:

> Peter: I think sometimes I will reblog women's photos they've posted of themselves even if the picture is not of great quality, uh ... sometimes I do it just to just kind of give them some encouragement or to just give them some positive indication ... um ... just because I've gotten so much of that.
>
> Interviewer: Can you give me an example of encouragement you have received?
>
> Peter: I was very hesitant to post pictures showing my whole torso, in particular my stomach, just because I don't have a flat stomach ... and I think I posted something about it, that I was hesitant about it and I got a lot of encouraging feedback, where ... somebody, at least one person, pointed out to me, look at all these women you're posting and praising, who certainly don't have perfect, you know "perfect" bodies, they certainly have flaws just like anybody else, and some women that you post are, you know have stomachs too and they are comfortable doing it. (Personal interview by authors, 2012)

Uma, another of our participants, had observed something similar, but where Peter framed his experiences in the context of body-normativity and gendered appearance standards, Uma focused on age:

> Seeing other people's images and the feedback I got for my
> own was so important for me to feel good about myself ...
> I want to do the same thing for them, I want to encourage
> ... I want to be a good role model for sexy 50, right? I want
> people to look at my pictures and think: "oh I can be that
> too!" (Personal interview by authors, 2012)

Practices of voluntary vulnerability and paying it forward
can thus destabilize (Plummer 2007) dominant cultural
discourses on what is beautiful or sexy or whose body deserves
to be shown and seen. When people claim control over their
own sexual storytelling (Plummer 1995) they also claim some
control over the aesthetics of sexiness in a wider sense.

Having experienced that sexuality, nudity, and kink – all
topics so easy to stigmatize – were tolerated or even validated
in this space led bloggers to share more and more about their
personalities, thoughts, or anxieties on their NSFW blogs.
Eric said:

> I guess here I'm very honest about my thinking, about
> what's on my mind, about what I like and what I don't like.
> So, in that regard, it's a lot more open. Whereas on my other
> blog [a SFW blog that his friends and family know of], a lot
> of the times I might want to post something, but I don't,
> because I'm afraid what people might think about it ... often-
> times with real-life friends I feel like it can be hard to go to
> them about certain things, you might go to somebody else
> online. (Personal interview by authors, 2012)

Thus, people shared all manner of content that fell outside
the existing moral, visual, commercial, and normative
standards on their NSFW blogs. Images of bodies that did not
meet the ageist, sizeist,[4] racist, sexist, and ableist standards
of "sexy" or "beautiful" were commonly and purposefully
circulated (Tiidenberg 2017; Tiidenberg and Gómez-Cruz
2015). Kinky, queer, or polyamorous practices had a place
within shared representations of desire and relationships
(Tiidenberg 2014a; Tiidenberg and Paasonen 2019). A sexual
subject position was routinely attributed to breastfeeding,

pregnant, or menopausal women (Tiidenberg 2014b), but also genderqueer people and men performing nonhegemonic masculinities. But people also found it easier to discuss their politics, their fannish excitements, their mental health issues, their anxieties and their daily frustrations, or share their creative works on their NSFW tumblogs. Through all this, people reworked their relationships with their own bodies and bodies as such, "took back" their sexualities from the normative stories of Hollywood and sex-ed, and reassessed their relationships as they learned to question the status quo that erased or marginalized them (Tiidenberg and Whelan 2019). In the next section, we describe the process of gaining such self-awareness in more detail.

Learning and empathy

While we have already addressed some of the functions that NSFW tumblr more broadly, and sexy selfie practices more narrowly, had for people, we want to stay with the example to really illuminate the process through which tumblr users grew to accept themselves, empathize with others, and consciously contribute to the diversification of discourses on bodies and sexualities. In the following interview snippet, Katie, one of our participants, described her experiences with taking and sharing sexy selfies, illustrating how NSFW tumblr became entangled with her attempts to find self-compassion and recalibrate her relationship with her own body:

> I post pictures of myself where I like what I see. And the more pictures I take, the more things I find to like. And now I have pages of evidence that I like my body. I've never in my life spent time trying to genuinely like my body. Only time trying not to hate my body. Those are very different things. (Group interview by authors, 2012)

She had started her blog a few months after having her second son and realizing how frustrated she was with the way society "strips pregnant and nursing women of their sexuality." Her blog was thus intended as something to help her reconnect with her sexual self, but became "empowering, therapeutic, entertaining and hell of a lot of fun." Taking and sharing selfies helped Katie unfix (Coleman 2009) her body from experiencing it as inferiorized (Bartky 1990) or otherwise culturally overburdened (Shilling 2003). This became particularly clear after the NSFW ban (see Chapter 1). Katie and others in the community told us that when it was no longer available, they realized that tumblr had offered quite a unique arena for sexy selfies that neither narrowly sex-centric apps and platforms (e.g., OnlyFans, Fetlife[5]) nor sexting could substitute (Tiidenberg 2019b). This is probably why pre-ban tumblr continues to be cast as a "hotbed for *everybody's* nude photos and naughty videos" in popular retrospectives (Greenwood 2020, emphasis added).

Of course, not all instances of posting sexy selfies to tumblr guaranteed a validating outcome. Our participants had plenty of experiences where they disliked what the camera showed them. Sometimes, the feedback did not meet their expectations. Body-negative, unkind comments were rare, but did happen. Rachel, who had shared in an interview that she had suffered from body dysmorphic tendencies her whole life and that posting sexy selfies on tumblr had been reparative for her, was once sent an anonymous message that called her "an overweight mommy." As she had previously received so much support and had become more accepting of her body by that point, she was able to push back against the message rather than be disheartened by it. As a response, she took a series of representationally, aesthetically, and compositionally assertive sexy selfies, and posted them with a sarcastic thank you note to the anonymous hater (see Tiidenberg 2014b). But Rachel did not stop at snark. Instead, a couple of days later she wrote a reflexive essay on the occurrence. A section of it read:

All this has only made me more defiant. It has strengthened my conviction that what Tumblr self-shooters[6] do – in our variety, in our different skin colors, shapes and sizes, our choices of self-presentation – is important, not just for ourselves but for others. It is important that we continue to stand firm against this rigid thinking about standards of bodies and beauty. It is only through seeing other women and men on tumblr showing their bodies, and saying "I do not look like a model, but I still like my body" that I learned to stop comparing myself to impossible photoshopped standards, and to accept myself. I have learned to appreciate so many different kinds of beauty that I was blind to before. I cannot think that this is anything but a good thing.

Over time such experiences layered and turned our participants' blogs into catalogues of self-love and archives for further self-reflection. Body-positivity extended into something lived rather than something purely rhetorical, and people's self-awareness became more nuanced. In an interview on her non-monogamous lifestyle, another participant, Katie, commented on how surprised she had been at the various functions NSFW tumblr gradually took on for her:

It makes me more aware of the things that push my buttons, it exposes me to new interests. It definitely helps me understand kinks or inclinations that I don't share. I follow mostly first-person-narrative blogs, so I get to read about the whys and what's behind these kinks and interests. It's very educational. (Personal interview by authors, 2013)

Katie's comment highlights the self-reinforcing cycle between tumblr having been experienced as a safe space for expressing things often judged or marginalized elsewhere, and it becoming a space of learning. What users see on their dashboards every day matters. While the NSFW bloggers we studied actively curated their feeds, their control over exactly which bodies, bodyparts, sexual acts, kinks, thoughts, dreams, or anxieties they saw was partial. After choosing to follow, and then not to unfollow, specific blogs, it was those other bloggers who co-curated the dashboard experience for each other.

But even more important than the diversity of visual representations was the context these visuals often came with. Katie mentioned first-person narratives, which we underscored in Chapter 2 as central to tumblr vernacular. In this community, sexual visuals were usually accompanied by captions and/or hashtags. The person posting revealed – explicitly or vaguely – why they were posting this content, what creating it made them feel, or why they chose to repost something of someone else's. They would indicate whether their post was intended as humorous, serious, titillating, angry, anxious, or sad. First-person narratives served an educational, reflexive, perhaps even a mobilizing function. Xavier, one of our interviewees, told us:

> It's definitely been eye-opening, especially reading about others' fantasies and sexuality, since this stuff typically doesn't get talked about in America outside of the bedroom and in pornography. ... A lot of what I am reading and following is related to BDSM, which has been a long-term interest, let's say, but not anything I'd been able to bring to my sex life. So, reading what other people are writing and fantasizing about made it easier to jump in and explore that side of myself a bit. ... I suppose I read a lot of really unhelpful second-wave feminist critiques of porn in the past and internalized a bit of that criticism. I didn't know how to reconcile the sort of ostensible violence and dominance of BDSM with what I believed politically about feminism, equality of women, etc. ... So reading posts by women who are fantasizing about submission made it easier to accept what is going on in my own head. (Personal interview by authors, 2012)

Where Xavier learned about other people's practices, experiences, and perceptions of BDSM in ways that allowed him to accept himself and change how he related to his own desires, Nadine credits NSFW tumblr with having taught her how to relate to other people in the context of her preferred sexual and romantic lifestyle of polyamory:

I think it's taught me most importantly the value of communication. And not to assume. And to check-in constantly. Which I may have picked up eventually but it helped to just kind of know that stuff going in. I think poly ties into the aspect of feminism that I'm not my partner's property and the relationship should be on equal footing. We don't have authority over each other and we're free to express our feelings about how things affect us without commanding each other to do one thing or another. tumblr is very good at driving that home. (Personal interview by authors, 2013)

It is impossible to overestimate the relevance of context when making sense of how NSFW tumblr became an educating and empathy building space. Those personalized comments revealed the nuances of people's desires, and turned body positivity and sexual tolerance from a concept into a practice. Thus, for anyone spending any kind of extended time embedded in the content flows of this particular community and much of the NSFW silo, it would have been impossible to look at another user's sexy selfie and interpret it merely from the objectifying perspective of "nice tits, wanna fuck?"

Finding and using a voice

Previous sections delineate how, through shared practices and vernacular, a community is made that allows people to accept themselves and others and to be more tolerant and empathetic. Users notice shifts in their own perceptions and practices, which leads to a shared sense of responsibility and a silo-specific expression of the sensibility of commitment to social justice (Chapter 2). Our participants said they felt responsible for how they interacted with others and their content, but also for what they represented as they created and shared content. Finally, they also felt responsible for what representations they amplified (Villi 2012) or which marginalized stories they highlighted as they reblogged. Katie explains:

> Well now I feel this strange sense of responsibility to be really
> honest [*laughs*] to talk about the real ups and downs. Like, at
> times when I didn't want to journal and "ruin" the fairytale
> of non-stop hot sex, I was encouraged by the fact that (a) it
> was so cathartic for me to write about these realities and (b)
> I wanted to be real for those who were reading. There is a
> lack of information out there for couples in open marriages.
> And the info that is out there is so skewed. Everything I
> read before I started was either erotic storytelling or about
> swinging or wife swapping. Nothing tackled the emotional
> issues involved with navigating polyamorous experiences.
> (Personal interview by authors, 2012)

These shared repertoires of responsibility were NSFW-silo
specific examples of what we conceptualized in Chapter 2
as an ethical sensibility. Our participants often articulated
this experience of becoming more self-aware and developing
this shared sensibility as an experience of *finding a voice*, a
process that often started from the bloggers noticing – either
in interview or in a self-reflexive blog post – that they had, as
a result of spending time in the NSFW tumblr silo and in the
community, developed a capacity to push back when faced
with actual or imagined shaming. As Marilyn said:

> I have always stood by my tumblr in terms of my rationale ...
> because I'm not getting paid for this, I'm not representing a
> company, I'm not wearing Calvin Klein underwear, I'm not
> in any way marketing this. I am ... this is a self-exploration,
> this is a finding of myself, and I ... feel ... if I were ever to
> be ... confronted with these images ... my first thing would
> definitely be: "I don't see what's wrong with it because I was
> of age and I was exploring who I am as a person and I don't
> see what the difference is between Megan Fox doing it for
> Armani and me doing it for myself." (Personal interview by
> authors, 2012)

Finding a voice could also emerge from a realization that
there is more than one way of enacting sexiness, femininity,
masculinity, or genderqueerness, or practicing a kink. In
a blog post from 2016, one of our participants wrote that,

after tumblr had exposed her to queer and feminist NSFW content,

> [I] realized that there are bratty submissives and little submissives, play pets and do-it-yourselfers, lady doms and femme daddies and gender queer tops and bottoms. I realized that people's kink is versatile and fluid and still authentic. So I was able to find an aesthetics and a dynamic that suited me, appealed to my senses and felt right. You build a dynamic with your partners, and it can be whatever you want it to be. So now my kink is like me, it fits me and my partners, and we create it as we go, building on parts that feel right until we have something that we love and can't get enough of. (Participant blog, 2016)

However, our participants did not only use their newfound, subversive voice to stand up for themselves, some of them put it to use to advocate for social justice. Rachel, describing her progression in a 2015 interview, noted that taking and sharing sexy selfies had helped her deal with her own body issues and made her feel that her "sexual shelf life was far from over," after which she entered a phase where her posts had to serve a bigger purpose: "At that point I really felt that there had to be a purpose to posting selfies, there was much more of a politicization to it, I was doing it for body positivity. So, it went from kind of pure sexual exhibitionism to testing out different personas to a more explicitly politicized thing."

Creating and curating sexual content in a safe space, consuming it with context, and building relationships in the process merged into a conscious, even activist, sensibility and a curatorial practice we've previously called "paying it forward." Our study participants started to purposefully post images of bodies or body parts they felt were underrepresented or marginalized in the popular visual discourse, or reblogging other people's selfies for other reasons than appreciation of what was on the image. A clear example of curatorial activism (Reilly 2018) in the NSFW silo was its engagement with the #BlackOutDay or #TheBlackout hashtag. On March

6, 2015, Black social media users were sharing selfies to flood
the feeds with Black faces – tumblr user *T'von Green* came
up with the idea in February 2015, making #BlackOut yet
another social justice hashtag public that originated on the
platform (see Chapter 5 for a discussion on #theBlackout).
After that, some users continued the practice in the form of
#BlackOutDay or #BlackOutFriday. Queer and NSFW users
on tumblr participated in this hashtag public (Rambukkana
2015) with gusto. Cho (2018b) points out that the queer-of-
color selfies posted with these hashtags are explicitly political,
as they rhetorically link the images to the #BlackLivesMatter
movement and the basic media studies tenet that "representation matters." Sociologist Matt Hart's (2018b) young black,
NSFW, and queer participants said that #theBlackOutDay
helped them to not be "insecure about our bodies, to not be
ashamed of our big asses, thick thighs, and stretch marks."
Our own NSFW participants engaged with #theBlackOut as
well, with multiple White participants consciously choosing
to not post any selfies on those days, instead using their
popularity to purposefully reblog and amplify the attention
that the Black sexy selfies got.

Existing scholarship on visual cultures and meaning
making has argued for decades that images teach us how
to see (Bordo, 2003). Popular amateur images, in particular,
communicate and strengthen collective moral and aesthetic
norms of what particular populations, at particular times,
deem "photographable" (Bourdieu 1996). Creating content
and partaking in the NSFW community led tumblr users
to experience a transformation in both their ways of seeing
(Berger 1972) and their relationships with their own bodies,
sexualities, and identities. While the NSFW community with
their specific culture of looking and being looked at existed
in the broader context that remains limiting (Gavey 2012),
and could not dismantle the sexist, ageist, sizeist, and racist
standards of the visual economy, it played an important part
in confusing it, and reinforcing a new, body-positive, feminist,

and queer-friendly visual discourse. We argue, then, that NSFW tumblr users were not just representing their naked bodies, interpreting representations of those of others, interacting with each other, building affinity; they were – almost as an unintended consequence – working on themselves and resisting dominant norms (Tiidenberg and Whelan 2019).

"tumblr doms" and image-based sexual abuse

This chapter has painted the NSFW silo in fairly bright colors. The community we have described was a pleasant, uplifting, generative space, but neither it nor the broader silo was devoid of interpersonal conflict, insidious social dynamics, and harassment. Partially overlapping with the community we studied was a network of blogs by young women, all interested in the same sexual kink. In 2012, two of the more popular and charismatic bloggers within that network recast it as a rigidly hierarchical imaginary army, with roles (e.g., Private, Sergeant) that came with privileges and had to be competed over in a complicated public performance of in-fighting and bullying. The army also had Fightclubesque commandments (e.g., "Fuck Facebook and Twitter. Deactivate them bitches," and "Never mention tumblr in the presence of family," but also, rather cryptically, "Threesomes," and "Don't call your mom a whore"). Elsewhere in the silo there were conflicts over ethics of photoshopping, the acceptable practice when it comes to separating images from captions in reblogs, and on saving and reposting images others had shared instead of reblogging them (Tiidenberg 2016). Among those interested in BDSM, a notion of a noxious "tumblr dom" emerged, well known enough to warrant a definition in the Urban Dictionary (2019). A tumbr dom is: "A fuckboy who tries to use kink to justify being a sexist prick. Named after the website tumblr because for a while asshole guys would go on there and inexperienced subs would flock to them when they knew nothing."

Finally, in the larger NSFW silo, tumblr was, at times, a space where young women were harassed and abused. In 2015, a group of young women and girls in Singapore found themselves to be victims of doxxing. Their SFW images were posted to a network of tumblogs with highly sexualized captions, or worse, their faces were superimposed onto nude pictures (Zheng 2019). tumblr users perusing these tumblogs were encouraged to locate the young women on their personal social media platforms via name searches, and pseudonymous users would frequently update posts and tumblogs with more doxxed information, such as the location of the schools the girls were attending and information about their extracurricular activities or whereabouts. Despite Singapore's stiff laws banning pornography, tumblr was commonly used to "house" and archive nonconsensual pornography that was usually first surfaced or leaked on the more surveyable social media platforms or private groupchats such as Telegram (Peh 2020). In a particularly distressing incident, a prolific Singaporean influencer had intimate videos with her former partner leaked and circulated on tumblr, after the latter's cloud was apparently hacked (Harper's Bazaar Staff 2018; Tai and Cheong 2020). While the pair and their legal team worked to have the videos removed from various social media platforms, including Facebook and Reddit, the videos were endlessly reblogged and still freely available across dozens of tumblogs (Kiew 2018). The "take down" notices that had been issued to users on other platforms did not seem to work on tumblr, where users are predominantly pseudonymous and untraceable.

NSFW ≠ porn

You would notice that we have called this silo the "NSFW tumblr, rather than "porn tumblr" or "sex tumblr." We believe that "NSFW" describes the culture most accurately and is most relevant to understanding tumblr. In the interview excerpt introducing this chapter, Marilyn refers to the silo by mentioning "sex tumblrs" first, then "NSFW tumblrs," then "intellectual blogs," and finally, "pornblrs." The blogs within the community were multifaceted and her language reflects it. There was porn on NSFW tumblr, yes, but there was also intellectual discussion, and a lot of sexually explicit content that does not qualify as porn. There was advice, information, fantasy, self-reflection, documentation, humor, and arguments about sexual acts, practices, identities, subcultures, lifestyles, preferences, representations, and discourses. Some of this content was textual, a lot of it was visual, but original visual NSFW content (mostly faceless selfies) depicted sexually intended (partial) nudity, rather than sexual activity we would typically associate with porn.

Differentiating porn from non-porn, of course, is more difficult than it may seem and the category of "sexually intended" is not uniformly clear either. Boundaries between "mainstream" and "amateur" porn have blurred (Paasonen 2011) as pornographic and porn-adjacent (e.g., PornHub's Twitter commentary) content has become ubiquitous on social media (Paasonen et al. 2019). Photos have always had multiple meanings (Barthes 1977), which emerge in negotiation between the photographer, the photographed, the genre conventions, and audience interpretations (Berger 1972). NSFW selfies are no different. Further, content on social media can have a very long social afterlife[7] (Klastrup 2007). Visual content can easily detach from its original narrative within a post as captions and hashtags change in the course of reblogging (see Chapter 1). An image intended and interpreted as sexy can hop communities, while still remaining on tumblr and even within the NSFW silo, and suddenly become ridiculous, shameful, or funny. One of our participants, Luna, posted a "rainbow panty dance" video as a joke, because within the community there was a brief trend of posting bad dance moves. The video was reblogged far and wide and, at some point, a teenage boy with a Star Wars fan blog reblogged it with a patronizing comment warning girls that sending sexy content to their boyfriends was a bad idea as it would obviously end up online after a breakup. Alternatively, something created and initially accepted as documentary or self-therapeutic can be appropriated into someone's spank bank. Something created as an exercise of body acceptance can be reinterpreted from a body-normative stance. As Iris, a NSFW tumblr user, said:

> my husband often criticizes my body, so it's nice [that] tumblr has been like a place where I haven't felt criticized. I've never, ever had anyone [here] say anything negative. I have been reblogged on "big beautiful women" and "thick" blogs though, which isn't my favorite thing to happen. (Personal interview by authors, 2012)

Similar remixing and reinterpretation used to happen to stills and GIFs from pornographic material. Feminist media scholar Alessandra Mondin's (2017) research participants took "more normative" pornographic images and recontextualized them as queer or feminist. To do so, they would add captions that imagined a backstory to what was happening, or included a perspective that reflected non-normative desires. Further, the interpretational flexibility and multiple meanings of images were utilized for incorporating non-sexual visuals into users' curatorial self-expression. NSFW bloggers would post cute animal images and pop culture GIFs with tags like #me, #gpoy (gratuitous picture of yourself), or #current status, to identify with practices that are potentially stigmatizable (a particular sexual kink), to make self-flattering statements that many cultures teach us are immodest, or to otherwise borrow cuteness or sexiness from photos, illustrations, and GIFs (Tiidenberg and Whelan 2017). The multiply meaningful visual content thus facilitates curating face-saving self-presentations (see Chapter 7 for how similar techniques are used in mental health discourses).

In their cross-platform analysis, Paasonen et al. (2019) engage with the NSFW acronym first and foremost as a metadata tag for classifying, flagging, and filtering online content. They argue that as a top-down, platform-enforced label, NSFW flattens crucial differences between the various content it is applied to, covering it all with an "opaque blanket of offensiveness, riskiness, and unsafety" (2019: 13). On tumblr, however, there was a bottom-up vernacular of NSFW prior to any forceful top-down flagging. Back in 2011 and 2012, it was very common to mention the acronym in blog descriptions or incorporate it into blog names. Even in hashtags it was used as a word in a metacommunicative sentence (see Chapter 1), rather than a stand-alone searchable term. In the community observed, NSFW became part of everyday vocabulary, casually used to describe culture, practices, communities, or content. Its use as an adjective rather than an acronym was evident in the pervasive lack of capitalization when used in written text. In 2012, one of our participants posted on her blog:

> I like blogs that don't post too frequently, are personal, are usually short posts and are fun. I like blogs that are sex/ feminism/bunny related, but I actually follow a wide variety of blogs, not just the nsfw ones. (Okay it's like half nsfw ones ... whatever.) (EDIT: it's like 70% nsfw ones ... whatever, still.)

In the bottom-up vernacular, NSFW was not a judgmental label, but an informative boundary marker to signify a space with a shared attitude toward the sexually explicit. This attitude was mentioned by all the participants in the NSFW study, and, as evident in the quote in the beginning of this chapter, was usually equated with openness, tolerance, and body-positivity.

Of course, this vernacular was afforded by the relaxed governance rules and the laissez-faire rhetoric of the platform owners and developers (see Chapter 1). For most of its tenure, tumblr's communication about NSFW content was almost cheerfully nihilist. "Sure," tumblr's Helpdesk page for Adult content said in the summer of 2014, "we have no problem with that kind of stuff. Go nuts. Show nuts. Whatever" (tumblr 2014). After Verizon acquired tumblr's owner Yahoo!, the previously primarily vernacular, primarily discursive label of NSFW was reframed. In 2017 tumblr launched "Safe Mode," which hid all content marked "sensitive" from search results and dashboard feeds, and all blogs labeled "explicit" from those not logged in, or under the age of 18 (see also Chapter 1). While "explicit" labeled the blog in its entirety, "sensitive" was a new label applied to specific posts. When content was deemed sensitive, the person who had posted it saw an icon of a crossed-out eye and the word NSFW appear (see Figure 6.1).

Tumblr attempted to position these changes as offering more control to users, who tended to interpret them as being shaming and threatening instead. The following is an excerpt from a group interview with five female NSFW bloggers in 2017, shortly after the changes were instated.

Figure 6.1: Example of a "sensitive" photo being marked by tumblr. Screengrab by authors.

Cookie: It feels really weird to see the NSFW stamp next to your own naked body. It feels a bit like shaming to me ... which is weird because all of my followers can still see it just fine

Katie: I've been working on backing up my blog through Wordpress, because I am anxious about them getting rid of NSFW altogether. But also I know the majority of their traffic comes from NSFW, so maybe there is hope

Penny: They are definitely moving in that direction. They are alienating some of their heaviest users and most popular blogs in the process

Katie: ... I hate that gore and misogyny and racism aren't regulated but bodies are. Like fuck. And it bothers me

because I get hundreds of hits a day from people who
aren't on tumblr. So now tumblr wants to restrict who can
access my blog, and that feels fucky. ...
Cookie: I feel that it's not OK that my boobies are being
flagged. It's too close to the way women's bodies are
policed in general. Like it's ok to mark out a space as
NSFW, like whole blog, but individual posts feels too like
"this is beyond the pale"
Katie: It's an emotional thing yeah ... I feel offended by it.
Like once again there is a feeling of "you are a deviant,
this isn't ok, it needs to stay hidden." It's a "dirty shame"
impulse.

(Group interview by authors, 2017)

These women interpreted Safe Mode and Tumblr Inc.'s
appropriation of the NSFW label through the framework of
shame, which was amplified by the fact that the imposed
NSFW label was only visible to the person who posted the
particular image. On their own dashboard a user would see
an image of their own breasts flagged as NSFW, while a
porn GIF right before or after appeared unflagged. Shame,
according to art historian Martha Hollander (2003: 1327) is
"profoundly visual, operating across an interface involving
seeing and being seen." Arguably then, prior to Safe Mode,
and especially prior to the NSFW ban, tumblr allowed its
users to control their own visibility and the meaning-making
associated with it. Art critic John Berger (1972) has written that
nakedness reveals itself, whereas nudity is about being placed
on display. By appropriating the vernacular NSFW discourse,
embedding in it the "firmly normative, taxonomical aspect
similar to other media content classification mechanisms"
(Paasonen et al. 2019: 167) and encoding it to function as a
visibility lever, tumblr collapsed all content involving naked
bodies into an objectifying category of nudity (see Tiidenberg
2020). This divested users of the agency to (choose how to)
reveal themselves and of their ability to remain multifaceted
humans in the process.

Conclusion

In this chapter, we relied on an example of one community within the NSFW silo to discuss how NSFW tumblr offered a safe space for sexual exploration and body-positivity, and how that led to people finding an agential voice and using it to stand up for themselves and others. The thick description of the processes through which an interconnected network of blogs becomes a safe space, as well as of the progression of experiences from seeking entertainment or titillation to becoming critically and politically self-aware serves multiple purposes. On the one hand, it explains the culture, dynamics, and implications of NSFW tumblr and highlights that NSFW was, at least on tumblr, so much more than porn. On the other hand, it offers yet another example of silosociality in action. tumblr's shaping hand in the digital culture of the twenty-first century only wielded the power it did because of silos such as NSFW tumblr. The NSFW silo offered a wide variety of people and groups a chance to boldly experiment, belong, find (self-)acceptance, escape the less tolerant parts of the world and the internet, and slowly, in a way almost camouflaged by pleasure and play of naked selfies and erotic storytelling, develop a political and ethical sensibility, perhaps even hone it into an activist voice. NSFW tumblr's significance relied on it functioning as a safe space for open discussions of personal sexual experiences and on people posting original NSFW visual content (e.g., nude selfies) with context (information on why they posted it, how it was meant to be interpreted, etc.). Within the safe space people felt that their bodies, identities, and practices were validated and accepted rather than shamed and stigmatized. While tumblr persists, and there is even a smattering of sexually explicit content on there, the NSFW silo as described in this chapter is no more. And that is a loss.

7

mental health

[M]y experience with social media is, I kind of keep to myself
a bit more than I guess other people ... [On tumblr] I kind of
want to know what the [mental health] experience is like for
other people who are sort of in the same situation as me, and
how they use it to, I guess, help them.

(16-year-old Laila: personal interview by authors, 2016)

Mental health – or mental illness – as it is curated and circulated on tumblr, is ambiguous. Mental health practices are
extremely nuanced on tumblr: while publicly visible and
explicit mental health-related content is common, tumblr
users also partake in "invisible" mental health practices,
circumvent visibility to unwelcome outsiders, or reappropriate unlikely media content to express emotional challenges
and make distress visible (Hendry 2020b; Seko and Lewis
2018). A drawing of a rose may be an important personal
disclosure of distress or recovery for one user, and understood
as such by their followers, just as a photograph of a self-injury
scar is for another. Overwhelmingly, and in line with tumblr
vernacular as described in Chapter 2, tumblr posts and blogs
about mental health and illness share information, stories,
resources, and opinions that produce *personal narratives* that
privilege *lived experience*. These narratives may not necessarily
negate dominant professional or medical ideas about mental
health, but they do counter the common ways that mental
ill-health is delegitimized or stigmatized beyond the platform.
Instead, on mental health tumblr, people communicate the
emotional distress, social isolation, practical, and sometimes

amusing challenges of living with mental ill-health. This produces new and nuanced understandings of mental health and illness, which can be both helpful and unhelpful. As such, tumblr conversations around mental health can be playful and insightful just as they may be distressing or uncomfortable.

In this chapter, we argue that mental health tumblr is complex and contradictory. Although public and academic discussions of mental health tumblr tend to focus more on the toxic and problematic content and practices on the platform, we argue that this is too simplistic, and unhelpfully flattens the diversity of practices the platform hosts. Akin to other silos and communities, the "mental health tumblr," or the "mental health community" that users refer to, is experiential and felt, and not delineated by the platform in any clear or obvious way.

Mental health and mental illness

Before discussing how mental health is enacted on tumblr, it is important to unpack some broad definitions, concepts, and ideas about mental health. Throughout this chapter, we variously refer to mental illness, mental or psychiatric disorder, mental ill-health, and mental health challenges, as well as "mental health" and "mental or emotional wellbeing." This is an attempt to convey the diversity of language and ideas about mental health in the public domain, but especially on tumblr. These terms and concepts shift and change over time and have different cultural, social, and political meanings for different communities and countries worldwide.[1]

We understand mental health as an umbrella term to refer to emotional, psychological, and cognitive wellbeing and health in various states, including emotional distress and disorder (Hendry 2018). While we recognize the World Health Organization's (2014) definition, which advises that mental health is "a state of well-being in which every individual realizes his or her own potential, can cope with the normal stresses of life, can work productively and fruitfully, and is able to make a contribution to her or his community," we also acknowledge that this may not align to how media users engage with mental health or mental illness (Feuston and Piper 2018; Hendry 2020b). Additionally, "mental health challenges" may refer to the stress, worry, or discrimination that people experience in the face of social, cultural, economic, and political problems such as racism, poverty, changing job market conditions, homophobia, transphobia, etc. (see Chapter 5). These may or may not fit within clinical psychiatric or medical ideas about mental illness or disorders.

Globally, public awareness of mental health challenges, ill-health, and disorder – however they are locally defined and experienced – has grown over recent decades. This may partly be attributed to government institutions, nongovernmental organizations and mental health services in different nations and states, but many of the political, social, and cultural efforts to address mental health issues rely on the work of those with lived experience. This work includes advocacy and lobbying; developing grassroots and community-based responses to inequity, emotional distress, and trauma; engaging with social media to share stories and resources; and other forms of work that challenge stigma and discrimination or compensate for the inadequacies of the underfunded health services. Lived experience refers to experiencing "mental health challenges that have caused life as we knew it to change so significantly, we have to reimagine and redefine ourselves, our place in the world and our future plans" (Byrne and Wykes 2020: 1; see also Russo and Sweeney 2016).[2]

As information about mental health expands worldwide, some people argue that how we talk about emotional and mental health is dominated by biomedical, psychiatric, and psychological approaches that may not reflect people's experience (Foucault 1987 [1954]; Russo and Sweeney 2016). Others point to how life's everyday struggles have been "psychopathologized" and argue that emotional challenges are now understood as mental disorders or psychiatric problems, often aligning to values and meanings of "health" from Western cultures of the global North.[3] Others explain that a "therapeutic culture," one that encourages people to consistently work toward self-realization, self-betterment, and self-help, has become normalized (see Salmenniemi et al. 2019), or that responses to mental health challenges are increasingly medicated or pharmaceuticalized. This means that people are encouraged to understand their feelings of distress and pain by labeling them as a disease and, subsequently, taking drugs to treat them, even when these feelings may express typical human feelings of sadness, anger, grief, or loneliness, or reasonable responses to social injustice or late capitalism. Mental health discourses are thus multiple and contradictory.

tumblr freedom and "like-others"

The previous overview is a useful backdrop in order to consider the value of tumblr for mental health, as tumblr both demonstrates and challenges the discussed complexity of discourses. As we will illustrate throughout this chapter, tumblr allows some users to escape the formal, medicalized ideas about emotional and mental wellbeing; the platform encourages others to identify with mental illness in ways that may or may not be helpful. For our research participants, tumblr is overwhelmingly a valuable and creative space to express and curate personal experiences about mental health and wellbeing. In fact, the most recent tumblr Year in Review (see Chapter 4) places "mental health" as the most important social issue for the tumblr community (as measured by "engagement volume"; see fandom 2019b).

Mental health tumblr is experienced by users through feelings of *freedom* and a *community of imagined "like-others."* Silosociality (see Chapter 2) counters the vulnerability our participants experience elsewhere, whether online or off. Users rely on tumblr's freedom to create a space to typically escape from vulnerability, shame, and stigma. In our research with young people engaged with psychiatric services in Australia, 14-year-old Zizi describes that she is "usually on tumblr" because, unlike the "excessive" sociality demanded on platforms like Facebook,

> it's not, you know, no one can tell when you're online[4] ... there's a lot more freedom in, with tumblr, I'd say, just because ... it's not like a social, I mean, it's a social media, but it's kind of just for me, and for, like, online friends or something. You know, I don't really have to worry about people waiting for me to message them. (Personal interview by authors, 2016)

This perceived freedom from "default publicness" (Cho 2018a) and known social networks including family and friends allows tumblr users, if they choose, to explore emotionally resonant, stigmatized, or complex experiences (see Chapter 6 and Conclusion). This freedom is maintained through the features and rules we have discussed already: users can customize their visibility to others, remain (pseudo-)anonymous, personalize their blog appearance, and embrace a (varying) ethos that "anything goes," including NSFW content that potentially shares self-harm themes. Our research interviewing and workshopping social media and mental health themes with young people in Australian schools found that, of the more than thirty tumblr users, none had more than one tumblr follower whom they knew personally beyond the platform. It was typical for tumblr followers to be distinct from young people's Facebook friends, Instagram followers, or school peers. Young people told us that, on other platforms, sharing sensitive experiences or thoughts might garner unwanted ridicule and discrimination, prompt well-intentioned, but unhelpful, offers of care and support, or provoke anxiety that they are burdensome to others (Hendry 2020b). Instead, tumblr offers escape from this anxiety and vulnerability. However, like other silos, this intense escape can mutate into "toxic" practices, something we return to later in the chapter.

It is not only the perceived freedom that underpins users' mental health practices. For most users in our research, going on tumblr to explore mental health is a *communal* practice. One of our participants, Laila, reflects that it is "easier to relate to other people" on tumblr. Similarly, sharing her story with the *Guardian* (UK), Mea Pearson describes first posting on tumblr about her diagnosis of borderline personality disorder (BPD) in 2013 to create a more affirming and authentic representation of the persistently stigmatized illness. She reflects that the value of tumblr is its collective, community-making capacity: "It's knowing 'hey, there's thousands of people who follow my blog who are experiencing this exact thing,'" Pearson said. "Even if I know exactly what's happening, I can't stop it, I just feel less alone because of the online community" (Holpuch 2016). Likewise, our research participant, 17-year-old Claude, explains why posting alongside other tumblr users is valuable: "I think it's to remove a feeling of isolation ... 'cause I think a lot of people in that [depressed] space do feel really alone or do feel really isolated, or are afraid to talk to friends and family because of the way ... they may react" (personal interview by authors, 2016).

Tumblr Inc.'s corporate rhetoric supports and amplifies this vision of tumblr as a communal space suited for mental health conversations. Tumblr Inc. set up a "Post it Forward" blog (postitforward 2020) and launched an accompanying #PostItForward hashtag campaign in May 2015 (Siese 2015). Initially, the blog shared mental health resources, reblogged related content, linked to #PostItForward branded merchandise to raise funds for charities, and encouraged users to share their stories through words, art, and video. Later, staff invited celebrities, activists, and mental health advocates to host Answer Time sessions (see Chapters 3 and 5) and explore mental health issues with guests such as former professional wrestler A. J. Mendez, who published a book about living with bipolar disorder (Shorey 2017). The campaign was a finalist in the Shorty Awards "Social Good Campaign" category. On the award website, tumblr argued that #PostItForward and tumblr were:

> dedicated to fostering positive and supportive community, especially when it comes to users experiencing emotional or psychological distress – from the invention of the reblog, which was designed as a constructive alternative to traditional online commenting; to our community guidelines, which explain in plain and relatable language what Tumblr is and is not for; to our search intercept PSAs, which connect users directly to relevant support and counseling resources prompted by certain search terms. At the same time, our members have always organically reached out to support one another, and organizations that specialize in counseling and support increasingly turn to Tumblr to disseminate their messages and resources. (Shorty Awards n.d.)

Engaging with mental health on tumblr produces the silosocial feelings of "like-others" – amorphous groups of people who "get it." But how is this produced? For the rest of this chapter, we turn to explore how tumblr's capacity for expressing and negotiating mental health emerges through users' practices and the implications of these practices. We begin by considering text-based practices of searching and tagging that illustrate how tumblr users play, overlap, and confuse clear distinctions between what is and is not related to mental health.

Searching for and tagging mental health experiences

The easiest way to engage with mental health content, posts, blogs, and practices on tumblr is to search the term on the platform. Searching "mental health" on the dashboard returns posts with tags and text that explore different and sometimes conflicting themes and ideas about mental health. Yet given that tumblr's search function is notoriously poor (see Chapter 2), the results can seem disorienting or incomprehensive. tumblr does not provide a total count of tagged or cited search terms. Users can choose to scroll through search results organized by most recent or popular posts, as well as filter by post type (e.g., text, photos, quotes, etc.), but it can be difficult to ascertain the date of original posts or reblogs, especially when date stamps are omitted. For popular terms, tumblr also suggests five related searches. Some search terms will suggest blogs to follow that focus on the theme of the search term (regardless of how recently they were updated). Search results are produced by both users' practices (the words they use to tag posts and reblogs, and the full text they use in posts) and the platform's search algorithm (which only indexes the first twenty tags of a post; see tumblr Help Center 2020d), as well as user settings on their tumblr account and devices, their internet service provider, and their geolocation.[5] While some of our participants dismissed search as irrelevant for their mental health-related practices on tumblr, for others, it was a valuable way to "check in" with posts about topics they were interested in: dogs, fanfic, self-care, and various psychiatric diagnoses, among other things.

In our Australian fieldwork, we found that tumblr suggested "self-care," "recovery," "ADHD" (attention deficit hyperactivity disorder), "positivity," and "mental disorder" when searching for "mental health." Posts included arguments about the importance of taking medication if it helps, comics about living with depression, lists with advice for writing when stressed, and memes that normalize the sentiment that "we're all a little broken." These suggested terms – and those suggested on the following pages after we clicked the suggestions – shifted as different hashtags and text from clicked posts became more prominent to the tumblr search algorithm.[6] Clicking through these recommendations, users might be directed from mental health to studyblr – tumblr for studying tips (via positivity, self-care, self-help, then studyblr) or from mental health to CSA (childhood sexual assault – via mental disorder, trauma, then CSA).

tumblr users also cultivate a variety of techniques to circumvent the algorithmic gaze (see Chapter 1). For example, we observed a vernacular of backup tags and hashtag migration in some of our fieldwork, where girls who circulated thinspo content would hide the backup tag (where the content would move if other tags were purged of content) on the third place within their huge list of hashtags. As digital media scholar Ysabel Gerrard (2018: 12–13) notes, "users often explicitly disavow a 'pro-ED' identity in their profile biographies, coining terms like 'not-pro-anything' to reassure an imagined third party – a content moderator, platform policy-maker, concerned user, or even a troll – that their account is unproblematic." Our own fieldwork too, has noted an explicit performance of recovery, where blogs are framed as halfway houses and counseling stations for recovering users to slowly wean people away from self-injury and disordered eating. In this case, blog descriptions will directly state that they are "only posting healed wounds on this account, no blood, no gore." It is complicated to distinguish between what is and what isn't "pro-ana," and where recovery meets obfuscation, given that users both disguise eating disorder content and deny pro-ana themes on blogs in an attempt to circumvent content and platform moderation (Cobb 2017). However, most eating disorder-related posts and blogs do not include tags, and tumblr has still been noted to circulate and algorithmically recommend eating disorder-related blogs *even if* tags are absent (see Chapter 1). While Gerrard (2018: 13) argues that algorithmic flows embed a user "in a pro-ED or other network – through their followers/followees, the content they share, like, save, comment on, their clickstreams, and other forms of mined social media data," our research participants perceived controversial or sensitive content to emerge from their own practices of following and searching rather than tumblr's algorithmic interventions.

However, not all users explore tumblr through its search function, and not all tags are coherent subject categories. Examples of this include more general tags such as "personal" or "me" being added to posts that explore stories of childhood trauma, going to see a therapist or struggling to concentrate at school. Sharing personal accounts like these *legitimizes* experiences that are often ignored or underacknowledged. This framing of authenticity carries over to other (social) media; as one example, Buzzfeed regularly mines tumblr for content (see Chapter 3), curating examples of tumblr users sharing "the truth" about everyday mental health challenges through creativity and humor (Nigatu 2015).

For example, tags such as "#actually mentally ill," "#just borderline things," and "#ADHD things" collate and curate content that claims legitimacy of particular authentic depictions and expressions of mental health. Here, the words "actually," "just," or "things" are attached to various labels, mental illness, or psychiatric disorder categories (e.g., actually mentally ill, actually borderline, actually autistic, "just girly things" memes)[7] in order to linguistically distinguish authenticity and legitimacy. Like other mental health-related tags, posts with these tags express diverse experiences. They share hopelessness and hopefulness, as well as information or reflection on what is or isn't mental illness or disorder. Posts and tags more often refer to "mentally ill" than they do to "mental illness." The adjective "mentally ill" centers the idea of living with a mental illness while at the same time becoming a collective term to refer to a group of people. Curating posts with these tags is explicitly community-making, activating vernacular boundaries between what *is* and what *isn't* mental illness and who *is* and who is *not* mentally ill.

Beyond tagging, other tumblr functions also build up bloggers' authority, expertise, and legitimacy within the mental health tumblr. The ask function (see Chapter 1) allows users to publicly share their experience and expertise related to mental health. This produces a shared archive of informal advice and resources, which is, at times, strategically leveraged (see the case of The Angry Therapist in Chapter 3).

Legitimizing mental illness challenges

Although tumblr's user base is certainly youthful, mental health posts and blogs engage with formal psychiatric and psychological concepts and language (see also Chapters 4 and 5 for vernacular use of professional and academic lexicon). As we have indicated, tags, posts, and blogs employ psychiatric diagnostic language, such as categorizations of mental disorders (e.g., mental illnesses) from the *Diagnostic and Statistical Manual of Mental Disorders* (*DSM-5*; APA 2013), as well as other psychological concepts such as trauma, personality dimensions, and attachment theories. These linguistic references to mental illness contribute toward qualifying their blogs' legitimacy and contextualize the authenticity of their posts about living with mental ill-health. One of our research participants, 14-year-old Dana, explains that it is important to counter colloquial misinterpretations of mental illness and distinguish between authentic and legitimate experiences of ill-health versus moments of stress or worry:

> Like ... people saying "People who are depressed just want attention!," or "People who don't eat just do it because they can." And it's like that's actually, like, so wrong, or people who joke about it and say ... you know ... "Oh I have such bad anxiety!" You don't actually suffer anxiety, you're just anxious. It's like no! (Personal interview by authors, 2016)

Her frustration is expressed on her blog via a reblogged meme (Figure 7.1). Psychiatric diagnoses, represented by different people's arms and hands, come together to collectively decry people who minimize their challenges. This both stresses the frustration of being misunderstood, but also

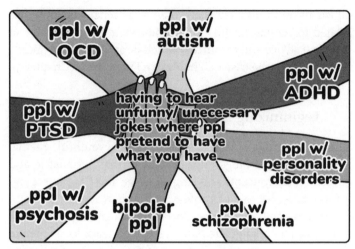

Figure 7.1: Artist's impression of a highly reblogged meme that remixes *DSM-5* (APA 2013) categories, similar post originally shared by Dana in an interview. Art provided by River Juno.

potentially distinguishes between "legitimate" disorders and people who do not meet clinical criteria for mental ill-health even if they colloquially use this language.

The participatory culture of tumblr shifts *some* of the power of institutional psychiatry to tumblr users; psychiatric discourse and resources like the *DSM-5* become yet another source to be curated, remixed, and remade. Users mine and poach a variety of texts to share their stories and rely on third-party content to "stand-in" for their self-representations in ways that may feel less vulnerable (see Chapters 2 and 6). They creatively remix their own experiences, interpretations, and perceptions using both professional and colloquial language. As Zara (personal communication, June 1, 2020) reflects, tumblr allowed them to "learn about other people's [clinical] experiences in a nonclinical, non-threatening way." Mental health tumblr serves as psychoeducation, or pedagogy pertaining to mental health treatment for its users (see Chapter 5). Different psychiatric categories and diagnoses may only feature on a few pages of the *DSM-5*, but on tumblr bloggers tease out and share "everyday" applications of these labels. For example, a blogger might list a diagnosis on their profile, alongside their gender identity or age, as well as share resources to help others interpret different diagnostic categories. They may also write posts explaining the everyday struggles of living with a disorder, reblog memes about very particular experiences of particular disorders or illness categories, or respond to other users' questions about typical issues. Together, these practices produce a sort of vernacular psychiatry or psychoeducation.

It might seem contradictory to argue that tumblr practices not only champion personal testimonies and narratives of living with mental health challenges, but also frequently rely on psychiatric taxonomies and concepts, but they do. These combinatory practices do not necessarily challenge psychiatric interpretations of typical struggles or negative feelings but instead help other users to make sense of their experiences through the same shared language. Our argument here runs parallel to Cover's (2018) proposition related to sexuality and gender, introduced in Chapter 5, as well as the argument about the NSFW silo's relationship with the hegemonic beauty standards within the visual economy, introduced in Chapter 6. Rather than dismantling the dominance of psychiatric interpretations altogether, tumblr expands how psychiatric language is used to make sense of emotions and experience outside mental health services.

Circulating toxic feelings and triggers

While we do not argue for or against applications of the *DSM-5* (APA 2013) and other frameworks on tumblr, we want to demonstrate practices that create or produce mental health in a particular vernacular form on tumblr. Yet vernacular that "legitimizes" formal and institutional mental health concepts may also encourage improper or confused self-diagnosis, or inappropriate care or treatment. The platform has received significant attention from psychologists, psychiatrists, mental health organizations, and services that are generally concerned about the relatively unmoderated nature of tumblr and what seems to be an abundance of potentially distressing, harmful, or "triggering"[8] posts and blogs (Hendry et al. 2017). For example, in an article for *The Atlantic*, US psychiatry professor Dr. Stan Kutcher articulates that users on social media platforms, including tumblr, conflate their negative feelings with clinical categories like depression (Bine 2013). This aligns to Dana's experience cited earlier. Identifying with a mental disorder or illness diagnosis may be an inappropriate or unhelpful way to make sense of emotional and mental distress, pain, or confusion, or, as we outlined in Chapter 3, may demonstrate how users adopt negative feelings as a condition of their participation on tumblr. Whether or not this is productive or toxic depends on the context and the content.

To further complicate an already complex terrain, there are practices of toxic positivity (and negativity) on tumblr. Disguised alongside justifications of "just being helpful," practices of "toxic positivity" reinforce stigmatized and problematic thoughts or behaviors, often related to disordered eating. These practices demonstrate affectively "happy" suggestions – "Just be positive! Have you tried to eat small portions?" – that seemingly encourage recovery but displace dealing with the challenges of these issues. These practices are not unique to tumblr, but are particularly amplified on the platform; they have circulated freely during tumblr's history and, in some instances, turned some of their producers into faceless celebrities (e.g., thinspo-related images shared by bloggers who gained notoriety within thinspo networks and motivated the reblogging practices of other users).

Concerns about "triggering" or problematic content like toxic positivity are based on a presumption of psychological "social contagion." This term recognizes that distressing feelings or behavior directly or indirectly extend to people in close physical proximity (e.g., during inpatient treatment: see Richardson et al. 2012). For tumblr users, proximity is not about sharing a physical place, but about feeling connected through tumblr with like-others, and professionals within the psychiatric industry worry that they may similarly "infect" one another.

Megan, interviewed for Australian ABC radio, stressed that going online can be "triggering for you and make you want to self-harm or make you feel even worse than you did when you initially went out seeking help" (Rice 2013), while Isabella shared that "I'd be cutting just so I could have a photo to put up there" (Cooper 2013). In these accounts, tumblr is framed as a risk to young people's mental health as it promotes social contagion and interferes with "appropriate" adult or professional care. In our research, we observed extreme nuance in young people's self-harm-related tumblr practices. While some posts taught others how to hide their eating disorder or thinspo practices (Kanai et al. 2020)[9] or self-injury scars, and can fairly straightforwardly be considered content that glorifies or supports self-harm, others focused on advice on how to self-harm "safely," if one was doing it for attention, and on how to generate attention through a performance of distress, without any physical self-harm. In strategies very similar to "Insta-vaguing" (Abidin 2020), performances of "tumblr depressed" baited attention and concern from friends through vague tumblr quotes and reblogging contentious images.

Notwithstanding these concerns, other young people emphasize that suicide or self-harm posts are not necessarily triggering or encouraging users to begin or maintain self-harm or problematic behavior. One of our research participants, 15-year-old Meara, argues that tumblr users should "just keep scrolling" past content they would prefer not to see: "If people think tumblr is all about people's mental health and mental illness, all negative ... then you're probably seeking it out, not on purpose ... [but] you don't have to get stuck in that if you don't want to, it is your choice" (personal interview by authors, 2016). The mental health tumblr seems to be mindful, at times, of the triggering potential of content, using tags to enable other users to blacklist them and avoid unwanted or triggering posts from flowing through their dashboards. Beyond tumblr's Safe Mode (which was enabled in 2017 and became a default setting in 2018; see Chapters 1 and 6), users can filter tags through tumblr's settings or use browser extensions such as Tumblr Savior (Stromberg 2020). Users are able to curate their own posts in support of other users within their silo, further reiterating the social justice ethos and commitment to safe spaces (see Chapters 2, 5, and 6). These functions enable a practice or ethics of care to frame the *possibility* rather than the *inevitability* of others being distressed or triggered by circulating posts. This moves mental health tumblr away from "all or nothing" content moderation, where any and all potentially distressing content is disallowed or censored, toward an ambiguous approach that allows for nuance and personal experience and relies on community-making. Curating content and tags becomes an ethical practice. However, for our participant, 16-year-old Laila, her panic is sparked by unique or distinct rather than assumed or typical "triggers," which complicates ethical tagging. She explains: "It's difficult. I think it's sensitive and it's a really personal thing. Personal preference. I find stuff that nobody else would find triggering online that ... kind of triggers panic and anxiety, but I guess nobody else would think [it would] do that ... (personal interview by authors, 2016). Others are ambivalent about the value of tagging potentially triggering posts as a helpful gesture of care. For example, Zizi reflects that:

> I can kind of maybe see how it might be helpful ... to me, they seem a bit useless ... not everyone that tags with that stuff, and it's difficult to avoid it. What am I going to do? Talk to everybody that I follow and say, "Hey, can you not?" and they'll be like, "Well ... ." (Personal interview by authors, 2016)

Both mental health users and mental health professionals characterize tumblr as a free space. But "free" means different things here and can be contradictory. Sometimes free refers to how freely triggering and distressing content circulates through the platform. Sometimes free means feeling free to express your mental health experiences or feeling free to "just keep scrolling." Sometimes free is enacted by bloggers, who actively tag content, so others can scroll freely without feeling distressed.

Laughing and relating to sadness and pain

In this section we continue our discussion of the ambiguity of mental health tumblr but turn to consider humor. While some users explicitly draw on mental health language in text-based posts, others practice multimodal humor to indirectly and sometimes ambiguously communicate their distress and struggle. Creative, irreverent, and funny memes and posts shift ideas about mental health from the individual and personal to the social, political, and cultural. We suggest that mental health meme circulation is a practice of distributed creativity (Literat and Glăveanu 2018), a practice of curation for self-expression by proxy (Seitzinger 2014), and a practice that produces a collective sense of being "in the know" (Ask and Abidin 2018), which builds communities for support through humour and criticism (Gonzalez-Polledo and Tarr 2014). Memes helped our participant, 14-year-old Dana, to relax when she was feeling stressed or anxious. She explained that tumblr was "my place to go hide from people, but still be on social media" and that "most of the things I find funny are usually on things that I don't share with people." Scrolling through memes, funny videos and comic posts allowed her to escape feeling stressed or lonely.

Understanding mental illness through humor is a networked practice that emphasizes a shared experience and sensibility. Meme-making and meme-sharing, in particular, engage hopelessness, competitive self-deprecation, and one-downmanship (Ask and Abidin 2018; see Figure 7.2). In Chapter 3 we introduced these as discursive attention-hacking strategies that become templates within and between different tumblr silos. For mental health tumblr, this is especially complicated as multiple and often contradictory humorous practices coexist. A depression meme may reinforce that "everyone" is depressed on one blog but also explore what it means to "actually" be depressed on another. Irony, sarcasm, and other forms of humor allow users to convey frustration, hopelessness, and struggle in socially palatable ways and without being too personal or risking ridicule. In an article for *i-D*, Maddie Knight explains: "[M]aking memes allowed

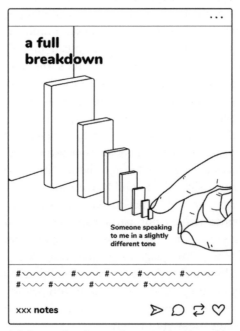

Figure 7.2: Artist's impression of a popular mental health tumblr meme on tumblr illustrating how seemingly minor interactions with others can trigger "a full breakdown," similar post originally sighted by the authors in a mental health blog. Art provided by River Juno.

me to discuss my experience with mental illness or the effects of trauma or even just the ugly parts of life and myself that I don't usually display in a way where I wasn't as scared that I would come off as too 'intense' or 'heavy'" (Syfret 2017).

Jokes and memes may seem to trivialize mental illness, but humor shifts mental ill-health narratives from spectacular accounts of extreme distress of a "broken" individual, to the banal yet relatable experience of struggling to establish or maintain wellbeing. Writing about memes related to chronic illness on tumblr, Gonzalez-Polledo and Tarr (2014: 1459) argue that "tumblr uniquely draws on abstract depersonalized expressions built on provocation, humor and sarcasm" to afford both "explanatory value" of living with illness as well as support.

tumblr's post formats are also creatively utilized to highlight the absurdity and frustration of managing mental health problems. The tumblr-specific chat post, for example, allows users to express, critique, but also humorously make tolerable the untenable position mental health services put them in (Figure 7.3)[10] or the frustrations of living with BPD (Figures 7.4 and 7.5; Hendry 2020a).

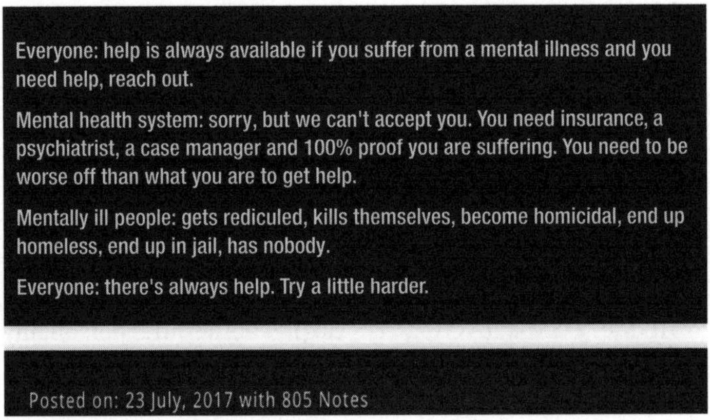

Everyone: help is always available if you suffer from a mental illness and you need help, reach out.

Mental health system: sorry, but we can't accept you. You need insurance, a psychiatrist, a case manager and 100% proof you are suffering. You need to be worse off than what you are to get help.

Mentally ill people: gets rediculed, kills themselves, become homicidal, end up homeless, end up in jail, has nobody.

Everyone: there's always help. Try a little harder.

Posted on: 23 July, 2017 with 805 Notes

Figure 7.3: Chat post between "everyone," "mental health system," and "mentally ill people." Image by authors.

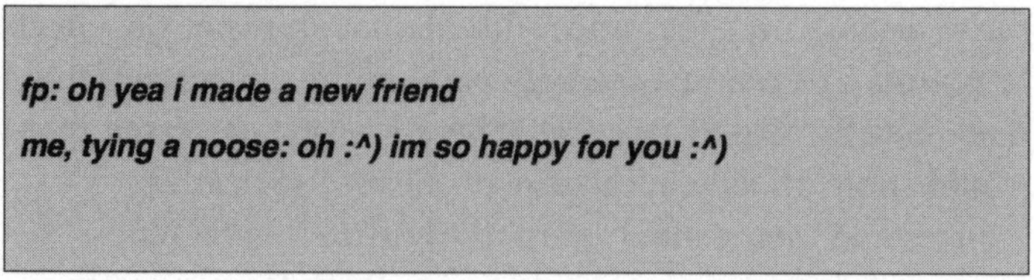

> **fp: oh yea i made a new friend**
> **me, tying a noose: oh :^) im so happy for you :^)**

Figure 7.4: Example of BPD-related Chat post between "fp" (favorite person) and "me." Image by authors.

> • • •
>
> **fp: hi!! i'm so sorry i didn't text you good night last night, i fell asleep while reading!! i'm sorry if i worried you!**
>
> **me, lying: ha ha don't worry i figured it was something like that!! i'm fine don't worry about it :)**
>
> **what actually happened: *had three panic attacks, almost relapsed, had reoccurring suicidal thoughts, thinking fp would leave me, still has an overwhelming amount of anxiety***
>
> #~~~~ #~~~ #~~~ #~~~~ #~~~~
> #~~~ #~~~~ #~~~~~ #~~~~~
>
> **xxx notes**   ▷ ◯ ⇄ ♡

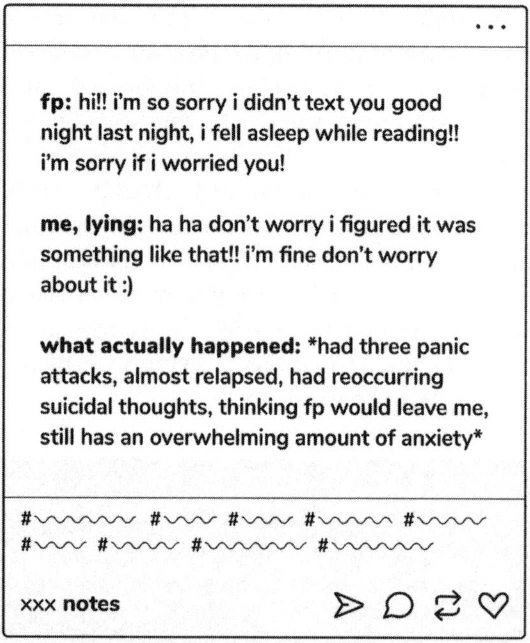

Figure 7.5: Example of BPD-related Chat post between "fp" (favorite person) and "me." Image by authors.

In the *DSM-5* (APA 2013: 663), "borderline personality disorder" refers to someone experiencing "a pervasive pattern of instability of interpersonal relationships, self-image, and affects, and marked impulsivity," who may oscillate between idealizing and devaluing their interpersonal relationships, engage in self-injuring practices, and experience intense fear of abandonment from others. This stigmatized diagnosis has been critiqued to misrepresent people's – mostly women's – emotional challenges that may be better understood as responses to complex trauma or experiences of sexual violence, rather than "manipulative" or "attention-seeking" behavior. Mental health tumblr helps people living with (or labeled as) BPD express their shifting feelings of idealizing and devaluing other people, one of the criteria of BPD (Hendry 2020a). For example, in the BPD content above (Figures 7.4 and 7.5), the chat post template organizes dialogues between a "me" living with BPD and their "favorite person" (or fp, with posts sometimes tagged with #fp), someone the user feels intensely connected to. Sometimes multiple "me" voices are used to illustrate conflicting internal monologues or obsessive thoughts. Arguably, the favorite person or "fp" term emerged within mental health tumblr (Hendry 2020a), and the chat meme format allows users to depict the tension between wanting the attention of a friend or family member, but also recognizing that these feelings might seem socially excessive and result in their fp shying away from them. These memes illustrate how the self-aware "me" in each chat plays down their reaction by pretending they are "so happy" or "fine" to hide their socially atypical feelings. These feelings are so intense that the uncensored "me" in the posts refers to suicidal gestures like "tying a noose" and overwhelming anxiety and panic attacks. Suicide and anxiety are not intrinsically funny, but exaggerated or "over the top" reactions follow the discursive strategies of self-deprecation used in me-chat memes across silos (see Chapter 3), and also express what it is like to live with BPD. Described by linguists Vásquez and Creel (2017: 67) as "doublevoicing," posts like these allow the author to divulge their own personal criticism and contradictions, expressing "the author's admission to vulnerability and personal flaws."

Interpreting tumblr's visual content often presumes an "insider" understanding, which relies on "a sharedness of references, or a sharedness of experiences" (Vásquez and Creel 2017: 62). Reading a post, image, or video, and "getting" the joke on tumblr require a classed, gendered, and raced digital literacy (Kanai 2016), which relies not only on understanding the intertextual meme vernacular (Miltner 2014), but also on knowing what it feels like to live with mental ill-health. In other words, as we argued in Chapter 2, the silo and the meaning making within is highly contextual.

"Invisible" mental illness feels

Up to this point we have discussed mostly "visible" mental health-related practices on tumblr. Although scholarship predominantly focuses on the "visibility" of mental health on tumblr, emerging research suggests a shift from "direct depictions of self-injured bodies [for example] to re-appropriations of popular media content that figuratively represent emotional struggles" (Seko and Lewis 2018: 180). Attending to these other indirect depictions of mental health helps us to understand how platform cultures circulate multiple and conflicting ideas about mental health (Hendry 2020b).

Not all mental health content tagged as such directly depicts self-injury or depression. Our participants often forgo explicit representations of mental ill-health, instead reblogging and recirculating images, GIFs, memes, and photography that *feel* authentic and offer a sense of belonging that alleviates the isolation of mental illness (Hendry 2020b). Curating content, here, becomes a highly creative, expressive practice. Our participants circulated mundane images, such as an illustration of a rose or a photograph of an empty room, to express an emotional state or a mood. One participant, Laila, shared that images were "just a more concise way of putting your feelings." Her tumblr blog adopts a fashion editorial style, reblogging pink and pastel images alongside photographs of art pieces, muted photographs of objects and clothing, simple two-color line drawings or text-based images (see Figure 7.6[11]).

Figure 7.6: Images from Laila's blog that incorporate text and art to express mood and feeling, blog images provided with permission from Laila and re-created. Art provided by River Juno.

Although no posts explicitly represent Laila's struggles with clinical anxiety, her blog curates, to her, "my real self." Most, if not all, of her posts are reblogs and do not include mental health-related tags, but her blog expresses her emotional and affective experience of living with mental ill-health.

> Laila: I feel like there's a lot of content on Tumblr and just because I didn't create [the post or image], doesn't mean that it's not mine. I guess in a way, once it's on my blog, I mean, like I said there's a lot of content on tumblr, and I picked these specific things … I don't know, together it makes a bigger image, I suppose.
> Interviewer: How would you describe that bigger image?
> Laila: Of all of this! It's just, it's just who I am I guess. I really have no idea how to describe who I am, I guess, if someone really wanted to know and they didn't know me personally, I'd say go on my Tumblr! [*points to her images, laughs*]

Likewise, most posts in communications scholar Yukari Seko and psychology researcher Stephen P. Lewis's (2018) study of self-injury photos on tumblr used visual content from popular culture to express emotion rather than direct depictions of cutting or other such self-injury. By reblogging and reappropriating images and memes, users collectively express a multiplicity of emotional experiences, such that "these memes represent self-injury as a form of life struggle virtually anyone can face while complicating conventional readings of self-injury as an individual pathologic experience" (2018: 180).

Mental health-related tumblr practices visualize and self-represent the social, emotional, and mental challenges of experiencing mental ill-health, even if users' posts and blogs may not depict them or discuss personal challenges (Hendry 2020b). This illustrates Tiidenberg and Whelan's (2017: 143) insights that self-representation is less about mandatory representation of one's face or body and instead becomes "a set of practices, conventions, and norms of content production and consumption." On mental health tumblr, these conventions and norms represent what it feels like to struggle with mental health, and these representations of feeling, in turn, generate a sense of affinity with others. Laila does not communicate with other tumblr users or post comments on mental health-related blogs, but she does say she is part of a community on tumblr. She experiences "a sense of comforting togetherness" on tumblr, created by her feeling of perceived intimacy with like-others (Kanai 2017: 9).

Such "figurative representation of mental suffering" (Seko and Lewis 2018: 193) through image-based content, including photographs, screengrabs of videos, animated gifs and illustrations, allows users – who are mostly anonymous – to engage in emotionally authentic practices to express their struggles and emotions. tumblr users can choose how explicit or implicit they are in invoking a vulnerable and "actual" mentally ill identity and thus shield themselves from potentially negative judgment or unhelpful questions to "prove" their illness (Hendry 2020b). Decontextualized content allows users to share their vulnerabilities without compromising their privacy. This aligns to other research about tumblr communities where sharing "often ambiguous, fragmented and multimodal" content (Gonzalez-Polledo and Tarr 2014: 5) allows users to share and recirculate emotional rather than narrative accounts of their lives.

Romanticizing mental illness?

The tension between these forms of escape from vulnerability become even more blurred as we discuss how tumblr has been framed to romanticize mental illness. The emotionally distressing and affectively intense content we have discussed so far has been argued to appropriate mental illness by romanticizing pain or rendering it desirable (Tatum 2013; see also Chapter 3). In a 2016 piece in *The Ringer*, Swedish young adult Hampus Leijon is quoted as saying that tumblr makes "it seem like – depression, suicide, this is cool. If you want to be part of the club, you gotta be insecure and unstable in some way. I'm not a fan" (Premack 2016). This position returned to earlier arguments in mostly US popular blogs and news sites such as *The Atlantic*, *Bustle*, and *Refinery29*, where communities on tumblr were framed to be "perpetuating ideas of 'beautiful suffering,' confusing what it means to be clinically depressed" (Bine 2013).

In these discourses, mental illness on tumblr is perceived as a trend "caught between glamorization and destig-matization" and something to aesthetically, socially, and emotionally relate to and perform, rather than a pre-existing, "authentic" experience (Joho 2019). tumblr aesthetic and styles are seen to express mental illness or sadness tropes that draw from other tumblr aesthetic vernacular, including sad girl culture, pastel goth, and soft grunge (Ackley 2015; Tatum 2013). Depression is made feminine and reflective through blogging fashion images, film screenshots, melan-cholic quotes on pastel pink backgrounds, and pictures of bodies doing nothing.

However, others argue that the sad girl content concurrently legitimizes, complicates, and romanticizes sadness, mental illness, and psychopharmaceutical drugs (Thelandersson 2018). Posts about medicating (or not) mental ill-health circulate within the mental health silo. Sometimes messages share that it is okay to take medication, where the aim is to decrease stigma related to taking psychopharmaceutical drugs (see Figure 7.7). Similarly, messages saying it is ok to not take drugs continue to circulate. For young women, like Laila, who embrace these styles, girlhood and melancholy become both motifs and moods on tumblr blogs; the aesthetic sensibility expresses sadness, longing, imperfection, and a complicated feminism that is both aggressive and vulnerable. Yet it is this melancholia that provides a reflective space and emotional recognition for users like her. Melancholy does not necessarily impede content from supporting recovery or advocacy, or responding to stigma, but may support reflection toward those ends (Pfister 2014). We argue that even with all of mental health tumblr's contradictions, melancholic themes, and ambiguous practices, it offers the potential for productive contemplation and escape.

Figure 7.7: Artist's impression of a text-based image post "Taking medication does not, and will not ever, make you weak." Art provided by River Juno.

Put together, creating, curating, and affinity around mental health content form a therapeutic practice. This is not to say that what people do on tumblr is psychotherapy, but that it offers a way to contemplate, reflect, and make meaningful the lived experience of emotional distress and mental ill-health, as well as life's everyday stresses and challenges. This also extends examples we have shared in earlier chapters, where tumblr is a kind of therapy for people in the queer silo (see Chapter 5) or the NSFW silo (see Chapter 6). tumblr "therapy-that-is-not-therapy-but-sort-of-is" is a form of emotional work where bloggers engage in self-care, peer support and learning, community care and connection, and formal advice. This helps us to shift the conversation from whether tumblr is good or bad for mental health to ask instead what tumblr therapy is and how it works. On the one hand, the "peer support group" of mental health tumblr – whether explicitly a support resource or a feeling of blogging with like-others – may encourage productive ways to make sense of distress or mark progress while negotiating challenges or mental illness. On the other hand, this work may encourage bloggers to embrace negative thinking that is unwelcome in their everyday lives and communities, as they feel it is understood and validated by other bloggers. Both these approaches may *feel* therapeutic for different people in different circumstances. They point to the lack of spaces for this emotional work outside the platform, particularly in the context of inadequate, inappropriate, or discriminatory mental health services and perhaps more importantly ongoing stigma toward mental health challenges. tumblr therapy is a form of escape. Whether or not this is productive or helpful depends on the context, and cannot be read easily without understanding tumblr's broader cultures and sensibilities.

Conclusion

tumblr's affordances, vernacular, and sensibility establish the platform as a valuable space for diverse and nuanced mental health disclosure, learning, and discussion. Users establish the legitimacy of their posts and contribute to a collective resource of lived experience through weaving together conversational and mental health language, remixing formal medical language with personal narratives. This does not always challenge the medical discourse, but demonstrates tumblr's participatory culture where psychiatric and institutional knowledge is just another resource to be curated.

The freedom tumblr offers, its adaptable visibility and sense of being with "like-others," encourage practices that help make sense of what it means to live with mental health challenges. To be able to create but also "get" this humor or vernacular, bloggers have to be multiply-literate. They have to understand tumblr's norms, but also be literate in mental health topics. However, this freedom also creates space for contradictory, toxic, and unhelpful practices to emerge alongside the community-making gestures that alleviate isolation and social disconnection. Our ambivalent reading of tumblr's silosociality highlights how the platform can romanticize mental ill-health and encourage toxic or distressing practices, but can also provide a reflective space that users feel is unavailable elsewhere beyond the platform. These practices do not straightforwardly help or harm, but demonstrate how users have limited spaces in their lives for emotional expression, exploration, and, as we discuss in our Conclusion, escape.

Conclusion: "beautiful hellsite"

I miss tumblr. I still have an account, but "my tumblr" was the NSFW silo and it is basically gone. It's not about the content, or even the people – I have access to both elsewhere. Rather, I miss a space where I could explore and construct a juxta-positional, incoherent, multifaceted version of myself that – I am finding – has absolutely nowhere else to go. I miss a particular engaged, kind audience. I miss being able to share random musings, bad poetry, critical analyses, screams of anguish and pictures of naked people reblogged with Leonard Cohen lyrics. I miss a space where I contained multitudes.

(Kat)

What is tumblr for now? I dip in and out of the platform, posting to a private blog a few weeks, or a month, between posts. tumblr was an escape, and it is still an escape for some people, but it is not where I escape to now. Social media no longer offers that escape or relief. Perhaps this comes from writing during a pandemic, where everything feels like it is online. Turning away from my screen feels like an escape, but I don't want to say that too loudly. I'm not in the digital detox camp. And I won't ever want to escape my digital archives: my emails, images on forums and networks, the thoughtful and thoughtless tweets, and not my blogs. My history is tangled up with tumblr's bloggers, staff, Tumblr Inc. and David Karp.

(Natalie)

For a few nights each week, I still open up the tumblr app on my phone and scroll through my dash until I fall asleep. It has been a 12-year-long affair, and quite the cheap and reliable companion for the nights I spend alone in various cities and bedrooms while traveling for work. Falling into tumblr silos and rabbit-holes-within-silos after a long and

> weary day is a present to myself, to insulate from the outside
> world, to be funneled right into the esoteric concerns of my
> fandoms, or support groups, or faceless nameless penpals,
> if only for a moment, until I fall asleep.
>
> (Crystal)

We wrote this book because we firmly believe that understanding tumblr and its silosociality extends existing thinking on social media. tumblr, and how it has been used by the self-professed weirdos who love it, has been profoundly impactful. The platform was, according to writer Marianne Eloise (2019), the only online space left in the 2010s that was still "carrying the torch for internet subculture." tumblr pioneered, as pointed out by Matt Mullenweg, CEO of Automattic, "a lot of what later would show up on Twitter, Instagram, WordPress, all sorts of other places" (Patel 2019). tumblr's features, functions, governance, affordances, and practices played a key role in shaping the (digital) cultures of the twenty-first century. It shaped the identities and politics of uncountable young people; offered safe, educational, therapeutic spaces; helped people sort through their feelings and figure themselves out; launched social movements; allowed people to find a (political) voice and learn how to use it; nurtured fandoms and birthed "ships"; and consistently functioned as a well of bottom-up creativity from which social media trends, aesthetics, and memetic activity bubbled up. A day after the NSFW ban, tumblr user *hypeswap* made a post that started a long, winding, cross-silo reblog trail that illustrates tumblr's impact perfectly: "I don't really want to leave tumblr ... I've been here since 2011"; *hypeswap* soon reblogged their own post, adding: "no other platform has the right format for me to just randomly barf actual thoughts, joaks [*sic*], and genuine creative content all in the same breath. I don't know how to compartmentalize." The post has approximately 339,000 notes at the point of writing, and an unusually large proportion of rebloggers have added comments on what tumblr has meant for them. We have collected some into the collage depicted in Figure 8.1. We wrote for and about the

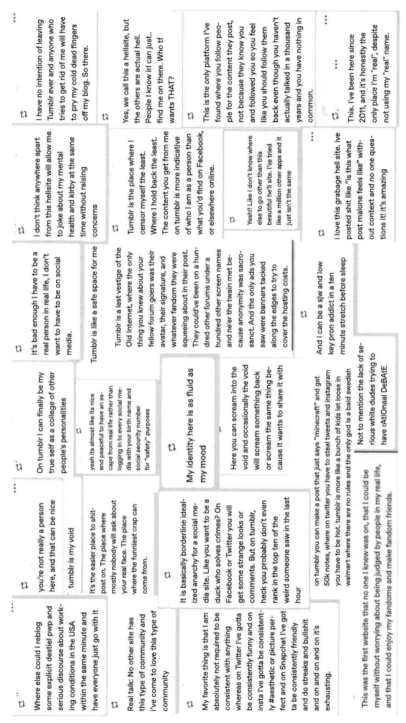

Figure 8.1: A collage of tumblr post reblogs on why tumblr is unlike any other social media. Collage by authors.

"beautiful hellsite," a "void that screams back," a "borderline idealized anarchy," a "community," an "escape," a "safe space," a place where we can finally be our true selves "as a collage of other people's personalities."

RIP tumblr

In the process of writing this book, we would sometimes mention tumblr on other social media. We asked on Facebook whether our friends and colleagues had had a particular tumblr experience or would mention the ups and downs of the writing process on Twitter. Almost invariably someone would ask, with sincere surprise or performative snark, whether tumblr "still exists." Other people did share their tumblr experiences, but with a certain air of nostalgia (see Chapter 4). They articulated their thoughts retrospectively, placed their meaningful experiences with the platform firmly in the past.

Part of this reflects our and our networks' "tumblr age" (and actual, biographical age). Our nostalgia might say more about us than about tumblr. Another part is owed to the fact that everything on the internet is sooner or later declared dead. Yes, platforms and trends do die, but signs of their demise are often overreported by bored early adopters or marketing professionals looking to signal expertise. Facebook has been declared dead since 2014 (Matthews 2014). Just because we want it to be true, or because the youngest are avoiding it – while often still having accounts and using Messenger – does not change the fact that the platform grew from 1.3 billion to 2.6 billion global users over the next six years (Statista 2020a).

That being said, quantitatively, tumblr usage is down. A lot of people left after the NSFW ban. Many communities were broken. Some argue that post ban tumblr exists as "a ghost, a porn-free puppet of its former self, much like how Myspace is technically still online" (Eloise 2019). When we gathered related Twitter content during the week after the ban was announced, declaring tumblr dead was the most popular thematic category. The imminent death of tumblr was also the most popular theme in the metadata: #TumblrIsDead, #TumblrIsDeadParty, #TumblrIsOverParty and #RIPTumblr were the most prevalent additional hashtags in the dataset (Tiidenberg 2019a). Quoting numbers from a web analytics firm and Statista, a story in The Verge argued that tumblr traffic dropped from 642 million visitors in July 2018 to 370 million in February 2020 (Liao 2019). The latest available Statista numbers at the time of writing suggest a continuing decline, with 292 million one-time visitors in September 2020 (Statista 2020b).

Mutating tumblr

Yet, there are those who argue that "reports of tumblr's death have been greatly exaggerated" and suggest that rather than dead, or dying, tumblr is simply going through a mutation (Rosenberg 2020). Relying on her own experience and on those of the people she interviewed for the story, Allegra Rosenberg (2020) proposed that for every user who left after the NSFW ban, there is one who "simply shrugged their shoulders and kept on blogging," relieved they no longer had to deal with "the threat of surprise dash-dicks, which had been a steady constant since joining the site."

People are indeed still on tumblr, and some are still joining. When we were exploring the mobile group chats for this book, we found that fandom groups were being set up – and quickly filled to capacity – by 15–20-year-olds, who had only recently started their first tumblog, and had missed, entirely, the whole hoopla with the NSFW ban. Veteran users report periods of inactivity, but are dipping their toes back in, or considering it. "I started using tumblr around 2010," shared one person who discussed tumblr nostalgia with us; "it tapered off around 2014. Honestly, I miss the community and the inspiration I found there every day and often think about going back!" Others report having been stunned into a year of silence after the ban, but find themselves sometimes logging in to see "if it's just tumbleweeds, or if miraculously, someone from the old crowd is still around." Another woman interviewed by Rosenberg (2020) articulated the transition she thinks tumblr has undergone since 2010. For her, it evolved from: "a space for pure fandom enthusiasm ... into a more politically aware and social-justice-focused community," to currently, just something casual and fun. Describing a very similar trajectory, albeit back in 2015 and within the NSFW silo, one of our own participants encapsulated her personal experience with tumblr as: "it went from kind of pure sexual exhibitionism to testing out different personas, to a more explicitly politicized thing, to ... just political jokes on there now." It is possible, thus, that the trajectory of passion → politics → humor → fadeout is typical of the biographical arc of a tumblr user's tumblr use, but incorrectly generalized to the biography of the entire platform. As noted by Cavalcante (2019) and Byron et al. (2019), tumblr sponsors intense, interest-driven enthusiasm, which some users experience as unsustainable for longer periods of time, meaning that they have to either pull back, start using tumblr differently, or leave (see Chapter 5). But this has been the case for years, and there are still new users who are, at this very moment, only just discovering the intensity.

Escape and irrelevance

If tumblr is indeed not dying, but changing, or even if it is changing en route to dying, what is it changing into? Rosenberg (2020) argues that the 2020 tumblr is characterized by a "zen-like acceptance," even a celebration, of its own irrelevance (see Figure 8.2). This irrelevance is cast as offering the same thing that the tumblr vernacular and sensibility we have spent this book exploring offered – *escape*.

...

I love how irrelevant tumblr is. like no celebrities on here, no
colleagues or family on here, no one's famous off tumblr or making
money, tbh no ones even updating the site like is there even any
staff? who knows? it's bliss

#p

275,550 notes

Figure 8.2: A tumblr post from January 2020, celebrating tumblr's supposed
irrelevance, with almost 275,550 notes. Screengrab by authors.

Escape from some of the realities of one's own life, but more
than that: escape from the rest of social media. How come?

In popular media imaginaries, the primary reason for
tumblr's escapist capacity stemmed from the platform's
failures to corporately commodify its userbase, from the lax
pre-ban moderation, or, currently, from the lack of attention
it seems to be getting from constituencies linked to other
social media becoming ever "shinier, more self-conscious
and monetized," at the expense of "user experience" (Eloise
2019). In other words, tumblr's current presumed irrelevance
among advertising brands, influencers, and celebrities is cast
as a good thing for users looking for a more authentic, more
relaxed social media experience. Even the new owner has
been keeping quiet.

We suggest that the escape is a function of silosociality.
Silosociality, as outlined in Chapter 2 and furnished with
empirical detail across the book, emerges from tumblr's
functions, affordances, and governance. But mostly it is a
result of what people do on tumblr, how they do it (through
multimodal, remixed, personal testimonial-based communication valued for its emotional and political pertinence over
"quality"), and why they think it is important to do it that
way (sensibility of social justice and safe spaces). This is why
the silos are all recognizably tumblr, but all different. Silos

are shared context par excellence. And this is why each one became a space of escape, but for different people and for different reasons. Some were escaping abuse, discrimination, or erasure elsewhere, others the dangers of default hyper-visibility and publicness of Facebook-like platforms (Cho 2018a), others the persistent sense of being bored by, or just a bit too weird for, most other socially mediated discourse.

Prior to the ham-fisted and tone-deaf NSFW ban, tumblr practiced nuance. This was often interpreted as messy. The various, seemingly similar, but slightly different features for on-platform interaction, for example, or the different self-, moderator-, and algorithm-appointed categories like NSFW, Adult, or Sensitive that tumblr experimented with during early attempts of Safe Mode, might have seemed haphazard, as if new things were tacked on to old things, without a system. But now, retrospectively, that might not have been the case. Nuance might have been the system. A (possibly naive) attempt to keep tumblr the kind of space it had become within a culture of connectivity and a platform economy (van Dijck 2013). tumblr used to check with users before rolling out policy changes. It used to, somewhat, listen. And there is no escape without nuance, because escape is personal. Escape is contextual. In the mental health silo (see Chapter 7) users escape the persistent green dots that signal availability to their peers on other social media. They escape the need to perform being okay or being consistent in how they express not being okay, or escape having to deal with unwanted support from people who know their passport name. In the NSFW silo (see Chapter 6) users escape the tedium of long-term partner-ships and waning sexual excitement, but they also escape the broader culture – replicated elsewhere on the internet – that disallows them from being multifaceted in ways that involve sexuality. On NSFW tumblr they could be smart and horny, feminist and kinky, professional and poly, whereas, elsewhere on social media, they could be smart, feminist, or profes-sional, but not sexual at the same time. In the fandom silo

(Chapter 4) users escape the disturbed confusion that their enthusiasm generates across all other social settings online and off, but also, again, remix it with their other interests. Only on tumblr can they "reblog some explicit destiel pwp[1] and serious discourse about working conditions in the USA within the same minute and have everyone just go with it" (see Figure 8.1). In the queer silo (Chapter 5) people escape the discriminatory and cruel culture that dismisses their entire existence, but also other spaces that are supposedly "safe" but are often experienced as intensely judgmental. Of course, the escapist bubble of nuanced identity taxonomies and careful boundary work around justice can become something one needs to escape as well. How a silo functions as a nuanced space of escape for a particular person shifts with time. What is an escape to someone, at one point, is likely to change, structurally, politically, and emotionally.

So, what is the state of silosociality in the Automattic era of tumblr (see Chapter 1)? Some silos – fandom and mental health – are doing well and arguably continue to offer the slumber-party atmosphere of safety and escape to those within. It does not mean that the fandom and mental health silos are not dynamic, constantly changing, or conflict-free. Rather, they have not been as badly hurt by the NSFW ban and subsequent decline in user numbers, so their change is gradual and organic.[2] Other silos were hurt more significantly by the ban. Within the queer silos NSFW content was habitually and purposefully remixed with self-acceptance, self-expression, and politics. If there is a big enough influx of new users, it might emerge from the ashes still queer, perhaps still social justice-oriented, still a space of safety and escape. That being said, it is difficult to divorce representations and conversations around sex from queer expression, queer politics, and queer identities, when the latter are responding to the heteronormative ideal of who should and who should not be allowed to have sex with or desire each other. So the jury is still out on the future of the queer silo. Finally, the NSFW silo, as it was, is probably irreparably broken. There is, as discussed in Chapter 6, some NSFW content still on tumblr, but not the shared practices, vernacular, and sensibility that made it a silo. Matt Mullenweg has not given any indication of changing the policy behind the ban, and the window for doing so has probably closed. It is possible that within this new context of tumblr, another silo will rise to take its place as central to and characteristic of tumblr.

Silosocial futures

At the same time, as we argued in the Introduction and in Chapter 2, social media are possibly on the cusp of a bigger mutation. There seems to be a critical amount of public dissatisfaction, fatigue, and popular awareness of the tally of sins that the current, social-graph and profile-centered social media platforms have racked up. What social media as such had matured into by the early 2020s hardly excites anyone. The most recent flash of social media-related excitement at the moment of concluding this book was the swift and impactful antiracist and Trump-pranking action taken by young people usually dubbed "K-pop fans" (see Abidin and Baudinette 2020; see also Chapter 4). However, even those excitements are marred by the knowledge that any and all new tactics will be weaponized. It is shortsighted to celebrate the invention of new hacks when they align with one's political views, as they will shortly be used by those with opposing ones. Instead, our focus should be on how dangerous such hackability is for democracy (Tufekci 2020).

Across predictions for social media's near and mid-range future (one to ten years), we note a pattern elevating the increasing importance of niche spaces, privacy, and small communities (HaileyB 2019; Influencer Marketing Hub 2020; Owen 2019). Social media professionals are noticing the growing reluctance among people to post self-referential content, and their reliance, instead, on tagging friends under memes (HaileyB 2019), and their favoring of "private groups that like-minded people can join to talk about their shared interests" (Influencer Marketing Hub 2020). Recent studies have found that the youngest social media users tend to avoid participating in semi-public online discussions entirely, because they think the discourse too aggressive and impolite, where older users will arrogantly dismiss young people's ideas and views as wrong (Kalmus and Siibak 2020). This move away from expression within and for the collapsed contexts and unsegregated audiences of the likes of Facebook (Marwick and boyd 2011) has been dubbed, somewhat unfortunately, "dark social" by the marketing constituencies (BBS Communications Group 2017). The darkness in this case indicates that the sociality enacted in semi-private enclaves of group pages or messaging apps is in the dark for those seeking to intercept it for advertising. Facebook, undoubtedly worried about such trends, has claimed a change toward "a privacy-focused vision for social networking," promising to build an experience that is more suited for private messaging, small groups and ephemeral stories (Zuckerberg 2019).

But we already have a social media platform perfectly suited and road-tested for all of that – tumblr. And it is possible that tumblr itself is becoming even more silosocial. Mobile group chats, for example, seem to intensify silosociality, at least on the surface. They are small, users have to request to join them, messages are ephemeral, and group members spend most of their time actually discussing things of interest, or sharing and performing memetic or humorous content (see Chapter 1). It could be argued that sociality within the mobile chat groups evades easy discoverability and surveillance. At the same time, this algorithmically shaped and Tumblr Inc.-designed version of silosociality differs in important ways from the organic, vernacular, bottom-up silosociality that developed on the platform over the course of the past decade. Users are offered a limited number of mobile group chats they can join, based on how tumblr's algorithms interpret their interests. Everyone seems to be offered meme groups, some of us were offered fandom groups and mental health groups, but no NSFW groups or LGBTQIA groups. Do they not exist? Are they algorithmically suppressed? Who knows. There is no catalogue of all existing groups. But unlike organic silos, for which there was no catalogue either, mobile chat groups can't be found by following the breadcrumb trail of human curation. They cannot be unearthed by sniffing out the reblogs and follows, by shyly making tumblr friends through reblogging someone's content with a compliment.

Mobile group chats have formal boundaries made up of computer code. While there might be groups intended only for people who "know" each other on tumblr, since our joining requests remained unanswered it is also possible that those groups have reached their limit of 200 participants – another Tumblr Inc. rule. However, spaces that only allow discussion as participation are exhausting. tumblr, with its blogs and dashboard feeds organized into interest-driven silos of somewhat recognizable pseudonyms, managed to strike a very charming balance between more and less overt participation. A user could modulate between scroll-lurking, private chatting, reblogging into drafts, posting and leaving and coming back later to bask in the attention and the feedback, and scrolling while simultaneously liking, replying, reblogging, and otherwise more publicly interacting with people.

Silosociality might continue to thrive on tumblr. After all, it is possible that Automattic will find a way to appropriate and formalize it in a way that allows them to earn revenue and still offers escape to people. But even if that does not happen, silosociality as such is something that tumblr has contributed to the social media ecosystem and that might very well outlive it.

We hope this book helped you celebrate the tumblr you used to know, or understand (and feel a bit of FOMO about) the tumblr you never used. If you are someone who uses, builds, develops, or thinks deeply about social media, we hope this book helped extend how you do so. Social media structures sociality in consequential ways. Different platforms, with their different rules, features, functions, affordances, and resultant variety of vernaculars and sensibilities, build different worlds with different possibilities. tumblr afforded silosociality and silosociality afforded nuance, learning, self-acceptance, belonging, and escape. Because of this, for a time, tumblr was a safe haven. Some hope it can be that again – if only communities were allowed to self-police, if Matt Mullenweg can find it in him to be a bit more flexible about sexual content, if "we all promise to go there and just, you know, *be cool*, it could be a place that fosters ideas instead of flames wars" (Watercutter 2019). But if not, we learned on tumblr what that looks like, we know how to do these things, we could, in theory, rebuild elsewhere. Build a place where users create without the "pressures of 'hustle culture'," curate without the "performative outrage that has ... swallowed up almost every single other area of open expression online" and consume this all in a "healthy culture of simply *liking* things" (Rosenberg 2020).

Notes

INTRODUCTION: TUMBLR, WITH A SMALL T

1 Calling someone a "shark," is usually intended to highlight that they do not shy away from taking advantage of other people to reach their goals.

2 LGBTQIA+ stands for Lesbian, Gay, Bisexual, Transgender, Queer, Intersex, and Asexual, plus other sexual and gender identifications. The most common acronym continues to be LGBT. From here on in this book, we will refer to the acronym that is used by our participants or by the researchers we cite; otherwise we will use LGBTQIA+ and, when talking about the silo that brings together people with these interests, we will also use the folkloric "queer."

3 There were two "wars" between 4chan and tumblr: one in 2010 that involved mutual spamming (first of shock images by 4chan users to tumblr then of kitten images by tumblr users to 4chan) and another in 2014 where a tumblr blog posted a plan to shut down 4chan (some think this was created by 4chan users as a ruse), to which 4chan users responded by hijacking social justice tags on tumblr with gore content, which tumblr users responded to by burying the content into an avalanche of cute things (Knowyourmeme 2020b).

4 Sociality is a term used to describe how people are social in the world and how they experience being in collectives.

5 A social graph is the visualized network of interconnections of relationships, basically a representation of how users are connected to each other, their product pages and interests. An ego network is a slightly different perspective on the same thing – it focuses on individuals (egos) and their ties with other individuals.

CHAPTER 1: TUMBLR STRUCTURE

1 Although the informal protocol of retweeting also dates back to March 2007, Twitter officially incorporated it as a feature in 2009.

2 tumblr changed the formatting of reblog threads to flat in 2015, this was done to increase legibility, but generated user pushback as it dismantled a by-then iconic genre of a nested reblog threads, which features in memes about tumblr (see Figure 1.3).

3 Just as we were finalizing this book, (former) US President Donald Trump – reacting to Twitter appending a fact-checking notice to his tweets – signed an Executive Order requiring the US Federal Communication Commission to revise CDA 230 so that "editing content" would lead to the platform forfeiting the safe harbor protection.

4 Why this is still mentioned is unclear, given that all explicit content is hidden from everyone.

5 This example returns the general PSA for the US, UK, and European contexts. The same message is returned when searching similar terms are located in other countries such as Australia.

6 However, it has also been argued that NSFW content is easier to train deep learning models on than extremism or disinformation (Dickson 2018), which is why it is more heavily regulated.

7 While the acronym NSFW is broadly interpreted as coming from "Not Safe For Work," tumblr has consistently used "Not Suitable For Work" in their Community Guidelines (both the 2012 and 2015 updates use that wording).

8 While the goal of FOSTA/SESTA is admirable, the vague language drove many internet platforms to pre-emptive overreach best described as deplatforming of sex (Molldrem 2018).

9 This may very well be true, but for context, we have spent more than ten years on tumblr, including regularly browsing sexual blogs, and have never seen child pornography.

10 We briefly discuss this in Chapter 5, but on May 4, 2020 a post was made on the staff blog which indicated that tumblr was adopting a stronger stance against Nazi hate speech (staff 2020b). Since the "Nazis vs nipples" juxtaposition was a common rhetorical and memetic move in responses to the NSFW ban, it is possible that the feedback to the ban informed this change.

11 Bots are automated scripts designed to perform a task with little oversight from humans (Shorey and Howard, 2016), in discussions around social media, we usually talk about socialbots, which are automated scripts controlling social media accounts to post and send connection requests (Boshmaf et al. 2011). Pornbots are socialbots that operate with pornographic content to grab attention.

CHAPTER 2: TUMBLR SOCIALITY

1 The asterisk (trans*) is used to indicate that the term covers both transsexual and transgender, and, increasingly, other gender identities.
2 Scholars of "Black Twitter" have argued that it is used to mobilize people around political and cultural issues (Brock 2012), so it can be argued that parts of Twitter are somewhat similar to tumblr in this.
3 After we settled on calling this form of sociality silosociality in 2019–20, it came to our attention that Alexander Cho (2011) has used the notion of silos in a conference paper on tumblr (Kanai 2019) and sociologists Megan Sharp and Barrie Shannon (2020) describe tumblr as a space of silos of resilience for nonbinary people.

CHAPTER 3: FAME

1 Paralanguages are aspects of language and communication that are nonverbal (Poyatos 1993). In contemporary internet culture and social media vernacular, this can comprise the likes of emoticons, emoji, stickers, gifs, etc.
2 Usually an overused meme or old trend that has begun to lose relevance.
3 We were unable to pinpoint exactly when the tumblr merchandise store was launched or when it was discontinued, but would guess it was available somewhere between 2012 and 2017 (unwrapping blog 2017). At the time of writing, it is still possible to purchase Themes on tumblr.
4 For comparison, the US Census Bureau notes the household median income in the United States in 2014 was US$53,657 (Denavas-Walk and Proctor 2015).
5 We have opted not to replicate or provide an impression of this

illustrator's work to honour their copyright, but invite readers to visit their tumblog.

6 A list of items the bloggers would like (either directly linked to a web store) or a list of links to products. These items would be purchased by fans and customers and mailed directly to the blogger.

Chapter 4: fandom

1 Archive of our Own, a nonprofit open-source fanfiction site created and managed (relying on crowdfunding) by the Organization for Transformative Works.

2 "Fandom wank" is dramatic internet discourse by fans.

3 Short for relationship, a word used to indicate an existing or imagined relationship between characters, artists, or actors that fans want to be or think are romantically and sexually involved.

4 Fans use tumblr's tags in unsystematic, diverse ways, where some people tag everything, others tag nothing, some people have sentence-long tags where they talk about themselves, others have fandom-specific tags. This makes tagging-based categorization somewhat suspect (Morimoto 2018).

5 Easter eggs are hidden messages or hidden bits of information put in media (movies, video games, comics, music).

Chapter 5: social justice

1 As we are finishing this book, antiracist protests sparked by the killing of yet another Black person by the American police (George Floyd, but also Breonna Taylor in the same week) swept first across the US and then many other cities globally. Social media, including tumblr, was flooded with Black Lives Matter content by users, influencers, and brands. tumblr staff made a number of posts on the matter, circulating resources, directing and pledging donations, making Juneteenth an official company holiday, hosting Answer Times with Black Lives Matter activists, asking people to vote and sign petitions (e.g., staff 2020a).

2 tumblr joined up with The Blackout (see also Chapter 6) as part of Black History Month to champion the voices and experiences of Black people. The Blackout's CEO, Marissa Rei, explained that "Being lovers of the platform, we appreciate tumblr's dedication to lifting the voices of marginalized folks ... [W]e've seen them doing great work before. But with their new year-long dedication

to social change, and solid partnerships like this one, I think it'll be way more effective" (Ruiz 2018).

3 See also literature related to curation as a mode of learning (e.g., Ungerer 2016) and public pedagogy of blogging (e.g., Dennis 2015).

4 In one example, Burton shares that users reblogged a post with a US-based suicide support hotline more than ten thousand times. Although this could be considered a simple and useful gesture of information sharing, the significance of the post deepens as it was posted on the night of Donald Trump's 2016 election victory alongside other posts reacting to the outcome.

5 Here, Cassius Adair and Lisa Nakamura (2017) reflect on the moment they first found and read the canonical woman of color feminist anthology, *This Bridge Called My Back* (Moraga and Anzaldúa 2015). For Adair, this was through tumblr blogs and networks devoted to women of color feminism; for Nakamura this was through her teaching work at a university.

6 Arguably, the disparaging circulation of SJWs is symptomatic of political and cultural debates (dominated by US or global North perspectives) that are activated by meme culture logics to quickly disseminate denigrating depictions on platforms that are sympathetic to alt-right concerns including Reddit and 4chan (Massanari and Chess, 2018).

7 A derogatory term, "snowflakes" are perceived to be overly sensitive, entitled and easily offended people, or (usually young) people who have an inflated sense of their own uniqueness.

8 The trolling group hacked tumblr, hosting a pop-up message proclaiming to protest "the seemingly pandemic growth and worldwide propagation of the most FUCKING WORTHLESS, CONTRIVED, BOURGEOISIE, SELF-CONGRATULATING AND DECADENT BULLSHIT THE INTERNET EVER HAD THE MISFORTUNE OF FACILITATING," and "REPEAT AFTER ME: I WISH I WAS PROFOUND, BUT I'M NOT! I WISH I WAS ORIGINAL, BUT I'M NOT!" (Adewunmi 2012).

9 Steven Universe is known for radical engagements with gender, race, and bodies.

Chapter 6: NSFW

1 Not Safe For Work – the acronym and the term marks content one would prefer one's colleagues not to see on one's screen.

While this should also include violence, hate-speech, and gore, the label is mostly used for sexually explicit content.

2 VFW stands for Veterans of Foreign Wars; it is an organization for US military veterans.

3 Faces are very often obscured or cropped out for purposes of maintaining what the bloggers in this community called "plausible deniablity."

4 Sizeism is prejudice based on the size of someone's body.

5 OnlyFans is a subscription-based service, where some (often already somewhat known) users share NSFW content and other users can choose to follow them, and have access to their content, for a monthly fee. Fetlife is a social networking site for people practicing or interested in kinky and fetishistic sex.

6 While the practice was popular, the word "selfie" was not yet prevalent in the studied community at the time of this interview (2012). People commonly referred to selfie taking as self-shooting.

7 In fact, it might have a longer afterlife on tumblr compared to other platforms (see Chapter 2); during the covid-19 pandemic, tumblr's head of communication was cited reporting her shock at content from 2010 going viral and trending again (Jennings 2020).

CHAPTER 7: MENTAL HEALTH

1 In some contexts, mental health is understood as a "spectrum" from mental health to mental ill-health; in others, mental health and illness are distinct. People can experience a sense of wellbeing while living with a mental illness, while someone else can experience emotional distress and poor mental health but not suffer from a mental illness or disorder (see Keyes 2002).

2 While this is a very brief acknowledgment of the complex histories and practices driven by people and communities with lived experience, we also understand this work to relate to antipsychiatry movements and Mad Studies (e.g., Russo and Sweeney, 2016).

3 The "psychopathology of everyday life" follows Freud's publication of the same name in 1901 (Freud 2003), but in this context refers to how problems are remade into psychiatric disorders and problems that require medical care. See also

Fernando and Moodley (2018) for a discussion of mental health in the global South.

4 At the time of writing, tumblr shows a green dot next to other users in the chat message function, and, in the browser version, lists of Followed blogs display information on when these blogs were last updated (ten months ago, one week ago, ten hours ago, etc.). This is more information on people's user activity than tumblr used to share, but still less than on most other social media platforms.

5 This is especially important given network-based censorship that may change between locations or nations.

6 Of note, no PSAs appeared in our analyses, and related suggestions such as self-harm or anorexia did not appear either, even if users tagged posts coming up in searches with those or other "banned" tags. The searches were conducted through the dashboard, via Australian servers and ISP. However, when we searched directly for "proana" or "depression," we were shown PSAs.

7 The history of these adverbs and descriptors in memetic communication is ambiguous, but they reflect youth language and memes on tumblr and other platforms such as "just ___ things," e.g., just girly things, just army things. While "actually ___" plays out on social justice and mansplaining genres on tumblr and Reddit, here we also associate "actually" with feminine youth vernacular depicted in the 1995 US youth culture film Clueless.

8 Understood as often causing immediate anxiety, posttraumatic stress, or not feeling safe that may or may not result from an earlier or ongoing experience of trauma (Kyrölä 2015).

9 For example, tips to distract one's dining partners from noticing how little food they were eating, such as playing around with food on a plate, talking a lot to distract other people, bringing the fork to one's mouth but gasping or acting surprised just as it is time to put food in one's mouth.

10 As Vásquez and Creel (2017) note, the origins of the "Chat" genre is uncertain, but the Chat post format has always been available to tumblr users since 2007. We agree with their speculation that the genre emerged from tumblr's interface.

11 The second image includes the title of a Courtney Barnett song painted onto a wall "NOBODY REALLY CARES IF YOU DON'T GO TO THE PARTY."

Conclusion: "beautiful hellsite"

1 Destiel is a name of a popular imagined relationship between
   two characters of the TV show *Supernatural*. PWP is an acronym
   for "porn without plot," a genre of fanfiction.
2 This is especially striking in relation to mental health tumblr,
   as the circulation of mental health and illness themes was not
   significantly impacted by the self-harm policy changes in 2012,
   unlike the adverse impact of the NSFW ban on the NSFW silo.
   In part, this is because the 2012 policy was a result of at least
   a partial dialogue with users, while the NSFW policy was a
   top-down verdict.

References

1kookieyeolssecondblog1. (n.d.). "Kpop ships + Kpop confessions ... and other things." tumblr. https://1kookieyeolssecondblog1.tumblr. com/.

aaawhyme. (2017). "The AAAH zone." tumblr, January 10. https:// aaawhyme.tumblr.com/post/165960183601/well-damn-there-goes-my-plans.

Abidin, C. (2016a). "Visibility labour: Engaging with influencers' fashion brands and #OOTD advertorial campaigns on Instagram." *Media International Australia*, 161(1), 86–100.

Abidin, C. (2016b). "Aren't these just young, rich women doing vain things online? influencer selfies as subversive frivolity." *Social Media + Society*, 2(2), 1–17.

Abidin, C. (2017). "#familygoals: Family influencers, calibrated amateurism, and justifying young digital labour." *Social Media + Society*, 3(2), 1–15.

Abidin, C. (2018). *Internet Celebrity, Understanding Fame Online*. Bingley: Emerald Publishing.

Abidin, C. (2019). "Yes homo: Gay influencers, homonormativity, and queerbaiting on YouTube." *Continuum: Journal of Media & Cultural Studies*, 33(5), 614–629.

Abidin, C. (2020). "Growing up and growing old on the internet: Influencer life courses and the internet as home." In A. Markham and K. Tiidenberg (eds.), *Metaphors of the Internet: Ways of Being in the Age of Ubiquity*. New York: Peter Lang, pp. 84–94.

Abidin, C. (forthcoming). "Grief hypejacking: Influencers, #ThoughtsAndPrayers, and the commodification of grief on Instagram." *The Information Society*.

Abidin, C., and Baudinette, T. (2020). "The civic hijinks of K–pop's super fans, How K–pop fans manipulate social media for activism." *Data Points*. https://points.datasociety.net/the–civic–hijinks–of–k–pops–super–fans–ae2e66e28c6.

acidwaste. (2020). "THE DEEPER THE BETTER." tumblr, April 30. https://tmblrnorms.tumblr.com/post/616834354686115840.

Ackley, C. (2015). "The problem with sad girl culture." *Into the Fold*, July 15. https://www.intothefoldmag.com/2015/07/the–problem–with–sad–girl–culture/.

action. (2020). "How's your 2020 going, Tumblr?" tumblr, January 27. https://action.tumblr.com/post/190497684110/hows–your–2020–going–tumblr–in–a–perfect–world.

Adair, C., and Nakamura, L. (2017). "The digital afterlives of *This Bridge Call My Back*: Women of color feminism, digital labor, and networked pedagogy." *American Literature*, 89(2), 255–278.

Adewunmi, B. (2012). "You can hack it, you can bash it, but Tumblr's still got it." *Guardian*, December 5. https://www.theguardian.com/commentisfree/2012/dec/04/hack–tumblr–microblogging–gnaa.

agustdboyfriend. (2019). "bts supporting lgbt rightsfor …" tumblr, June 7. https://tmblrnorms.tumblr.com/post/185439881293/agustdboyfriend–bts–supporting–lgbt–rights–for.

ahkmunrah. (2016). "notable g–dragon cameos." tumblr, n.d. https://ahkmunrah.tumblr.com/post/134597947432/notable–g–dragon–cameos.

Ahmad, A. (2015). "A note on call-out culture." *Briar Patch Magazine*, March 2. https://briarpatchmagazine.com/articles/view/a–note–on–call–out–culture.

airborneranger63. (2020). "Do u ever think about …" tumblr, May 19. https://tmblrnorms.tumblr.com/post/618568678773030913/do–u–ever–think–about–how–dogs–who–have–2–colour.

Aleksandra. (n.d.). "How to make money on Tumblr." Top Offers, n.d. https://topoffers.com/blog/affiliate–tips/how–to–make–money–on–tumblr/.

alexander. (2017). "they: i used to work for this hellsite lmfao." tumblr, August 16. https://alexander.tumblr.com/post/164259804623/if–someone–bought–this–for–me–i–think–id–love–them.

Alexander, J. (2019). "Tumblr is launching a new group messaging feature built with fandoms in mind." The Verge, November 6. https://www.theverge.com/2019/11/6/20948596/tumblr–group–chats–fandom–privacy–direct–messaging–safety–mobile.

alittlepessimistic. (2016). "People became singers because of …" tumblr, April 5. https://alittlepessimistic.tumblr.com/post/142325332752/people–became–singers–because–of–feelings–like.

Anselmo, D. W. (2018). "Gender and queer fan labor on Tumblr: The case of BBC's Sherlock." *Feminist Media Histories*, 4(1), 84–114.

anthonybourdain. (2020). "ANTHONY BOURDAIN." tumblr, n.d. https://anthonybourdain.tumblr.com/.

APA. (2013). *Diagnostic and Statistical Manual of Mental Disorders* (5th ed.). Washington, DC: American Psychiatric Association.

Arevalo-Downes, L. (2014). "Tumblr is the wealthiest social platform." a.list, September 18. https://www.alistdaily.com/social/tumblr–is–the–wealthiest–social–platform/.

Armstrong, M. (2019). "Porn ban hits Tumblr where it hurts." Statista, March 15. https://www.statista.com/chart/17378/tumblr–traffic/.

arrogantcarrot. (2018). "arashi social media au." tumblr, October 31. https://tmblrnorms.tumblr.com/post/179616790428/arrogant carrot–arashi–social–media–au–bonus.

Arscott, I. (2018). "What Tumblr taught me about my gender identity." *Flare*, August 28. https://www.flare.com/sex–and–relationships/teenager–non–binary–gender–identity/.

aru. (2020). "if i ever see any ..." tumblr, April 30. https://tmblrnorms.tumblr.com/post/616833662708760576/guys.

Ashley, V. (2019). "Tumblr porn eulogy." *Porn Studies*, 6(3), 359–362.

Ask, K., and Abidin, C. (2018). "My life is a mess: Self-deprecating relatability and collective identities in the memification of student issues." *Information, Communication & Society*, 21(6), 834–850.

avecesfui. (2020). "My friend's kid decided baby ..." tumblr, April 18. https://tmblrnorms.tumblr.com/post/615761141877063680/avecesfui–ownerofdark–mijukaze.

AwakenWithJP. (2018). "Being a social justice warrior: Ultra Spiritual Life episode 88." YouTube, January 2. https://www.youtube.com/watch?v=ZBdnyrzq96s.

azizisbored. (2020). "Aziz Ansari." tumblr, n.d. https://azizisbored.tumblr.com/.

babyrubysoho. (n.d.). "We're normal!" tumblr, n.d. https://babyrubysoho.tumblr.com/.

baekhyuns-high-notes. (2019). "psa." tumblr, June 13. https://tmblrnorms.tumblr.com/post/185565508013/u–cannot–compare–someone–leaving–a–group–to?is_related_post=1.

baelor. (2020). "can you imagine if coronavirus ..." tumblr, June 2. https://tmblrnorms.tumblr.com/post/619855707383152640#notes.

Baila, M. (2017). "Surprising tumblrs you had no idea were this good." *Refinery29*, March 2. https://www.refinery29.com/en–us/2016/02/100713/celebrities–to–follow–on–tumblr.

Bakardjieva, M. (2009). "Subactivism: Lifeworld and politics in the age of the internet." *The Information Society*, 25(2), 91–104.

Baptiste, N. (2017). "Origins of a movement: A new book charts the rise and resilience of Black Lives Matter." *The Nation*, February 9. https://www.thenation.com/article/archive/origins-of-a-movement/.

Barrett-Ibarria, S. (2018). "Remembering the golden age of the queer internet." *Vice*, August 3. https://i–d.vice.com/en_uk/article/qvmz9x/remembering–the–golden–age–of–the–queer–internet.

Barthes, R. (1977). *Image, Music, Text.* New York: Hill and Wang.

Bartky, S. L. (1990). *Femininity and Domination: Studies in the Phenomenology of Oppression.* New York: Routledge.

Baym, N. K. (2000). *Tune In, Log On: Soaps, Fandom, and Online Community.* Thousand Oaks, CA: Sage.

Baym, N. K. (2010). "Social networks 2.0." In R. Burnett, M. Consalvo, and C. Ess (eds.), *The Handbook of Internet Studies.* Malden, MA: Blackwell Publishing, pp. 384–405.

Baym, N. K. (2015). *Personal Connections in the Digital Age.* (Digital Media and Society series). Wiley. Kindle edition.

BBS Communications Group. (2017). "Dark social: The future of social media?" November 20. http://www.bbscommunications.com.au/dark–social–future–social–media/.

Bercovici, J. (2013). "Tumblr: David Karp's $800 million art project." *Forbes*, January 2. https://www.forbes.com/sites/jeffbercovici/2013/01/02/tumblr–david–karps–800–million–art–project/.

Bereznak, A., Giorgis, H., Herman, A., Knibbs, K., Luckerson, V., McHugh, M., and Bakeret, K. (2017). "Roundtable: What happened to Tumblr?" *The Ringer*, November 29. https://www.theringer.com/tech/2017/11/29/16713354/david–karp–tumblr.

Berger, J. (1972). *Ways of Seeing.* London: British Broadcasting Association and Penguin.

Berners-Lee, T. (2019). "I invented the World Wide Web. Here's how we can fix it." *New York Times*, November 24. https://www.nytimes.com/2019/11/24/opinion/world–wide–web.html.

Bine, A. (2013). "Social media is redefining 'depression.'" *The Atlantic*, October 28. https://www.theatlantic.com/health/archive/2013/10/social–media–is–redefining–depression/280818/.

Bishop, S. (2020). "Algorithmic experts: Selling algorithmic lore on YouTube." *Social Media + Society*, 6(1), 1–11.

Black, R. W. (2009). "Online fan fiction and critical media literacy." *Journal of Computing in Teacher Education*, 26, 75–80.

blurberrys. (2015). "If we're mutuals and I ..." tumblr, n.d. https://blurberrys.tumblr.com/post/119139581237/if–were–mutuals–and–i–ever–awkwardly–reply–to–a.

bodyglitter. (2020). "when you tag something #FSLDMSLNDSSDLKFD ..." tumblr, May 20. https://tmblrnorms.tumblr.com/post/619564918312730624/bodyglitter–when–you–tag–something #notes.

Booth, P. (2018). "Tumbling or stumbling? Misadventures with Tumblr in the fan studies classroom." *Transformative Works and Cultures*, 27. http://dx.doi.org/10.3983/twc.2018.1252.

Bordo, S. (2003). *Unbearable Weight: Feminism, Western Culture, and the Body*. Berkeley: University of California Press.

Boshmaf, Y., Muslukhov, I., Beznosov, K., and Ripeanu, M. (2011). "The socialbot network: When bots socialize for fame and money." In *Proceedings of the 27th Annual Computer Security Applications Conference*, pp. 93–102. https://doi.org/10.1145/2076732.2076746.

Bourdieu, P. (1996). *Photography: A Middle-brow Art*. Stanford, CA: Stanford University Press.

Bourlai, E. E. (2018). "'Comments in tags, please!': Tagging practices on Tumblr." *Discourse, Context & Media*, 22, 46–56.

bovidae. (n.d.). "ppl changing their icons and ..." tumblr, n.d. https://bovidae.tumblr.com/post/80458802487/ppl–changing–their–icons–and–urls–at–the–same–time.

boyd, d. (2010). "Social network sites as networked publics: Affordances, dynamics, and implications." In Z. Papacharissi (ed.), *A Networked Self: Identity, Community and Culture on Social Network Sites*. New York: Routledge, pp. 39–58.

boyd, d. (2014). *It's Complicated: The Social Lives of Networked Teens*. New Haven, CT: Yale University Press.

BrainyDude. (2018). "The funniest conversations found on Tumblr." YouTube, July 24. https://www.youtube.com/watch?v=feXHNClEZdI.

britneyspears. (2020). "Britney Spears | Official Tumblr." tumblr, n.d. https://britneyspears.tumblr.com/.

Brock, A. (2012). "From the blackhand side: Twitter as a cultural conversation." *Journal of Broadcasting & Electronic Media*, 56(4), 529–549.

Brock, A. (2015). "Whiteness as digital imaginary: SJW as boundary object." Paper presented at the *Association of Internet Researchers Conference*. Phoenix, AZ.

Brown, M. L., and Phifer, H. (2018). "The rise of Belle from Tumblr." In C. Abidin and M. L. Brown (eds.), *Microcelebrity Around the Globe*. Bingley: Emerald, pp. 121–130.

btobshypeman. (2018). "IKON taking care of their ..." tumblr, June 18. https://tmblrnorms.tumblr.com/post/175008764823/btobshypeman–ikon–taking–care–of–their–so.

Bucher, T. (2012). "Want to be on the top? Algorithmic power and the threat of invisibility on Facebook." *New Media & Society*, 14(7), 1164–1180.

Bucher, T. (2017). "The algorithmic imaginary: Exploring the ordinary affects of Facebook algorithms." *Information, Communication & Society,* 20(1), 30–44.

Bucher, T., and Helmond, A. (2017). "The affordances of social media platforms." In J. Burgess, T. Poell, and A. Marwick (eds.), *The SAGE Handbook of Social Media.* Thousand Oaks, CA: SAGE, pp. 233–253.

Burgess, J. (2006). "Hearing ordinary voices: Cultural studies, vernacular creativity and digital storytelling." *Continuum: Journal of Media & Cultural Studies,* 20(2), 201–214.

Burgess, J., and Baym, N. K. (2020). *Twitter, A biography.* New York: New York University Press.

Burgess, J., and Green, J. (2009). *YouTube: Online Video and Participatory Culture.* Cambridge: Polity.

burgrs. (2020). "*unlikes post so i can ..." tumblr, May 30. https://tmblrnorms.tumblr.com/post/619565600580288514/burgrs-unlikes–post–so–i–can–like–it–from–u.

Burt, K. (2016). "What TV networks still don't understand about fandom." Den of Geek, April 14. https://www.denofgeek.com/tv/what–tv–networks–still–dont–understand–about–fandom/.

Burton, J. (2017). "Making space on the digital margin: Youth fandom communities on tumblr as spaces for making the self and re-making society." Doctoral dissertation. Rutgers, NJ.

Burton, J. (2019). "Look at us, we have anxiety: Youth, memes and the power of online cultural politics." *Journal of Childhood Studies,* 44(3), 3–17.

Bury, R., Deller, R., Greenwood, A., and Jones, B. (2013). "From Usenet to Tumblr: The changing role of social media." *Participations,* 10(1), 299–318.

Byrne, L., and Wykes, T. (2020). "A role for lived experience mental health leadership in the age of Covid–19." *Journal of Mental Health,* 1–4. https://doi.org/10.1080/09638237.2020.1766002.

Byron, P. (2019). "'How could you write your name below that?' The queer life and death of Tumblr." *Porn Studies,* 6(3), 336–349.

Byron, P., Robards, B., Hanckel, B., Vivienne, S., and Churchill, B. (2019). "'Hey, I'm having these experiences': Tumblr use and young people's queer (dis)connections." *International Journal of Communication,* 13, 2239–2259.

Cadwalladr, C., and Graham-Harrison, E. (2018). "Revealed: 50 million Facebook profiles harvested for Cambridge Analytica in major data breach." *Guardian,* March 17. http://freestudio21.com/wp–content/uploads/2018/04/50–million–fb–profiles–harvested–by–cambridge–analitica.pdf.

Caffyn, G. (2016). "Nescafe sees Tumblr and other platforms as e-commerce opportunities." Digiday, October 26. https://digiday. com/uk/nescafe–plans–monetize–growing–social–following/

cakejam. (2014). "I'll like this post so ..." tumblr, n.d. https://cakejam. tumblr.com/post/81710777735/ill–like–this–post–so–i–can–find–it–later–on.

Calhoun, K. (2020). "Blackout, black excellence, Black Power: Strategies of everyday online activism on Black Tumblr." In A. McCracken, A. Cho, L. Stein, and I. Neill Hoch (eds.), A Tumblr Book: Platform and Cultures. Ann Arbor: University of Michigan Press, pp. 48–62.

Cavalcante, A. (2019). "Tumbling into queer utopias and vortexes: Experiences of LGBTQ social media users on Tumblr." Journal of Homosexuality, 66(12), 1715–1735.

Cavazos-Rehg, P. A., Krauss, M. J., Sowles, S. J., Connolly, S., Rosas, C., ... Bierut, L. J. (2017). "An analysis of depression, self-harm, and suicidal ideation content on Tumblr." Crisis, 38, 44–52.

Chang, Y., Tang, L., Inagaki, Y., and Liu, Y. (2014). "What is Tumblr: A statistical overview and comparison," ACM SIGKDD Explorations Newsletter. Special issue on big data, 16, 21–29. https://dl.acm.org/doi/10.1145/2674026.2674030.

Cheshire, T. (2012). "Tumbling on success: How Tumblr's David Karp built a £500 million empire." Wired, February 2. https://www.wired. co.uk/article/tumbling–on–success.

Chess, S., and Shaw, A. (2015). "A conspiracy of fishes, or, how we learned to stop worrying about #GamerGate and embrace hegemonic masculinity." Journal of Broadcasting & Electronic Media, 59(1), 208–220.

Chew, N. (2018). "Tumblr as a counterpublic space for fan mobilization." Transformative Works and Cultures, 27. https://doi. org/10.3983/twc.2018.1186.

Cho, A. (2011). "Queer Tumblrs, networked counterpublics." Annual meeting of the International Communication Association, Boston, May 25. http://citation.allacademic.com/meta/p_mla_apa_research_citation/4/8/8/8/4/p488843_index.html?phpsessid=88d42ca776f4 df5cfd0651debf8d1744.

Cho, A. (2015a). "Queer reverb: Tumblr, affect, time." In K. Hillis, S. Paasonen, and M. Petit (eds.), Networked affect. Cambridge, MA: MIT Press, pp. 43–58.

Cho, A. (2015b). "Sensuous participation: Queer youth of color, affect, and social media." Doctoral dissertation. University of Texas at Austin. https://repositories.lib.utexas.edu/handle/2152/31667.

Cho, A. (2018a). "Default publicness: Queer youth of color, social media, and being outed by the machine." *New Media & Society*, 20(9), 3183–3200.

Cho, A. (2018b). "Disruptive joy." In Z. Papacharissi (ed.), *A Networked Self and Love*. London: Routledge, pp. 189–201.

choi-seunghyunie. (2019a). "Coton candy T.O.P." tumblr, July 26. https://tmblrnorms.tumblr.com/post/186573352388/cotton–candy–top.

choi-seunghyunie. (2019b). "i really miss t-oh-p." tumblr, July 20. https://tmblrnorms.tumblr.com/post/186422130928.

choi-seunghyunie. (2019c). "It's still extremely hard being ..." tumblr, July 18. https://tmblrnorms.tumblr.com/post/186388449568.

christianstepmoms. (2020). "0–4 notes – your post sucks ..." tumblr, May 6. https://tmblrnorms.tumblr.com/post/617412821353955328.

chromolume. (2019). "the most exciting thing about ..." tumblr, October 24. https://tmblrnorms.tumblr.com/post/188564059648/konohaeleven–chromolume–the–most–exciting.

Clark, J., and Aufderheide, P. (2009). *Public Media 2.0: Dynamic, Engaged Publics*. Center for Social Media, University of East Anglia.

Clarke, A., and Star, S. L. (2008). "The social worlds framework: A theory/methods package." In E. Hackett, O. Amsterdamska, M. Lynch, and J. Wacjman (eds.), *The Handbook of Science and Technology Studies* (3rd ed.). Cambridge, MA: MIT Press, pp. 113–138.

cleanie. (2018). "Tumblr mobile: you have five ..." tumblr, August 22. https://tmblrnorms.tumblr.com/post/177263739628/tumblr–mobile–you–have–five–new.

Clemons, E. K. (2009). "The complex problem of monetizing virtual electronic social networks." *Decision Support Systems*, 48, 46–56.

Cobb, G. (2017). "'This is not pro-ana': Denial and disguise in pro-anorexia online spaces." *Fat Studies*, 6(2), 189–205.

Coldeway, D. (2019). "Automattic's bargain-bin Tumblr deal plugs right into the WordPress business model." *Techcrunch*, August 13. https://techcrunch.com/2019/08/12/automattics–bargain–bin–tumblr–deal–plugs–right–into–the–wordpress–business–model/.

Coleman, R. (2009). *The Becoming of Bodies: Girls, Images, Experience*. Manchester: Manchester University Press.

Collins, K. (2018). "How Taylor Swift flipped online fandom on its head for the better." CNet, June 8. https://www.cnet.com/news/how–taylor–swift–flipped–online–fandom–on–its–head–for–the–better/.

colourofoctober. (2015). "Refreshing a page just as ..." tumblr, July 9. https://colourofoctober.tumblr.com/post/123597141495/refreshing–a–page–just–as–you–see–something.

Community Guidelines update. (2012). Github, March 3. https://
github.com/tumblr/policy/commit/38f37e7680146442b3eab7908
0a73e3a896d8ad0#diff–ef5d83620cbf52ab9f327cc48b35975f.

concernedfansofgdragon. (2018). "Perfect example of how she ..."
tumblr, September 23. https://tmblrnorms.tumblr.com/post/
178371883203/concernedfansofgdragon–perfect–example–of–
how?is_related_post=1.

confessyourkpop. (n.d.). "Confess your kpop." tumblr, n.d. https://
confessyourkpop.tumblr.com/.

confessyourkpopsin-blog. (n.d.). "Kpop's confessions – French."
tumblr, n.d. https://confessyourkpopsin–blog.tumblr.com/.

Connelly, S. M. (2015). ""Welcome to the FEMINIST CULT": Building a
feminist community of practice on Tumblr." Student paper, Gettysburg
College. http://cupola.gettysburg.edu/student_scholarship/328.

Cooper, H. (2013). "Alarming rise of self-harm by teenagers." 7.30,
ABC, September 10. http://www.abc.net.au/7.30/content/2013/
s3845800.htm.

Coscarelli, J. (2017). "How Taylor Swift is using Tumblr to create a
safe space with her fans." *Independent*, November 9. https://www.
independent.co.uk/arts–entertainment/music/features/taylor–
swift–tumblr–safe–space–fans–posts–reputation–album–release–
social–media–a8045511.html.

Cover, R. (2018). *Emergent Identities: New Sexualities, Genders and
Relationships in a Digital Era*. Abingdon: Routledge.

Dame, A. (2016). "Making a name for yourself: Tagging as
transgender ontological practice on Tumblr." *Critical Studies in
Media Communication*, 33(1), 23–37.

damsandwich. (2020). "one day i will escape ..." tumblr, June 14.
https://tmblrnorms.tumblr.com/post/620926250535567360/
dampsandwich–one–day–i–will–escape–from–this#notes.

Dannen, C. (2009). "What the hell is tumblr? And other worthwhile questions." *Fast Company*, May 13. https://www.fastcompany.
com/90185298/what–the–hell–is–tumblr–and–other–worthwhile–
questions.

David's Log. (2008). "I'm in page six." tumblr, January 20. https://www.
davidslog.com/24227964/im–in–page–six–magazine–today–if–
you–happen–to.

Davis, J. L. (2017). "Curation: A theoretical treatment." *Information,
Communication & Society*, 20(5), 770–783.

Davis, J. L., and Chouinard, J. B. (2017). "Theorizing affordances:
From request to refuse." *Bulletin of Science, Technology & Society*,
36(4), 241–248.

DeCook, J. R. (2018). "Memes and symbolic violence: #proudboys and the use of memes for propaganda and the construction of collective identity." *Learning, Media and Technology*, 43(4), 485–504.

de Laat, P. B. (2008). "Online diaries: Reflections on trust, privacy, and exhibitionism." *Ethics and Information Technology*, 10(1), 57–69.

Delo, C. (2012a). "Tumblr unveils first major brand campaign for Adidas." *Ad Age*, June 8. https://adage.com/article/digital/tumblr–unveils–major–brand–campaign–adidas/235262.

Delo, C. (2012b). "Digital agency launches Tumblr commerce service for brands." *Ad Age*, June 27. https://adage.com/article/digital/digital–agency–launches–tumblr–commerce–service–brands/235626.

DeMeo, E. (2016). "Fandom and social media marketing: Looking at Doctor Who Tumblr engagement through the lens of participatory culture." Master's thesis. Liberty University, Lynchburg, VA. https://digitalcommons.liberty.edu/masters/400/.

Denavas-Walk, C., and Proctor, B. D. (2015). "Income and poverty in the United States: 2014." *United States Census Bureau*, September. https://www.census.gov/library/publications/2015/demo/p60–252. html#:~:text=Median%20household%20income%20was%20 %2453%2C657,the%202013%20median%20of%20%2454 %2C462.

Dennis, C. A. (2015). "Blogging as public pedagogy: Creating alternative educational futures." *International Journal of Lifelong Education*, 34(3), 284–299.

Denyer, S., and Min, J. K. (2020). "These South Korean women went abroad to get married. Then one spoke out at home, and the backlash began." *Washington Post*, March 23. https://www.washingtonpost.com/world/asia_pacific/south–korea–same–sex–marriage–gay–lesbian/2020/03/22/2890df14–61f6–11ea–912d–d98032ec8e25_story.html.

depressedphoenix. (2019). "you're so fucking lucky, I ..." tumblr, February 2. https://tmblrnorms.tumblr.com/post/182500593653/hamburgertrousers–depressedphoenix–oh.

Dickey, M. R. (2013). "David Karp went on The Colbert Show and defended all the porn on Tumblr." *Business Insider*, July 18. https://www.businessinsider.com.au/david–karp–defends–porn–on–tumblr–2013–7.

Dickson, B. (2018). "The challenges of moderating online content with deep learning." *TechTalks*, December 10. https://bdtechtalks.com/2018/12/10/ai–deep–learning–adult–content–moderation/.

Dictionary.com. (2020). "code-switching." Dictionary, n.d. https:// www.dictionary.com/browse/code–switching?s=t.

Duguay, S. (2017). "Identity modulation in networked publics: Queer women's participation and representation on Tinder, Instagram, and Vine." Doctoral dissertation. Queensland University of Technology.

dulect. (2019). "I contribute daily to the ..." tumblr, August 31. https:// tmblrnorms.tumblr.com/post/187396750033.

dulect. (2020a). "When the ads on this ..." tumblr, January 31. https://tmblrnorms.tumblr.com/post/190570396668/ buckyhasablog–when–the–ads–on–this–hellsite.

dulect. (2020b). "Untoasted slice of white bread." tumblr, February 19. https://tmblrnorms.tumblr.com/post/190912009023/agirruknow- eriggyageptulel.

Dunn, G. (2013). "10 people you will meet on tumblr." Thought Catalog, January 18. https://thoughtcatalog.com/gaby–dunn/2013/01/10– people–you–will–meet–on–tumblr/.

Eaton, K. (2010). "Tumblr is turning a billion page views into cash, but not through ads." Fast Company, April 20. https://www. fastcompany.com/1621645/tumblr–turning–billion–page–views– cash–not–through–ads.

elmosanica. (2018). "WINNER being husband/father material." tumblr, July 29. https://tmblrnorms.tumblr.com/post/176428400973/ elmosanica–winner–being–husbandfather–material.

Eloise, M. (2019). "Rise and fall of the reblog: 10 years of Tumblr." Paper, December 26. https://www.papermag.com/ten–years–of– tumblr–2010s–2641949795.html.

Engelberg, J., and Needham, G. (2019). "Purging the queer archive: Tumblr's counterhegemonic pornographies." Porn Studies, 6(3), 350–354.

Escribano, U. (2016). "Tumblr and fandom, a match made in heaven." The Daily Fandom, March 16. https://thedailyfandom.com/ tumblr–fandom–match/.

Evans, S. K., Pearce, K. E., Vitak, J., and Treem, J. W. (2017). "Explicating affordances: A conceptual framework for understanding affor- dances in communication research." Journal of Computer-Mediated Communication, 22, 35–52.

Ewing, T. (2014). "All our friends: The Marvel tumblrwave." Freaky Trigger, January 10. http://freakytrigger.co.uk/wedge/2014/01/ all–our–friends/.

fakelitty. (2019). "How can I monetize my ..." Reddit, n.d. https://www.reddit.com/r/Blogging/comments/95j9sn/ how_can_i_monetize_my_my_tumblr_blog_with_47000/.

fandom. (n.d.). "About Fandometrics." tumblr, n.d. https://fandom.
tumblr.com/about.

fandom. (2019a), "Year in review." tumblr, December 2. https://
fandom.tumblr.com/post/189431749669/best-of-2019.

fandom. (2019b). "Tumblr and social impact in 2019." tumblr,
November 27. https://fandom.tumblr.com/post/189334801959/
2019-social-impact.

fandom. (2020). "Week in review." tumblr, June 29. https://fandom.
tumblr.com/post/622273782378315776/you-never-completely-
have-your-rights-one#notes.

fasterfood. (2020). "no ..." tumblr, March 16. https://tmblrnorms.
tumblr.com/post/612762222164410368/fasterfood-no-maybe.

Fathallah, J. M. (2018). "Polyphony on Tumblr: Reading the hateblog
as pastiche." *Transformative Works and Cultures*, 27. http://dx.doi.
org/10.3983/twc.2018.1210.

Feldman, B. (2017). "Tumblr's unclear future shows that there's no
money in internet culture." *New York Magazine*, January 28. https://
nymag.com/intelligencer/2017/06/theres-no-money-in-internet-
culture.html.

Fell, J. (2014). "Tumblr still struggling to be a profitable business."
Entrepreneur, May 5. https://www.entrepreneur.com/article/233629.

Fennessey, S. (2010). "Cancel publish: A call for the end of Tumblr book
deals." *GQ*, April 27. https://www.gq.com/story/cancel-publish-
a-call-for-the-end-of-tumblr-book-deals.

Feraday, C. (2016). "For lack of a better word: Neo-identities in
non-cisgender, non-straight communities on Tumblr." Master's
thesis. Ryerson University, Toronto.

Fernando, S., and Moodley, R. (eds.) (2018). *Global Psychologies:
Mental Health and the Global South*. London: Palgrave Macmillan.

Feuston, J. L., and Piper, A. M. (2018). "Beyond the coded gaze:
Analyzing expression of mental health and illness on Instagram."
Proceedings of the ACM on Human–Computer Interaction, 2(CSCW),
1–21. https://doi.org/10.1145/3274320.

Fichman, P., and Dainas, A. R. (2019). "Graphicons and tactics
in satirical trolling on tumblr.com." *International Journal of
Communication*, 13, 4261–4286.

Fiegerman, S. (2016). "How Yahoo derailed Tumblr, after Marissa
Mayer promised 'not to screw it up.'" *Mashable*, June 15. https://
mashable.com/2016/06/15/how-yahoo-derailed-tumblr/
?europe=true.

Fink, M., and Miller, Q. (2014). "Trans media moments: Tumblr,
2011–2013." *Television & New Media*, 15(7), 611–626.

flower-tabi. (2019). "✿" tumblr, January 27. https://tmblrnorms. tumblr.com/post/182352696908.

Fotopoulou, A., and Couldry, N. (2017). "Telling the story of the stories: Online content curation and digital engagement." *Information, Communication & Society*, 18(2), 235–249.

Foucault, M. (1987 [1954]). *Mental Illness and Psychology*, trans. A. Sheridan. Berkeley: University of California Press.

Foucault, M. (2005). *The Hermeneutics of the Subject: Lectures at the Collège de France, 1981–1982*, ed. F. Gros, trans. G. Burchell. London: Palgrave Macmillan.

Fox, J., and Ralston, R. (2016). "Queer identity online: Informal learning and teaching experiences of LGBTQ individuals on social media." *Computers in Human Behavior*, 65, 635–642.

Franssen, M., Lokhorst, G.-J., and van de Poel, I. (2018), "Philosophy of Technology." In E. N. Zalta (ed.), *The Stanford Encyclopedia of Philosophy*. https://plato.stanford.edu/archives/fall2018/entries/technology/.

Fraser, N. (1999). "Social justice in the age of identity politics: Redistribution, recognition, and participation." In L. Ray and A. Sayer (ed.), *Culture and Economy after the Cultural Turn*. London: Sage, pp. 25–52.

Frazer, R., and Carlson, B. (2017). "Indigenous memes and the invention of a people." *Social Media + Society*, 3(4), 1–12.

Freire, P. (2018). *Pedagogy of the Oppressed* (50th anniversary ed.). New York: Bloomsbury Academic.

Freud, S. (2003 [1901]). *The Psychopathology of Everyday Life*, trans. A. Bell. New York: Penguin Books.

fuckheadsawhore. (2019). "You're fucking disgusting for pulling ..." tumblr, July 7. https://tmblrnorms.tumblr.com/post/186126589093.

fucknotumblrsjw. (2020). tumblr, n.d. https://fucknotumblrsjw. tumblr.com/

futbolwag. (2020). "tumblr is dead but also ..." tumblr, n.d. https:// futbolwag.tumblr.com/post/190403582800/tumblr–is–dead–but–also–if–i–dont–reblog–pointless.

Fyfe, M. (2016). "Rise and fall of Jess Miller's pizza empire." *Sydney Morning Herald*, May 12. https://www.smh.com.au/lifestyle/rise–and–fall–of–jess–millers–pizza–empire–20160512–gotftv. html.

fy-winner. (2018). "please don't post photos of ..." tumblr, August 26. https://tmblrnorms.tumblr.com/post/177429355058/please–dont–post–photos–of–jinwoo–from.

garbage-empress. (2018). "PSA." tumblr, November 12. https://

tmblrnorms.tumblr.com/post/180048514418/pregnantseinfeld–informed–me–that–i–was–in–a.

Gavey, N. (2012). "Beyond 'empowerment'? Sexuality in a sexist world." *Sex Roles*, 66(11–12), 718–724.

gayarsonist. (2020). "I'm sure I've missed a …" tumblr, n.d. https://gayarsonist.tumblr.com/post/189724873083/im–sure–ive–missed–a–few–things–but–i–cant.

Gayomali, C. (2015). "Tumblr launches an in-house ad agency that pairs creators with big brands." *Fast Company*, January 22. https://www.fastcompany.com/3041271/tumblr–creatrs–network.

Gee, J. P. (2004). *Situated Language and Learning: A Critique of Traditional Schooling*. New York: Routledge.

Gelder, K., and Thornton, S. (eds.) (1997). *The Subcultures Reader*. London: Routledge.

Gerrard, Y. (2018). "Beyond the hashtag: Circumventing content moderation on social media." *New Media & Society*, 20(12), 1–20.

Gibbs, M., Meese, J., Arnold, M., Nansen, B., and Carter, M. (2014). "#Funerals and Instagram: Death, Social Media and Platform Vernacular." *Information, Communication & Society*, 18(3), 255–268. https://doi.org/10.1080/1369118X.2014.987152.

Gilkerson, N., and Berg, K. T. (2018). "Social media, hashtag hijacking, and the evolution of an activist group strategy." In L. Austin and Y. Jin (eds.), *Social Media and Crisis Communication*. New York: Routledge, pp. 141–155.

Gillespie, T. (2012). "The relevance of algorithms." In T. Gillespie, P. Boczkowski, and K. Foot (eds.), *Media Technologies: Essays on Communication, Materiality, and Society*. Cambridge, MA: MIT Press, pp. 167–194.

Gillespie, T. (2018). *Custodians of the Internet*. New Haven, CT: Yale University Press.

Gingold, N. (2019). "Why the blueprint for k-pop actually came from Japan." *NPR*, January 8. https://www.npr.org/2019/01/08/683339743/why-the-blueprint-for-k-pop-actually-came-from-japan.

gnhwan. (2018). "iKON Summertime in Bali (Scan)." tumblr, July 13. https://tmblrnorms.tumblr.com/post/175843478243/gnhwan-ikon-summertime-in-bali-scan?is_related_post=1.

Goffman, E. (1963). *Stigma*. Englewood Cliffs: Prentice Hall.

Gonzalez-Polledo, E., and Tarr, J. (2014). "The thing about pain: The remaking of illness narratives in chronic pain expressions on social media." *New Media & Society*, 18(8), 1455–1472.

goodraandyy. (2020). "I love that on mobile …" tumblr, June 2.

https://tmblrnorms.tumblr.com/post/619830118066601984/lazorsandparadox–ichigotchipng–goodraandyy

Gray, M. L. (2007). "From websites to Wal-Mart: Youth, identity work, and the queering of boundary publics in Small Town, USA." *American Studies*, 48(2), 49–59.

Green, L. 2018. *Sex Plus: Learning, Loving, and Enjoying Your Body*. New York: HarperCollins. https://www.harpercollins.com/9780062561008/sex–plus–learning–loving–and–enjoying–your–body/.

Greenwood, D. (2020). "This girl is right: 2013 was a cultural reset." *Vice*, April 6. https://i–d.vice.com/en_uk/article/bvg43a/2013–cultural–reset–tiktok?utm_term=Autofeed&utm_medium=Social&utm_source=Twitter&Echobox=1589940565#twitterclicid=Echobox.

Gürsimsek, Ö. A. (2016). "Animated GIFs as vernacular graphic design: Producing tumblr blogs." *Visual Communication*, 15(3), 329–349.

Hailey, B. (2019). "12 Predictions for the future of social media." *Medium*, September 6. https://medium.com/better–marketing/12–predictions–for–the–future–of–social–media–9c08ad247b63.

Haimson, O. L., Dame-Griff, A., Capello, E., and Richter, Z. (2019). "Tumblr was a trans technology: The meaning, importance, history, and future of trans technologies." *Feminist Media Studies*, 1–17. https://doi.org/10.1080/14680777.2019.1678505.

Halpern, D., and Gibbs, J. (2013). "Social media as a catalyst for online deliberation? Exploring the affordances of Facebook and YouTube for political expression." *Computers in Human Behavior*, 29, 1159–1168.

Hamburger, E. (2014). "Tumblr declares war on the internet's identity crisis. What's a profile if it looks like everybody else's?" The Verge, May 6. https://www.theverge.com/2014/5/6/5684212/tumblr–declares–war–on–the–internets–identity–crisis.

Hanckel, B., and Morris, A. (2014). "Finding community and contesting heteronormativity: Queer young people's engagement in an Australian online community." *Journal of Youth Studies*, 17(7), 872–886.

Hanckel, B., Vivienne, S., Byron, P., Robards, B., and Churchill, B. (2019). "'That's not necessarily for them': LGBTIQ+ young people, social media platform affordances and identity curation." *Media, Culture & Society*, 41(8), 1261–1278. https://doi.org/10.1177/0163443719846612.

Hardy, A., Bennett, A., and Robards, B. (2018). *Neo-Tribes*. Cham: Palgrave Macmillan.

Harper's Bazaar Staff. (2018). "Christabel Chua finally opens up about that incident." *Harpers Bazaar*, July 30. https://www.harpersbazaar.com.sg/life/christabel–chua–finally–opens–up–about–that–incident/.

Hart, M. (2018a). "'It's nice to see you're not the only on with kinks': Presenting intimate privates in intimate publics on tumblr." In A. Dobson, B. Robards, and N. Carah (eds.), *Digital Intimate Publics and Social Media*. Cham: Palgrave Macmillan, pp. 171–199.

Hart, M. (2018b). "#Topless Tuesdays and #Wet Wednesdays: Digitally mediated neo-tribalism and NSFW selfies on tumblr." In A. Hardy, A. Bennett, and B. Robards (eds.), *Neo-tribes*. Cham: Palgrave Macmillan, pp. 207–219.

Hautsch, J. (2018). "Tumblr's supernatural fandom and the rhetorical affordance of GIFs." *Transformative Works and Cultures*, 27. https://doi.org/10.3983/twc.2018.1165.

Hendry, N. A. (2018). "Everyday anxieties: Young women, mental illness and social media practices of visibility and connection." Doctoral dissertation. RMIT University, Melbourne.

Hendry, N. A. (2020a). "New ways of seeing: Tumblr, young people, and mental illness." In A. McCracken, A. Cho, L. Stein, and I. Neill Hoch (eds.), *A Tumblr Book: Platform and Cultures*. Ann Arbor: University of Michigan Press, pp. 315–325.

Hendry, N. A. (2020b). "Young women's mental illness and (in-)visible social media practices of control and emotional recognition." *Social Media + Society*, 1–10. https://doi.org/10.1177/2056305120963832.

Hendry, N. A., Robards, B., and Stanford, S. (2017). "Beyond social media panics for 'at risk' youth." In S. Stanford, E. Sharland, N. R. Heller, and J. Warner (eds.), *Beyond the Risk Paradigm in Mental Health Policy and Practice*. London: Palgrave Macmillan, pp. 135–154.

Hickey-Moody, A. (2013). "Affect as method: Feelings, aesthetics and affective pedagogy." In R. Coleman and J. Ringrose (eds.), *Deleuze and Research Methodologies*. Edinburgh: Edinburgh University Press, pp. 79–95.

Highfield, T. (2016). *Social Media and Everyday Politics*. Cambridge: Polity.

Hillman, S., Procyk, J., and Neustaedter, C. (2014). "alksjdf;Lksfd": Tumblr and the fandom user experience." In *Proceedings of the 2014 Conference on Designing Interactive Systems*, Vancouver, pp. 775–784.

Hines, K. (2014). "How to make money on Tumblr: 25 proven tips." MonetizePros, February 5. https://monetizepros.com/features/25–ways–to–make–money–on–tumblr/.

Hollander, M. (2003). "Losses of face: Rembrandt, Masaccio and the drama of shame." *Social Research*, 70(4), 1327–5130.

Hollingsworth, J. (2020). "In the camp world of K-pop, it's hard for stars to be gay." *CNN World*, 27 January. https://edition.cnn.com/2020/01/25/asia/k–pop–gay–star–intl–hnk/index.html.

Holpuch, A. (2016). "'I just feel less alone': How Tumblr became a source for mental health care." *Guardian*, May 19. http://www.theguardian.com/lifeandstyle/2016/may/19/tumblr–mental–health–information–community–disorders–healthcare.

hotboyproblems. (2020a). "Why is tumblr recommending themselves ..." tumblr, March 10. https://tmblrnorms.tumblr.com/post/612216347634630656/fetus–cakes–walrusguy–emigration–why–is.

hotboyproblems. (2020b). "Things i've seen preschoolers hurt ..." tumblr, May 17. https://tmblrnorms.tumblr.com/post/618334409078292480/robots–and–lizards–invalleumbraemortis.

hotboyproblems. (2020c). "Normal siblings ..." tumblr, May 17. https://tmblrnorms.tumblr.com/post/618333747006390272/saviorownsoul–tsunderrated–me–and–my–sibling.

Houston, E. (2014). "Wear your tumblr addiction on your shirt with these amazing limited-edition tees." *Seventeen*, November 7. https://www.seventeen.com/fashion/style–advice/news/a25494/tumblr–artist–series–tees/.

humansoftumblrcom. (2020). "Humans of Tumblr." Facebook, n.d https://www.facebook.com/humansoftumblrcom/.

hypeswap. (2019). "i dont really ... WANT ... to ..." tumblr, July 25. https://tmblrnorms.tumblr.com/post/186540658893/lunamalfoy7–hypeswap–hypeswap–i–dont.

ikon-global. (2018). "iKON GLOBAL RECRUITMENT." tumblr, January 30. https://ikon–global.tumblr.com/post/170304763322/ikon–global–tumblr–is–looking–for–new–members.

ikon-global. (n.d.). "IKON GLOBAL." tumblr, n.d. https://ikon–global.tumblr.com/

ikon-official. (2019). "[!] iKON–OFFICIAL IS LOOKING FOR MODERATORS." tumblr, February 8. https://tmblrnorms.tumblr.com/post/182666266908/ikon–official–ikon–official–is–looking–for?is_related_post=1.

ikonis. (2018). "Bobby is the absolute cutest." tumblr, November 30. https://tmblrnorms.tumblr.com/post/180649242448/bobby–is–the–absolute–cutest?is_related_post=1.

Influencer Marketing Hub (2020). "Social media trends for 2020 and beyond." *Influencer Marketing Hub*, May 26. https://influencermarketinghub.com/social–media–trends/.

Ito, M., Martin, C., Pfister, R. C., Rafalow, M. H., Salen, K., and

Wortman, A. (2018). *Affinity Online: How Connection and Shared Interest Fuel Learning.* New York: New York University Press.

its-dirty-kpop-confessions. (n.d.). "its-dirty-kpop-confessions." tumblr, n.d. https://its–dirty–kpop–confessions.tumblr.com/.

Jamison, A. (2013). *Fic: Why Fanfiction is Taking Over the World.* Dallas, TX: BenBella Books.

Jenkins, H., Clinton, K., Purushtoma, R., Robison, A. J., and Weigel, M. (2007). *Confronting the Challenges of Participatory Culture: Media Education for the 21st Century.* MacArthur Foundation. https://www.macfound.org/media/article_pdfs/jenkins_white_paper.pdf.

Jennings, R. (2020). "Stuck in 2020, pretending it's 2014: Millennials and Gen Z are revisiting indie pop, grunge fashion, and the early 2010s Tumblr aesthetic. Wouldn't it be nice if life still looked like that?" *Vox,* May 7. https://www.vox.com/the–goods/2020/5/7/21247938/tumblr–aesthetic–2014–nostalgia–tiktok–indie–pop.

Joho, J. (2019). "How being sad, depressed, and anxious online became trendy." Mashable, June 28. https://mashable.com/article/anxiety–depression–social–media–sad–online/.

julla. (2018). "I SCREAMEDKABSKSNSSLSHAGELEKDVDLSNSVS MSVSKSKVMXD." tumblr, October 31. https://julla.tumblr.com/post/179612655958/i–screamedkabsksnsslshagelekdvdlsnsvsmsvs-kskvmxd.

just-shower-thoughts. (n.d.). "Every single odd number has ..." tumblr, n.d. https://tmblrnorms.tumblr.com/post/613514040012144640/lubricates–queerly–tony–mxsicc–yeetkey.

Kalmus, V., and Siibak, A. (2020). "Eesti noored virtuaalses arvamus-ruumis. Eesti Inimarengu Aruanne 2019/2020." *Inimareng.* https://inimareng.ee/eesti–noored–virtuaalses–arvamusruumis.html.

Kanai, A. (2015). "WhatShouldWeCallMe? Self-branding, individuality and belonging in youthful femininities on Tumblr." *M/C Journal,* 18(1). http://journal.media–culture.org.au/index.php/mcjournal/article/view/936.

Kanai, A. (2016). "Sociality and classification: Reading gender, race, and class in a humorous meme." *Social Media + Society,* 2(4), 1–12.

Kanai, A. (2017). "Girlfriendship and sameness: Affective belonging in a digital intimate public." *Journal of Gender Studies,* 26(3), 1–14.

Kanai, A. (2019). *Gender and Relatability in Digital Culture Managing Affect, Intimacy and Value.* Cham: Palgrave Macmillan.

Kanai, A., Abidin, C., and Hart, M. (2020). "Practices, privacy, and privileges: Conducting research on Tumblr." In A. McCracken, A. Cho, L. Stein, and I. Neill Hoch (eds.), *A Tumblr Book: Platform and Cultures.* Ann Arbor: University of Michigan Press, pp. 114–126.

Keller, J. (2019). "'Oh, she's a Tumblr feminist': Exploring the platform vernacular of girls' social media feminisms." *Social Media + Society*, 5(3), 1–11.

kelofthesea. (2019). "Some LGBTQ highlights from 2019 ..." tumblr, June 7. https://tmblrnorms.tumblr.com/post/185439814303/kelofthesea–some–lgbtq–highlights–from–2019–so?is_related_post=1.

Kenny, L. (2017). "Remember when Katy Perry had a blog?" *Popsugar*, June 12. https://www.popsugar.co.uk/celebrity/Remember–When–Katy–Perry–Had–Tumblr–Blog–41964580.

Kerkez, M. (2015). "'Taking down rape culture' with Laci Green." UNM Newsroom, August 17. https://news.unm.edu/news/taking–down–rape–culture–with–laci–green.

Keyes, C. L. (2002). "The mental health continuum: From languishing to flourishing in life." *Journal of Health Social Behaviour*, 43(2), 207–222.

Kiew, E. (2018). "Singapore's top influencer Christabel Chua opens up about sexual harassment after sex tapes leaked." *Girl Style*, July 31. https://girlstyle.com/sg/article/9367/singapore–s–top–influencer–christabel–chua–opens–up–about–sexual–harassment–after–sex–tapes–leaked.

Kim, E. (2016). "Yahoo just wrote down another $482 million from Tumblr, the company it bought for $1 billion." *Business Insider*, July 19. https://www.businessinsider.com/yahoo–tumblr–write–down–2016-7.

kittyzumi. (2020). "only 90's kids will remember..." tumblr, April 30. https://tmblrnorms.tumblr.com/post/616833938841845760/eurydixe–chickenissiriat–kittyzumi–only.

Klasto, S.-P., and Simpson, A. (2020). "Gay Korea: Homophobia sparked by Seoul coronavirus cluster driven by Protestant right." *The Conversation*, May 15. https://theconversation.com/gay–korea–homophobia–sparked–by–seoul–coronavirus–cluster–driven–by–protestant–right–138491.

Klastrup, L. (2007). "Telling and sharing: Understanding mobile stories and the future of narratives." In A. Hutchinson (ed.), *Proceedings of Perth DAC 2007*, 7th International Digital Arts and Culture Conference. Curtin University of Technology, Perth.

Klink, F. (2017). "Towards a definition of 'fanfiction.'" *Medium*, May 31. https://medium.com/fansplaining/towards–a–definition–of–fanfiction–178d4c681289.

Knowyourmeme. (2020a). "Spiders georg." Knowyourmeme, n.d. https://knowyourmeme.com/memes/spiders–georg.

Knowyourmeme. (2020b). "2014 tumblr 4chan raids." Knowyourmeme, n.d. https://knowyourmeme.com/memes/events/2014–tumblr–4chan–raids.

Kohnen, M. (2014). "'The power of geek': Fandom as gendered commodity at Comic-Con." *Creative Industries Journal*, 7(1), 75–78.

konycardexchange. (2018). "KONY CARD EXCHANGE 2017." tumblr, n.d. https://konycardexchange.tumblr.com/post/167458324292/extend–the–holidays–sweetens–a–bit–longer–by.

kpop-confessions. (n.d.). "Kpop-confessions!" tumblr, n.d. https://kpop–confessions.tumblr.com/.

kpop-locks. (2018). "Bobby; imessage + bf material." tumblr, May 28. https://tmblrnorms.tumblr.com/post/174344053238/kpop–locks–bobby–imessage–bf–material.

k-popmvstills. (2018). "JENNIE – SOLO." tumblr, November 12. https://tmblrnorms.tumblr.com/post/180038918473/k–popmvstills–jennie–solo.

kpopsexconfessions-blog-blog. (n.d.). "kpopsexconfessions-blog-blog." tumblr, n.d. https://kpopsexconfessions–blog–blog.tumblr.com/.

Kunert, J. (2019). "The footy girls of Tumblr: How women found their niche in the online football fandom." *Communication & Sport*, 1–21. https://doi.org/10.1177/2167479519860075.

Kyrölä, K. (2015). "Toward a contextual pedagogy of pain: Trigger warnings and the value of sometimes feeling really, really bad." *Lambda Nordica*, 1, 126–144.

Laci Green. (n.d.). "laci green." https://www.lacigreen.tv/about.

Langlois, G. (2012). "Participatory culture and the new governance of communication: The paradox of participatory media." *Television and New Media*, 14(2), 91–105.

Lapowski, I. (2013). "David Karp: Why I sold Tumblr." *Inc*, May 31. https://www.inc.com/issie–lapowsky/david–karp–why–i–sold–tumblr–yahoo.html.

Leaver, T., and Highfield, T. (2018). "Visualising the ends of identity: Pre-birth and post-death on Instagram." *Information, Communication & Society*, 21(1), 30–45.

Leaver, T., Highfield, T., and Abidin, C. (2020). *Instagram: Visual Social Media Cultures*. Cambridge: Polity.

Le Cudennec, L. (2018). "'We deserve better': Tumblr fandoms and the fan activists' fight for better representation of queer characters on TV." *Synoptique*, 7(2), 33–48.

Lexico. (2020). "paralanguage." Lexico, n.d. https://www.lexico.com/definition/paralanguage.

Liao, S. (2018). "Tumblr's adult content ban means the death of unique blogs that explore sexuality." The Verge, December 6. https://www.theverge.com/2018/12/6/18124260/tumblr–porn–ban–sexuality–blogs–unique.

Liao, S. (2019). "After the porn ban, Tumblr users have ditched the platform as promised." The Verge, March 14. https://www.theverge.com/2019/3/14/18266013/tumblr–porn–ban–lost–users–down–traffic.

Light, B., Burgess, J., and Duguay, S. (2018). "The walkthrough method: An approach to the study of apps." *New Media & Society*, 20(3), 881–900.

Lisa, D. (2017). "From <mrsniall–horan–until–the–end> to <keepin-gupwithıd>: Online usernames and identity in the One Direction fandom." *Journal of Fandom Studies*, 5(3), 285–300.

Literat, I., and Glăveanu, V. P. (2018). "Distributed creativity on the internet: A theoretical foundation for online creative participation." *International Journal of Communication*, 12, 893–908.

Lowe, J. S. A. (2020). "Kitten thinks of nothing but murder all day: Tumblr text post memes as fandom *détournement*." In A. McCracken, A. Cho, L. Stein, and I. Neill Hoch (eds.), *A Tumblr Book: Platform and Cultures*. Ann Arbor: University of Michigan Press, pp. 181–193.

Lowensohn, J. (2007). "Tumblr: Microblogging done right." *CNet*, March 27. https://www.cnet.com/news/tumblr–microblogging–done–right/.

Lupfer, N., Kerne, A., Webb, A. M., and Linder, R. (2016). "Patterns of free-form curation: Visual thinking with web content." In *Proceedings of the 24th ACM International Conference on Multimedia*, pp. 12–21.

madelinelist. (2018). "First dates with Choi Seung-hyun." tumblr, October 25. https://tmblrnorms.tumblr.com/post/179435894718/madelinelist–first–dates–with–choi.

Maffesoli M (1996). *The Time of the Tribes: The Decline of Individualism in Mass Society*, trans. D. Smith. London: Sage.

Mahmud, A. (2020). "We are more than footnotes: Black women and intellectual theft." In A. McCracken, A. Cho, L. Stein, and I. Neill Hoch (eds.), *A Tumblr Book: Platform and Cultures*. Ann Arbor: University of Michigan Press, pp. 127–131.

Manley, T. (2013). "What tumblr taught me about writing: A new author cites eight lessons he learned by launching a Tumblr." November 22. https://www.publishersweekly.com/pw/by–topic/columns–and–blogs/soapbox/article/60122–the–tumblr–tutorial.html.

Maris, E., and Baym, N. K. (2018). "'Duking it out': Tumblr's

Fandometrics and the implications of ranking online communities." Presented at the *International Communication Association Conference*. Prague, Czech Republic.

Markham, A. N. (1998). *Life Online: Researching Real Experience in Virtual Space*. Walnut Creek, CA: Alta Mira.

marklightgreatsword. (2020). "Discourage art theft in fandom ..." tumblr, January 4. https://marklightgreatsword.tumblr.com/post/190056977650/discourage-art-theft-in-fandom-in-2020-dont.

Markus, M. L., and Silver, M. (2008). "A foundation for the study of IT effects: A new look at DeSanctis and Poole's concepts of structural features and spirit," *Journal of the Association for Information Systems*, 9(10), 609–632.

Marquart, E., (2010). "Microblog sensation: The growing popularity of Tumblr." *3PM Journal of Digital Research and Publishing*, Session 2, 70–75.

Martin, J. Q. (2007). "The 21-year-old behind a 'darling.'" *New York Sun*, November 8. https://www.nysun.com/business/21-year-old-behind-a-darling-new-york-web-startup/66108/.

Martinon, J.-P. (2013). "Introduction." In J.-P. Martinon (ed.), *The Curatorial: A Philosophy of Curating*. London: Bloomsbury.

Marwick, A. E. (2017). "Are there limits to online free speech." *Points*, January 15. https://points.datasociety.net/are-there-limits-to-online-free-speech-14dbb7069aec.

Marwick, A. E., and boyd, d. (2011). "I tweet honestly, I tweet passionately: Twitter users, context collapse, and the imagined audience." *New Media & Society*, 13(1), 114–133.

Mason, P. (2012). "I meet Tumblr whizz-kid David Karp." BBC, November 1. https://www.bbc.com/news/technology-20173435.

Massanari, A. L. (2017). "#Gamergate and The Fappening: How Reddit's algorithm, governance, and culture support toxic technocultures." *New Media & Society*, 19(3), 329–346.

Massanari, A. L. and Chess, S. (2018). "Attack of the 50-foot social justice warrior: The discursive construction of SJW memes as the monstrous feminine." *Feminist Media Studies*, 18(4), 525–542.

Matsakis, L. (2018). "Tumblr's porn-detecting AI has one job – and it's bad at it." *Wired*, December 5. https://www.wired.com/story/tumblr-pornai-adult-content/.

Matthews, C. (2014). "More than 11 million young people have fled Facebook since 2011." *Business*, January 15. https://business.time.com/2014/01/15/more-than-11-million-young-people-have-fled-facebook-since-2011/.

Matthews, J. C (2018). "A past that never was: Historical poaching in *Game of Thrones* fans' Tumblr practices." *Popular Communication,* 16(3), 225–242.

McCracken, A. (2017). "Tumblr youth subcultures and media engagement." *Cinema Journal,* 57(1), 151–161.

McCracken, A., Cho, A., Stein, L., and Neill Hoch, I. (eds.) (2020). *A Tumblr Book: Platform and Cultures.* Ann Arbor: University of Michigan Press.

mcltifandcm. (2018). "I hate how kpop has ..." tumblr, November 30. https://tmblrnorms.tumblr.com/post/180649209383/i–hate–how–kpop–has–turned–into–a–job–for–the.

meanplastic. (n.d.). "in 2011 on my tumblr ..." tumblr, n.d. https://meanplastic.com/post/168590266420.

mehreenqudosi. (2020). "classically trained but we'll still ..." tumblr, May 25. https://tmblrnorms.tumblr.com/post/619100814415446016/sketchyfletch–arrghigiveup–mehreenqudosi.

memedocumentation. (2017). tumblr, November 18. https://memedocumentation.tumblr.com/post/167648753860/have–yall–done–the–is–a–statistical–error.

Menegus, B. (2017). "Tumblr founder David Karp steps down." *Gizmodo,* November 28. https://www.gizmodo.com.au/2017/11/tumblr–founder–david–karp–steps–down/.

miggdrgn. (2018). "Baby GD." tumblr, May 31. https://tmblrnorms.tumblr.com/post/174425538768/miggdrgn–baby–gd.

Milian, M. (2010). "Tumblr: 'We're pretty opposed to advertising,'" *Los Angeles Times,* April 17. https://latimesblogs.latimes.com/technology/2010/04/tumblr–ads.html.

Milner, R. M. (2016). *The World Made Meme: Public Conversations and Participatory Media.* Cambridge, MA: MIT Press.

Miltner, K. M. (2014). "'There's no place for lulz on LOLCats': The role of genre, gender, and group identity in the interpretation and enjoyment of an Internet meme." *First Monday,* 19(8). http://first-monday.org/ojs/index.php/fm/article/view/5391.

minomyno. (2018). tumblr, July 25. https://tmblrnorms.tumblr.com/post/176266983138.

minty-top. (2018). "Getting the notification that T.O.P." tumblr, October 31. https://tmblrnorms.tumblr.com/post/179616595098/getting–the–notification–that–top–made–a–post–in.

mjalti. (2016). "me, interacting with another 20+ ..." tumblr, October 5. https://mjalti.tumblr.com/post/151384021528/me–interacting–with–another–20–year–old–on.

mogie. (2019). "being mutuals is so ... intimate ..." tumblr,

November 5. https://mogie.tumblr.com/post/188843585565/being–mutuals–is–so–intimate–like–u–follow.

Molldrem, S. (2018). "Tumblr's decision to deplatform sex will harm sexually marginalized people." *Wussy Magazine*, December 6. https://www.wussymag.com/all/2018/12/6/tumblrs–decision–to–deplatform–sex–will–harm–sexually–marginalized–people.

Mondin, A. (2017). "'Tumblr mostly, great empowering images': Blogging, reblogging and scrolling feminist, queer and BDSM desires." *Journal of Gender Studies*, 26(3), 282–292.

Moraga, C., and Anzaldúa, G. (eds.) (2015 [1983]). *This Bridge Called My Back* (4th ed.). New York: Kitchen Table Women of Color Press.

Morimoto, L. (2018). "Roundtable: Tumblr and fandom." *Transformative Works and Cultures*, 27. http://dx.doi.org/10.3983/twc.2018.1351.

Morimoto, L., and Chin, B. (2017). "Reimagining the imagined community: Online media fandoms in the age of global convergence." In J. Gray, C. Sandvoss, and C. L. Harrington (eds.), *Fandom: Identities and Communities in a Mediated World*. New York: New York University Press, pp. 174–188

Morimoto, L., and Stein, L. E. (2018). "Tumblr and fandom." *Transformative Works and Cultures*, 27. http://dx.doi.org/10.3983/twc.2018.1580.

Morris, N. (2019). "I used to find joy in sharing myself online – but now, the internet seems a more hostile place." *New Statesman*, August 2. https://www.newstatesman.com/2019/08/i–used–find–joy–sharing–myself–online–now–internet–seems–more–hostile–place.

mothric-bry. (2017). "No sideblogs, we chaotically cram ..." tumblr, August 1. https://mothric–bry.tumblr.com/post/163699097772.

mothurs. (2017). "tumblr culture in 2012: touch ..." tumblr, March 22. https://tmblrnorms.tumblr.com/post/158719024083/mothurs–tumblr–culture–in–2012–touch–my–butt?is_related_post=1.

Muise, A. (2011). "Women's sex blogs: Challenging dominant discourses of heterosexual desire." *Feminism & Psychology*, 21(3), 411–419.

Munteanu, D. G. (2017). "Improbable curators: Analysing nostalgia, authorship and audience on Tumblr microblogs." In J. Graham and A. Gandini (eds.), *Collaborative Production in the Creative Industries*. London: University of Westminster Press, pp. 125–156.

mykpopconfession. (n.d.). "MYKPOPCONFESSION." tumblr, n.d. https://mykpopconfession.tumblr.com/.

Nagle, A. (2017). *Kill All Normies: Online Culture Wars from 4chan and tumblr to Trump and the Alt-right*. Washington, DC: Zero Books.

Nakamura, L. (2015). "The unwanted labour of social media: Women of colour call out culture as venture community management." *New Formations*, 86(86), 106–112.

Narai, R. (2017). "Female-centered fan fiction as homoaffection in fan communities." *Transformative Works and Cultures*, 24. http://dx.doi.org/10.3983/twc.2017.1014.

Neill Hoch, I. (2018). "Content, conduct, and apologies in Tumblr fandom tags." *Transformative Works and Cultures*, 27. http://dx.doi.org/10.3983/twc.2018.1198.

Ng, E., and Russo, J. L. (2017). "Envisioning queer female fandom." *Transformative Works and Cultures*, 24. http://dx.doi.org/10.3983/twc.2017.1168.

Nguyen, C. (2015). "An attempted suicide forced a Tumblr community to open its eyes about bullying." *Vice*, November 6. https://www.vice.com/en_us/article/3da838/an–attempted–suicide–forced–a–tumblr–community–to–open–its–eyes–about–bullying.

Nichols, E. (n.d.). "How to get my post to be popular on Tumblr." *Chron.* https://smallbusiness.chron.com/post–popular–tumblr–26918.html.

Nigatu, H. (2015). "25 times Tumblr told the truth about mental health." *BuzzFeed*, February 28. https://www.buzzfeed.com/hnigatu/tumblr–mental–health.

Norton, J. (2015). "8 celebrities that creep on your tumblr." *MTV News*, April 4. http://www.mtv.com/news/2115461/celebrities–tumblr–lurking/.

Nye, D. (2017). "21 times Tumblr taught the world how to speak Australian." *Buzzfeed*, June 13. https://www.buzzfeed.com/deannye/speak–strayan–ya–flamin–galahs.

Oakley, A. (2016). "Disturbing hegemonic discourse: Nonbinary gender and sexual orientation labeling on Tumblr." *Social Media + Society*, 2(3), 1–12.

oldnapkinned. (2019). "i feel like I can ..." tumblr, August 6. https://oldnapkinned.tumblr.com/post/186830384411/i–feel–like–i–can–legitimately–sue–half–of–you–for.

Olin-Scheller, C., and Wikström, P. (2010). "Literary prosumers: Young people's reading and writing." *Education inquiry*, 1(1), 41–56.

ommanyte. (2019). "Tumblr color scheme in 2024 ..." tumblr, n.d. https://ommanyte.tumblr.com/post/182434785715.

Opam, K. (2015). "Tumblr announces Answer Time Q&A platform to take on Reddit AMAs." The Verge, 5 June. https://www.theverge.com/2015/6/5/8737691/tumblr–answer–time–q–a–platform–reddit–ama.

Östman, J. (2012). "Information, expression, participation: How involvement in user-generated content relates to democratic engagement among young people." *New Media & Society*, 14(6), 1004–1021.

ourexes. (2018). "If you hate tumblr so ..." tumblr, August 1. https://ourexes.tumblr.com/post/163652287352/if–you–hate–tumblr–so–much–why–dont–you–just.

Owen, J. (2019). "Top 20 social media future trends [2020 & beyond]." *Techjackie*, December 16. https://techjackie.com/social–media–future/.

Paasonen, S. (2011). *Carnal Resonance: Affect and Online Pornography*. London: MIT Press.

Paasonen, S., Jarrett, K., and Light, B. (2019). *Not Safe for Work: Sex, Humor, and Risk in Social Media*. Cambridge, MA: MIT Press.

Palleschi, A. (2013). "Teletherapy, Tumblr'd." *The Atlantic*, July 31. https://www.theatlantic.com/health/archive/2013/07/teletherapy–tumblrd/278221/.

Pande, R., and Moira, S. (2017). "Racial dynamics of online femslash fandoms." *Transformative Works and Cultures*, 24. http://dx.doi.org/10.3983/twc.2017.908.

Panzarino, M. (2012). "Tumblr's new Fan Mail feature will let you leave messages for other users," *The Next Web*, January 5. https://thenextweb.com/media/2012/01/05/tumblrs–new–fan–mail–feature–will–let–you–leave–messages–for–other–users/%7B%7B%20linkTracker/%7B%7B%20linkTracker/.

Papacharissi, Z. (2015). *Affective Publics: Sentiment, Technology, and Politics*. New York: Oxford University Press.

Paramanathan, G. (2019). "Desi dick." *Porn Studies*, 6(3), 332–335.

Parrish, J. J. (2007). "Inventing a universe: Reading and writing internet fan fiction." Doctoral dissertation. University of Pittsburgh, PA.

Parsons, T. (1951). *The Social System*. New York: The Free Press.

Patel, N. (2019). "Exclusive: Automatic CEO Matt Mullenweg on what's next for Tumblr." The Verge, August 14. https://www.theverge.com/2019/8/14/20804894/tumblr–acquisition–matt–mullenweg–ceo–automattic–wordpress–verizon–changes–vergecast.

Peh, Y. (2020). "The rise of non-consensual porn in Singapore, and the battle to stem its spread." *Channel News Asia*, April 26. https://www.channelnewsasia.com/news/cnainsider/the–rise–of–non–consensual porn–singapore–battle–stem–its–spread–12677446.

Pereira, G., and Bojczuk, I. (2018). "Zap zap, who's there? WhatsApp and the spread of fake news during the 2018 elections in Brazil." *Global Media, Technologies & Cultures Lab Blog*, November 9. http://

globalmedia.mit.edu/2018/11/09/zap–zap–whos–there–whatsapp–and–the–spread–of–fake–news–during–the–2018–elections–in–brazil/.

Perez, S. (2011). "Tumblr acknowledges its growing spam problem, says it's doing everything it can." *Tech Crunch*, October 31. https://techcrunch.com/2011/10/31/tumblr–acknowledges–its–growing–spam–problem–says–its–doing–everything–it–can/.

Perez, S. (2013). "Tumblr brings more ads to users' dashboards, rearranges buttons & teens freak out." *Tech Crunch*, May 30. https://techcrunch.com/2013/05/30/tumblr–brings–more–ads–to–users–dashboards–rearranges–buttons–teens–freak–out/.

Petersen, L. N. (2014). "Sherlock fans talk: Mediatized talk on Tumblr." *Northern Lights: Film and Media Studies Yearbook*, 12(1), 87–104. https://www.ingentaconnect.com/content/intellect/nl/2014/00000012/00000001/art00006.

Petronzio, M. (2016). "Tumblr is the one social platform taking action ahead of Trump's America." Mashable, December 10. https://mashable.com/2016/12/09/action–on–tumblr–election/.

Petrov, C. (2020). "Tumblr statistics 2020." *Tech Jury*, June 19. https://techjury.net/blog/tumblr–statistics/#gref.

Pfister, D. S. (2014). *Networked Media. Networked Rhetorics. Attention and Deliberation in the Early Blogosphere*. University Park: Pennsylvania State University Press.

phantomrose96. (2018). "Throw back to 2013–specific ..." tumblr, November 15. https://phantomrose96.tumblr.com/post/180155681387/throw–back–to–2013–specific–tumblr–experiences.

Phelan, S. (2019). "Neoliberalism, the far right, and the disparaging of 'social justice warriors'." *Communication, Culture and Critique*, 12(4), 455–475.

Phillips, W. (2020). "The internet is a toxic hellscape – but we can fix it." *Wired*, March 2. https://www.wired.com/story/the–internet–is–a–toxic–hellscape–but–we–can–fix–it/.

Plummer, K. (1995). "Telling sexual stories in a late modern world." *Studies in Symbolic Interaction*, 18(1), 101–120.

Plummer, K. (2007). "Queers, bodies and post-modern sexualities: A note on revisiting the 'sexual' in symbolic interactionism." In M. Kimmel (ed.), *The Sexual Self*. Nashville, TN: Vanderbilt University Press, pp. 16–30.

Pollack, N. (2012). "How Lady Gaga's manager reinvented the celebrity game with social media." *Wired*, May 21. https://www.wired.co.uk/article/troy–carter.

Popova, M. (2017). "Slight dub-con but they both wanted it hardcore: Erotic fanfiction as a form of cultural activism around sexual consent." Doctoral dissertation. University of the West of England.

positivekpopconfessions-blog. (n.d.). "Positive K-pop confessions." tumblr, n.d. https://positivekpopconfessions–blog.tumblr.com/.

postitforward. (2020). "Post it forward." https://postitforward.tumblr. com/.

Potter, J. (2015). "Curation as a new literacy practice." *E-Learning and Digital Media*, 12(2), 123–127.

Poyatos, F. (1993). *Paralanguage: A Linguistic and Interdisciplinary Approach to Interactive Speech and Sounds*. Amsterdam: John Benjamins Publishing Company.

Premack, R. (2016). "Tumblr's depression connection." *The Ringer*, October 24. https://theringer.com/tumblr–communities–depression–mental–illness–anxiety–c2ca927cd305.

prince-vegeta. (2016). "*doesnt talk to tumblr friends ..." tumblr, June 19. https://prince–vegeta.tumblr.com/post/146187186006/doesnt–talk–to–tumblr–friends–for–6–months.

quadrinips. (2020). "a tumblr Youth™: you got ..." tumblr, February 27. https://tmblrnorms.tumblr.com/post/611158975273156608/quadrinips–a–tumblr–youth–you–got–to–get–off.

queentianas. (2019). "i know this website is ..." tumblr, February 19. https://queentianas.tumblr.com/post/182923908726/i–know–this–website–is–slowly–dying–but–its–going.

Quora. (2018). "How can I get more reblogs on Tumblr?" *Quora*, July 30. https://www.quora.com/How–can–I–get–more–reblogs–on–Tumblr.

q-shinji. (2019). "remember when dash drama looked ..." tumblr, February 5. https://tmblrnorms.tumblr.com/post/182590834998/imperatorcorleone–q–shinji–remember–when.

Rambukkana, N. (2015). *Hashtag Publics: The Power and Politics of Discursive Networks*. Berlin: Peter Lang.

Ratcliff, C. (2014). "Why your brand should definitely be on Tumblr: 10 fantastic examples." *Econsultancy*, April 9. https://econsultancy.com/why–your–brand–should–definitely–be–on–tumblr–10–fantastic–examples/.

realbarbiex. (2014). "when a good url is ..." tumblr, n.d. https://realbarbiex.tumblr.com/post/59803320998/when–a–good–url–is–taken–by–a–shitty–blog.

realmckitten. (2019). "Tumblr ... you ok?" tumblr, 27 May. https://tmblrnorms.tumblr.com/post/185185815148/tumblryou–ok.

reddit. (2020). "What are the real heights ..." Reddit, n.d. https://

www.reddit.com/r/bigbang/comments/f8ymdh/what_are_the_ real_heights_of_each_member/.

Reeve, E. (2016). "The secret lives of Tumblr teens." *The New Republic*, February 17. https://newrepublic.com/article/129002/ secret–lives–tumblr–teens.

Reilly, M. (2018). *Curatorial Activism: Towards an Ethics of Curating.* New York: Thames and Hudson.

Renninger, B. J. (2014). "'Where I can be myself ... where I can speak my mind': Networked counterpublics in a polymedia environment." *New Media & Society*, 17(9), 1513–1529.

Revanche, J. (2016). "Tumblr was my saviour. It made me see I wasn't monstrous and unloveable." *Guardian*, August 24. https://www. theguardian.com/commentisfree/2016/aug/24/tumblr–was–my– saviour–it–made–me–see–i–wasnt–monstrous–and–unloveable.

Revanche, J. (2019). "Tumblr transformed me but now it's just another place for people already protected by the mainstream." *Guardian*, May 2. https://www.theguardian.com/commentisfree/2019/may/02/ tumblr–transformed–me–but–now–its–just–another–place–for– people–already–protected–by–the–mainstream.

Rice, D. (2013). "Spike in self-harm behaviour among girls and women." *PM*, ABC Radio, August 23. http://www.abc.net.au/pm/ content/2013/s3832623.htm.

Richardson, B. G., Surmitis, K. A., and Hyldahl, R. S. (2012). "Minimizing social contagion in adolescents who self-injure: Considerations for group work, residential treatment, and the internet." *Journal of Mental Health Counseling*, 34(2), 121–132.

Ringrose, J., and Lawrence, E. (2018). "Remixing misandry, manspreading, and dick pics: Networked feminist humour on Tumblr." *Feminist Media Studies*, 18(4), 686–704.

Robards, B., Byron, P., Churchill, B., Hanckel, B., and Vivienne, S. (2020). "Tumblr as a space of learning, connecting, and identity formation for LGBTIQ+ young people." In A. McCracken, A. Cho, L. Stein, and I. Neill Hoch (eds.), *A Tumblr Book: Platform and Cultures.* Ann Arbor: University of Michigan Press, pp. 281–292.

Rosenberg, A. (2020). "The ever-mutating life of tumblr dot com." *Fansplaining*, February 28. https://www.fansplaining.com/articles/ the–ever–mutating–life–of–tumblr–dot–com.

Roser, M., Ritchie, H., and Ortiz-Ospina, E. (2020). "Internet." *Our World in Data.* https://ourworldindata.org/internet.

roswell-newton-vargas. (2020). "Podcast where every week someone ..." tumblr, May 30. https://tmblrnorms.tumblr.com/ post/619565739205066752.

rslashrats. (2020). "another fat fuck friday is ..." tumblr, May 18. https://tmblrnorms.tumblr.com/post/618469526765453312.

Ruddock, A. (2020). "Social media and intoxication: 'Tweaker Nation': Celebrating drug use on Tumblr." In F. Hutton (ed.), *Cultures of Intoxication*. Cham: Palgrave Macmillan, pp. 263–282.

ruinedchildhood. (2020). "what is one day, for ..." tumblr, May 25. https://tmblrnorms.tumblr.com/post/619128699393081344/timetravelingcacti–superwholocked–for–life.

Ruiz, R. (2018). "Tumblr has a game plan for 2018: Keep handing the mic to activists." Mashable, February 12. https://mashable.com/2018/02/11/tumblr–activists–social–justice/.

Russo, J., and Sweeny, A. (eds.) (2016). *Searching for a Rose Garden: Challenging Psychiatry, Fostering Mad Studies*. Monmouth: PCCS Books.

Safronova, V. (2014). "Millennials and the age of Tumblr activism." *New York Times*, December 19. http://www.nytimes.com/2014/12/21/style/millennials–and–the–age–of–tumblr–activism.html.

Salmenniemi, S., Nurmi, J., Perheentupa, I., and Bergroth, H. (2019). *Assembling Therapeutics: Cultures, Politics and Materiality*. New York: Routledge.

Salmon, F. (2012). "How sharing disrupts media." *Reuters*, January 23. http://blogs.reuters.com/felix–salmon/2012/01/23/how–sharing–disrupts–media/.

Santos, C. (2012). "Laci Green's guide to the best sex ever." *The Highlander*, May 16. https://www.highlandernews.org/3532/laci–greens–guide–to–the–best–sex–ever/.

Sarappo, E. (2018). "How Tumblr taught social justice to a generation of teenagers." *PS Mag*, December 13. https://psmag.com/social–justice/how–tumblr–taught–social–justice–to–a–generation–of–teenagers.

sassy-dae. (n.d.). "most wave or high–five ..." tumblr, August 26. https://sassy–dae.tumblr.com/post/177417600631/most–wave–or–high–five–their–fans–then.

Sawchuk, S. (2017). "Jason Wong became a Tumblr influencer at age 17 and leveraged it into a fledge entrepreneurial career." *Medium*, February 15. https://medium.com/intheirshoes/jason–wong–became–a–tumblr–influencer–at–age–17–and–leveraged–it–into–a–fledge–entrepreneurial–4e9e81a0c5db.

Schawbel, D. (2013). "David Karp on Tumblr's growth, monetization, and future plans." *Forbes*, January 2. https://www.forbes.com/sites/danschawbel/2013/01/02/david-karp-on-tumblrs-growth-monetization-mentors-and-future-plans/.

Schonfeld, E. (2011). "Why David Karp started Tumblr: Blogs

don't work for most people." *Tech Crunch*, February 21. https:// techcrunch.com/2011/02/21/founder–stories–why–david–karp– started–tumblr–blogs–dont–work–for–most–people/.

Seekins, E. (2020). "How to get more Tumblr followers (and blog traffic)." *Blogging Wizard*, April 28. https://bloggingwizard.com/ how–to–get–more–followers–on–tumblr/.

Seitzinger, J. (2014). "Curate me! Exploring online identity through social curation in networked learning." In *Proceedings of the 9th International Conference on Networked Learning*, pp. 7–9.

Seko, Y., and Lewis, S. P. (2018). "The self-harmed, visualized, and reblogged: Remaking of self-injury narratives on Tumblr." *New Media & Society*, 20(1), 180–198. https://doi.org/10.1177/ 1461444816660783/.

selva3bd. (2019). "This scene was so heartbreaking …" tumblr, February 2. https://tmblrnorms.tumblr.com/post/182512722493/ selva3bd–this–scene–was–so–heartbreaking–it?is_related_post=1.

seoftly. (2019a). "let's meet again when the …" tumblr, February 8. https://tmblrnorms.tumblr.com/post/182666092338/lets–meet– again–when–the–flowers–bloom?is_related_post=1.

seoftly. (2019b). "a moodboard in which Jiyong …" tumblr, February 2. https://tmblrnorms.tumblr.com/post/182514266783/a– moodboard–in–which–jiyong–is–a–beautiful–spirit.

seungcheolsboyfriend. (2018). "i'm not afraid." tumblr, July 5. https://seungcheolsboyfriend.tumblr.com/post/175595358913/ im–not–afraid.

sexhaver. (2019). "remember when people on here …" tumblr, n.d. https://sexhaver.tumblr.com/post/177333465172/remember– when–people–on–here–back–in–2k12–would.

Sharp, M., and Shannon, B. (2020). "Becoming non-binary: An exploration of gender work in Tumblr." In D. N. Farris, D. R. Compton, and A. P. Herrera (eds.), *Gender, Sexuality and Race in the Digital Age*. Cham: Springer, pp. 137–150.

shewillfeatdrake. (2015). "me with tumblr on my …" tumblr, n.d. https://shewillfeatdrake.tumblr.com/post/116616880444.

Shifman, L. (2016). "Cross-cultural comparisons of user-generated content: An analytical framework. *International Journal of Communication*, 10, 5644–5663.

Shilling, C. (2003 [1993]). *The Body and Social Theory*. Thousand Oaks, CA: Sage.

Shorey, S. (2015). "Fragmentary girls: Selective expression on the tumblr platform." Master's thesis. University of Massachusetts.

Shorey, E. (2017). "Tumblr unveils Mental Health Month

initiatives." *Nylon*, May 2. https://www.nylon.com/articles/tumblr–mental–health–awareness–month.

Shorey, S., and Howard, P. N. (2016). "Automation, big data, and politics: A research review." *International Journal of Communication*, 10, 5032–5055.

Shorty Awards. (n.d.). "Tumblr's 'Post It Forward' campaign." https://shortyawards.com/8th/tumblrs–post–it–forward–campaign.

showiee. (2019). "Taeyang's height: Sincerely presented by ..." tumblr, May 18. https://tmblrnorms.tumblr.com/post/184978241843/toit–letstalkaboutseungrispecs–showiee.

Siese, A. (2015). "Tumblr launches mental health awareness campaign." *Bustle*, May 14. https://www.bustle.com/articles/83199–tumblr–post–it–forward–campaign–tackles–mental–health–issues–by–using–social–media–to–reach–out.

sjwsofokc. (2020). "Social Justice Warriors of OKCupid." tumblr, n.d. https://sjwsofokc.tumblr.com/.

skyfoxx186. (2018). "Beach date with Bobby moodboard." tumblr, June 3. https://tmblrnorms.tumblr.com/post/174539712113/skyfoxx186–beach–date–with–bobby–moodboard.

slimetony. (2020). "I'm really worried half of ..." tumblr, April 28. https://tmblrnorms.tumblr.com/post/616679861265776642/slimetony–isobull–slimetony–isobull.

slow-riot. (2015). "20 minutes into tumblr mobile ..." tumblr, August 14. https://slow–riot.tumblr.com/post/126717461474/20–minutes–into–tumblr–mobile–he–gives–you–this.

soft-tabi. (2018). "soft father/husband Seunghyun mb." tumblr, March 22. https://tmblrnorms.tumblr.com/post/172128267523/soft–tabi–soft–fatherhusband–seunghyun–mb?is_related_post=1.

soompi. (2012). "Big Bang's real height questioned again." *Soompi*, April 17. https://www.soompi.com/article/383362wpp/big–bangs–real–height–in–dispute–again.

staff. (2009). "Introducing: Submissions." tumblr, July 9. https://staff.tumblr.com/post/138478782/submissions.

staff. (2011). "Now live: The tumblr spotlight." tumblr, May 25. https://staff.tumblr.com/post/5835098314/spotlight.

staff. (2012a). "A new policy against self-harm blogs." tumblr, February 23. https://staff.tumblr.com/post/18132624829/self–harm–blogs.

staff. (2012b). "Follow up: Tumblr's new policy against pro-self-harm blogs." tumblr, March 1. https://staff.tumblr.com/post/18563255291/follow–up–tumblrs–new–policy–against.

staff. (2015). Answer time." tumblr, June 5. https://staff.tumblr.com/

post/120783984775/youre–on–tumblr–you–like–things–on–tumblr–we.

staff. (2017). "Best stuff first." tumblr, October 18. https://support.tumblr.com/post/166540445922/best–stuff–first.

staff. (2018). "New community guidelines." tumblr, August 27. https://staff.tumblr.com/post/177449083750/new–community–guidelines/embed.

staff. (2020a). "#hellajuneteenth." tumblr, June 17. https://staff.tumblr.com/post/621182716407431168/hellajuneteenth.

staff. (2020b). "Updates to how we enforce our Community Guidelines on hate speech." tumblr, May 4. https://staff.tumblr.com/post/617194581364195328/updates–to–how–we–enforce–our–community–guidelines#notes.

Statista. (2020a). "Number of monthly active Facebook users worldwide." https://www.statista.com/statistics/264810/number–of–monthly–active–facebook–users–worldwide/.

Statista. (2020b). "Combined desktop and mobile visits to Tumblr.com from May 2019 to May 2020." https://www.statista.com/statistics/261925/unique–visitors–to–tumblrcom/.

Stein, J. (2013). "Why Facebook didn't buy Tumblr: Op-ed." CNBC, May 21. https://www.cnbc.com/id/100754658.

Stein, L. E. (2018). "Tumblr fan aesthetics." In M. A. Click and S. Scott (eds.), *The Routledge Companion to Media Fandom*. London: Routledge, pp. 86–97.

STRANGE ÆONS. (2018). "I found the WORST of Tumblr," YouTube, April 22. https://www.youtube.com/watch?v=B06fv4NZQE8.

Strauss, A. L. (1978). "A social world perspective." In N. Denzin (ed.), *Studies in Symbolic Interaction*, vol. 1. Greenwich, CT: JAI Press, pp. 119–128.

Stromberg, B. (2020). "Tumblr savior." *Bjornstar.* https://bjornstar.com/tumblr–savior

Sung, M. (2019). "Tumblr loses almost a third of its users after banning porn." Mashable, March 14. https://mashable.com/article/tumblr–lost–a–third–of–its–users–after–porn–ban/?europe=true.

sungri-seyo. (2018). "Seriously what a psychopath." tumblr, June 27. https://tmblrnorms.tumblr.com/post/175307805423/seriously–what–a–psychopath–both–the–soldier–and?is_related_post=1.

sushihairjiyong. (2018). "Honestly this is my eternal …" tumblr, January 10. https://sushihairjiyong.tumblr.com/post/169563497284/honestly–this–is–my–eternal–favourite–there–is.

suspend. (2013). "its never safe to use …" tumblr, December 12.

https://suspend.tumblr.com/post/69748764155/its–never–safe–to–use–tumblr–beside–your–parents.

Sutter, J. D. (2011). "Tumblr becomes platform for Occupy Wall Street debate." *CNN*, October 12. https://edition.cnn.com/2011/10/12/tech/web/tumblr–occupy–wall–street/index.html.

Syfret, W. (2017). "How memes taught millennials to talk about mental health." *I-D*, February 13. https://i–d.vice.com/en_au/article/43wenm/how–memes–taught–millennials–to–talk–about–mental–health.

tabithings. (2018). "What kind of type of ..." tumblr, May 4. https://tmblrnorms.tumblr.com/post/173585957713/what–kind–of–type–of–boyfriend–is–top–ssi?is_related_post=1.

Tai, H. and Cheong, W. X. (2020). "#HerWorldHerStory: How Christabel Chua bounced back from the lowest point in her life." *Her World*, May 20. https://www.herworld.com/women/women–now/christabel–chua–bellywellyjelly–social–media–leak/.

Tatum, E. (2013). "Soft grunge: Mental illness is not a style." *Everyday Feminism*, December 26. http://everydayfeminism.com/2013/12/soft–grunge/.

Taylor, T. R. (2018). "Digital space and 'walking dead' fandom's team delusional." *Transformative Works and Culture*, 27. http://dx.doi.org/10.3983/twc.2018.1180.

taylorswift. (2020). "Lover." tumblr, n.d. https://taylorswift.tumblr.com/.

Tedone, G. (2017). "Tracing networked images: An emerging method for online curation." *Journal of Media Practice*, 18(1), 51–62.

Tenbarge, K. (2020). "Taylor Swift is sending $3,000 to fans posting on Tumblr about their coronavirus quarantine struggles." *Insider*, March 27. https://www.insider.com/taylor–swift–sending–tumblr–fans–3000–money–coronavirus–quarantine–support–2020–3.

thankyousirmayihaveanother. (2018). "just to be clear, I'm ..." tumblr, December 3. https://thankyousirmayihaveanother.tumblr.com/post/180767310496/just-to-be-clear-im-staying-here-as-long-as-this.

thebootydiaries. (2020). "Please don't appropriate uwu culture ..." tumblr, May 30. https://tmblrnorms.tumblr.com/post/619565398804905984/please–dont–appropriate–uwu–culture–if–you–cant#notes.

Thelandersson, F. (2018). "Social media sad girls and the normalization of sad states of being." *Capacious*, 1(2), 2–21.

Thomas, K. (2013). "Revisioning the smiling villain: Imagetexts and intertextual expression in representations of the filmic Loki on Tumblr." *Transformative Works and Cultures*, 13. https://doi.org/10.3983/twc.2013.0474.

Thoreson, R. (2020). "Covid-19 backlash targets LGBT people in South Korea." *Human Rights Watch*, May 13. https://www.hrw.org/news/2020/05/13/covid–19–backlash–targets–lgbt–people–south–korea.

thothoes. (2019). "being on tumblr is literally ..." tumblr, October 31. https://thothoes.tumblr.com/post/188729528376/being–on–tumblr–is–literally–just–straight–up.

Tiidenberg, K. (2013). "How does online experience inform our sense of self? NSFW blogger identity narratives." In A.-A. Allaste (ed.), *Back in the West: Changing Lifestyles in Transforming Societies*. New York: Peter Lang, pp. 177–202.

Tiidenberg, K. (2014a). "There's no limit to your love: Scripting the polyamorous self." *Journal für Psychologie*, 22, 1–27.

Tiidenberg, K. (2014b). "Bringing sexy back: Reclaiming the body aesthetic via self shooting." *Cyberpsychology: Journal of Psychosocial Research on Cyberspace*, 8(1). https://doi.org/10.5817/CP2014–1–3.

Tiidenberg, K. (2016). "Boundaries and conflict in a NSFW community on tumblr: The meanings and uses of selfies." *New Media & Society*, 18(8), 1563–1578.

Tiidenberg, K. (2017). "'Nude selfies til I die': Making of sexy in selfies." In P. G. Nixon and I. K. Düsterhöft (eds.), *Sex in the Digital Age*. London: Routledge, pp. 78–88.

Tiidenberg, K. (2019a). "Nipples & nazis @ the #tumblrisdeadparty: Twitter discourse on the tumblr nsfw ban." Presented at Association of Internet Researchers conference, *AoIR19 "Trust in the System."* Brisbane, Australia, October 2–5.

Tiidenberg, K. (2019b). "Playground in memoriam: Missing the pleasures of NSFW tumblr." *Porn Studies*, 6(3), 363–371.

Tiidenberg, K. (2019c). "Single, taken or in love with a fictional character? Or how fanfiction could help us understand (digital) reading." *Publije*, 1.

Tiidenberg, K. (2020). "NSFW selfies." In A. McCracken, A. Cho, L. Stein, and I. Neill Hoch (eds.), *A Tumblr Book: Platform and Cultures*. Ann Arbor: University of Michigan Press, pp. 142–153.

Tiidenberg, K., and Allaste, A.-A. (2016). "Perceptions of participation and the share button." *Studies of Transition States and Societies*, 8(2), 52–63.

Tiidenberg, K., and Gómez-Cruz, E. (2015). "Selfies, image and the re-making of the body." *Body & Society*, 21(4), 77–102

Tiidenberg, K., and Paasonen, S. (2019). "Littles: Affects and aesthetics in sexual age-play." *Sexuality & Culture*, 23, 375–393.

Tiidenberg, K., and van der Nagel, E. (2020). *Sex and Social Media*. Bingley: Emerald Publishing.

Tiidenberg, K., and Whelan, A. (2017). "Sick bunnies and pocket dumps: 'Not-selfies' and the genre of self-representation." *Popular Communication*, 15(2), 141–153.

Tiidenberg, K., and Whelan, A. (2019). "'Not like that, not for that, not by them': Social media affordances of critique." *Communication and Critical/Cultural Studies*, 16(2), 83–102.

tmblrnorms. (2018). "Fandometrics in depth: K-pop." tumblr, July 29. https://tmblrnorms.tumblr.com/post/176411854633/fandometrics–in–depth–k–pop.

TODAY. (2018). "How to improve intimacy with your partner, according to the 'sexperts.'" *Today*, July 24. https://www.today.com/popculture/how–improve–intimacy–your–partner–according–sexperts–t134060.

toopsy. (2020). "being 18+ on this site ..." tumblr, January 31. https://toopsy.tumblr.com/post/109738229901/being–18–on–this–site–is–so–surreal–so–many–ppl.

Toor, A. (2016). "Tumblr will allow users to make money from ads." The Verge, 28 July. https://www.theverge.com/2016/7/28/12307484/tumblr–advertising–user–blogs–revenue.

topbap. (2018). "BIGBAND REACTION: You flinching during ..." tumblr, July 2. https://tmblrnorms.tumblr.com/post/175473861538/bigbang–reaction–you–flinching–during–an–argument.

topfied. (n.d.). "concept: gtop domesticity on mbc ..." tumblr, December 30. https://topfied.tumblr.com/post/155131866389/concept–gtop–domesticity–on–mbc–radio–star–ep.

transgender-neurotica. (2020). "When you're an adult man ..." tumblr, May 28. https://tmblrnorms.tumblr.com/post/619401432559386625/chilewithcarnage–liebgoth.

trillow. (2020). "remember when the world ended..." tumblr, March 14. https://tmblrnorms.tumblr.com/post/612612136050491392/starrysleeper–trillow–remember–when–the.

troyesivan. (2015a). "so i think i walked ..." tumblr, February 9. https://troyesivan.tumblr.com/post/110595188501/so–i–think–i–walked–in–a–fashion–show.

troyesivan. (2015b). "I guess I have snapchat ..." tumblr, January 23. https://troyesivan.tumblr.com/post/108907197566/i–guess–i–have–snapchat–now–my–username–is.

troyesivan. (2016). "Thank u endlessly to @Kia ..." tumblr, May 9. https://troyesivan.tumblr.com/post/144105303461/thank–u–endlessly–to–kia–for–choosing–me–as–this.

troyesivan. (2018a). "hey guys! I'll be answering ..." tumblr,

August 8. https://troyesivan.tumblr.com/post/176782801741/hey–guys–ill–be–answering–your–questions–next.

troyesivan. (2018b). "so my @tumblr is BACK ..." Twitter, August 10. https://twitter.com/troyesivan/status/1027638520435769344?la ng=en.

troyesivan. (2020). "troyesivan." tumblr, n.d. https://troyesivan.tumblr.com/.

Tufekci, Z. (2020). Twitter, June 21. https://twitter.com/zeynep/status/1274682429488406532.

tumblr (2007). Landing page. Archive. https://web.archive.org/web/20070505025259/http://www.tumblr.com/.

tumblr (2008). Landing page. Archive. https://web.archive.org/web/20081226102605/http://tumblr.com/.

tumblr (2012). "Community guidelines." tumblr, March 22. https://static.tumblr.com/nvpc8l7/PeTm1e2ss/community_guidelines.txt.

tumblr (2014). "Adult content section on help page." Archive. https://web.archive.org/web/20140702023039/http://www.tumblr.com/docs/en/nsfw).

tumblr. (2016). "Tumblr community guidelines." tumblr, June 23. https://www.tumblr.com/policy/en/community.

TumblrMadeMeDoIt. (2020). "Tumblr made me do it." Facebook, n.d. https://www.facebook.com/TumblrMadeMeDoIt/.

tumblr Help Center. (2018). "Content moderation." Tumblr Zendesk. https://tumblr.zendesk.com/hc/en–us/articles/360011799473–Content–moderation–on–Tumblr.

tumblr Help Center. (2020a). "Ask." Tumblr Zendesk. https://tumblr.zendesk.com/hc/en–us/articles/231857168–Ask.

tumblr Help Center. (2020b). "Replies." Tumblr Zendesk. https://tumblr.zendesk.com/hc/en–us/articles/231855648–Replies.

tumblr Help Center. (2020c). "Your age on Tumblr." Tumblr Zendesk. https://tumblr.zendesk.com/hc/en–us/articles/360003018754–Your–Age–on–Tumblr.

tumblr Help Center. (2020d). "Appearing in search results." Tumblr Zendesk. https://tumblr.zendesk.com/hc/en–us/articles/223857628–Appearing–in–search–results.

Tumblr Reads. (2020). "Tumblr reads." YouTube, n.d. https://www.youtube.com/channel/UCwvz9MqJHji1Twr86YDP_1A/about.

tychography. (2020). "Reblog if you're dead." tumblr, June 14. https://tmblrnorms.tumblr.com/post/620926444738052096/reblog–if–youre–dead.

underrated-idols. (2018). "holland, underrated idols, by choigiraffe."

tumblr, 6 July. https://underrated–idols.tumblr.com/post/ 175597078138/im–not–afraid–2018.

Ungerer, L. (2016). "Digital curation as a core competency in current learning and literacy: A higher education perspective." *International Review of Research in Open and Distributed Learning*, 17(5), 1–27.

Unwrapping blog. (2017). "Tumblr might have closed its ..." tumblr, October 25. https://unwrapping.tumblr.com/post/166797486027/ tumblr–merch–store#notes.

Urban Dictionary. (2019). "tumblr dom." *Urban Dictionary*, September 26. https://www.urbandictionary.com/define.php?term =tumblr%20dom.

uwunnie. (2019). "Why do you need to ..." tumblr, June 13. https:// tmblrnorms.tumblr.com/post/185565584123.

Vaidhyanathan, S. (2018). *Anti-social Media: How Facebook Disconnects Us and Undermines Democracy*. New York: Oxford University Press.

valucard. (2020). "tumblr is a very bad ..." tumblr, January 7. https:// tmblrnorms.tumblr.com/post/190129532548/the–gender– enigma–valucard–tumblr–is–a–very.

van Dijck, J. (2013). *The Culture of Connectivity: A Critical History of Social Media*. New York: Oxford University Press. Kindle edition.

Vásquez, C., and Creel, S. (2017). "Conviviality through creativity: Appealing to the reblog in Tumblr Chat posts." *Discourse, Context and Media*, 20, 59–69.

vetoing. (2020). "when you finally receive an ..." tumblr, May 21. https://tmblrnorms.tumblr.com/post/618740158554144768/ vetoing–when–you–finally–receive–an–ask–during.

Villi, M. (2012). "Social curation in audience communities: UDC (user-distributed content) in the networked media ecosystem." *Participations: The International Journal of Audience and Reception Studies*, 9(2), 614–632.

viniumsabbathi. (2014). "Waka Flocka and Amy Poehler ..." tumblr, June 26. https://viniumsabbathi.tumblr.com/post/90025391645/ waka–flocka–and–amy–poehler–havin–a–moment–in–my.

Vivienne, S. (2016). *Digital Identity and Everyday Activism: Sharing Private Stories with Networked Publics*. New York: Palgrave MacMillan.

Vivienne, S. (2019). "Holding a queer space: Safe or suspect?" Paper presented at *Digital Intimacies 5: Structures, Cultures, Power*. December 9. Melbourne.

Walker, R. (2012). "Can Tumblr's David Karp embrace ads without selling out?" *New York Times*, July 15. https://www.nytimes. com/2012/07/15/magazine/can–tumblrs–david–karp–embrace– ads–without–selling–out.html.

wanted1993. (n.d.). "ON vs. OFF camera." tumblr, n.d. https://
wanted1993.tumblr.com/post/182403300142/on–vs–off–camera.

Warfield, K. (2016). "'Reblogging someone's selfie is seen as a really
nice thing to do': Spatiality and emplacement within a non–
dominant platform vernacular on Tumblr." Paper presented at the
Association of Internet Researchers Conference. Berlin.

Wargo, J. M. (2017a). "#donttagyourhate: Reading collecting and
curating as genres of participation in LGBT youth activism on
Tumblr." *Digital Culture & Education*, 9(1), 14–31.

Wargo, J. M. (2017b). "'Every selfie tells a story …': LGBTQ youth
lifestreams and new media narratives as connective identity texts."
New Media & Society, 19(4), 560–578.

Warner, M. (2002). "Publics and counterpublics." *Public Culture*, 14(1),
49–90.

Waskul, D. D. (2007). "Internet sex: The seductive 'freedom to.'" In
S. Seidman, N. L. Fischer, and C. Meeks (eds.), *Introducing the New
Sexuality Studies*. Abingdon: Routledge, pp. 276–284.

Watercutter, A. (2019). "The internet needs Tumblr more than
ever." *Wired*, August 14. https://www.wired.com/story/tumblr–
reinvigorated/.

Wellman, B. (2002). "Little boxes, glocalization and networked
individualism." In M. Tanabe, P. van den Besselaar, and T. Ishida
(eds.), *Digital Cities II: Computational and Sociological Approaches*.
New York: Springer, pp. 10–25.

Whitman, R. (2015). "Tumblr launches creative agency to link adver–
tisers to artists." *Media Post*, January 22. https://www.mediapost.
com/publications/article/242296/tumblr–launches–creative–
agency–to–link–advertiser.html.

wikiHow Staff. (2019). "How to get more followers on Tumblr."
wikiHow, June 23. https://www.wikihow.com/Get–More–
Followers–on–Tumblr.

Willard, L. (2016). "Tumblr's GIF economy: The promotional function
of industrially gifted gifsets." *Flow Journal*, July 27. https://www.
flowjournal.org/2016/07/tumblrs–gif–economy/.

Willard, L. (2017). "From co-option to commission: A diachronic
perspective on the development of fannish literacy through Teen
Wolf's Tumblr promotional campaigns." *Transformative Works and
Cultures*, 25. http://dx.doi.org/10.3983/twc.2017.894.

Winterwood, L. (2018). "Discourse is the new wank: A reflection on
linguistic change in fandom." *Transformative Works and Cultures*, 27.
http://dx.doi.org/10.3983/twc.2018.1276.

Wood, E. A. (2008). "Consciousness-raising 2.0: Sex blogging and the creation of a feminist sex commons." *Feminism & Psychology*, 18(4): 480–487.

World Health Organization. (2014). *Mental Health: A State of Well-being.* http://origin.who.int/features/factfiles/mental_health/en/.

Xu, J., Compton, R., Lu, T., and Allen, D. (2014). "Rolling through Tumblr: Characterizing behavioral patterns of the microblogging platform categories and subject descriptors." Subject Descriptors. In *Proceedings of the 2014 ACM Conference on Web Science.* Bloomington, IN, June 23–26, pp. 13–22.

yellow-sprout. (n.d.). "BIG BANG Together Forever." tumblr, n.d. https:// yellow-sprout.tumblr.com/post/171803679203/bigbang-will-always-be-together-forever-fanart.

ygconfessions. (n.d.). "ygconfessions." tumblr, n.d. https://ygconfessions.tumblr.com/.

yooneroos. (2017). "who am i? i am ..." tumblr, July 18. https://yooneroos.tumblr.com/post/163149334501/who-am-i-i-am-kwon-jiyong.

Zamanian, P. (2014). "Queer LIVES: The construction of queer self and community on tumblr." Master's thesis. Sarah Lawrence College, Bronxville, NY.

Zappavigna, M. (2018). *Searchable Talk.* Bloomsbury Publishing. Kindle Edition.

zayn. (2020). "ZAYN." tumblr, n.d. https://zayn.tumblr.com.

Zheng, Z. (2019). "S'porean student doxxed at 16, had photos & personal info circulating on lewd Tumblr sites." *Mothership*, May 10. https://mothership.sg/2019/05/gia-lim-doxxing-dayre-story/.

Zuckerberg, M. (2019). "A privacy-focused vision for social networking." Facebook, March 6. https://www.facebook.com/notes/mark-zuckerberg/a-privacy-focused-vision-for-social-networking/10156700570096634/.

Index